ON THE ROOF OF THE WORLD

READER'S DIGEST

Travels & Adventures

ON THE ROOF OF THE WORLD

Published by The Reader's Digest Association Limited

LONDON • NEW YORK • SYDNEY • CAPE TOWN • MONTREAL

♦ COVER:

Main picture: **Three mountaineers in Everest's Western Cwm, with Lingtren (22,142 feet) rising dramatically in front of them.**

Smaller pictures, from top to bottom: **Peter Somerville-Large and Caroline beside their tent on the Nepal–Tibet border. Lhasa's most famous landmark: the Potala Palace. A Tibetan woman wearing her finest jewellery. The magnificent, rare Himalayan snow leopard. Devotional lamps, fuelled by yak butter, inside a Buddhist shrine.**

Spine: **The head of the Buddha, 'The Awakened One', from a shrine in Kathmandu.**

♦ FRONTISPIECE:

Early morning, with a fresh dusting of snow, at Dingboche, on the Everest trail.

♦ TITLE PAGE:

A Tibetan pilgrim woman in typical local dress.

♦ OPPOSITE:

The wise eyes of the Buddha gaze out from a shrine in Kathmandu.

♦ CONTENTS PAGES:

Left: **Terraced rice fields on the slopes of the Himalayas in eastern Nepal.**

Right: **Peter Somerville-Large and Caroline beside their tent on the Nepal–Tibet border.**

♦ PAGES 8–9:

The Gurla range of mountains in Tibet, seen across the holy lake Manasarowar. In the foreground is a mani wall, made of stones carved with prayers and religious texts.

♦ PAGES 42–43:

A Nepalese villager and her two yaks meet a Buddhist monk beneath snow-covered Tramserku (21,680 feet), near Namche Bazar.

ON THE ROOF OF THE WORLD was edited and designed
by The Reader's Digest Association Limited, London

The Reader's Digest Association Limited
Berkeley Square House, Berkeley Square, London W1X 6AB.

To the Navel of the World: Original full-length version published by
Hamish Hamilton Ltd, 1987 and Sceptre, an imprint of Hodder and Stoughton
Paperbacks, 1988. © 1987 by Peter Somerville-Large. British condensed version
© The Reader's Digest Association Limited, 1994, published by arrangement
with Hamish Hamilton Ltd.

Contributors

Consultant Editor: Donald Payne
Special Advisers: Elaine Brook, John Cleare

Editor: David Scott-Macnab
Associate Editors:
David Compton, Mary Gibson, David Blomfield
Copy Editor: Jenny Baines
Designer: Louise Dick
Assistant Designer: Rick Lecoat
Picture Researcher: Cathy Stastny
Assistant Picture Researcher: James Robinson
Additional material by:
Elaine Brook, John Cleare, Tim Locke,
George Lowe, Sita Narasimhan
Watercolour illustrations: Mark Entwisle
Cartography: Malcolm Porter
Index: Barbara Nash

♦ The publishers and project team would like to express
their gratitude to the Royal Geographical Society for its
ongoing help and advice. They would also like to thank
the many individuals who have contributed to the
preparation of this volume. In particular, they are grateful
to Nicky Sherriff of the Royal Geographical Society and
Jane Moore of the Tibet Image Bank for their expert and
enthusiastic advice on photographs.

Contents

TO EVEREST AND BEYOND

Condensed from TO THE NAVEL OF THE WORLD by Peter Somerville-Large

— page 42 —

♦ *with special features:*

Index and Acknowledgments

— page 186 —

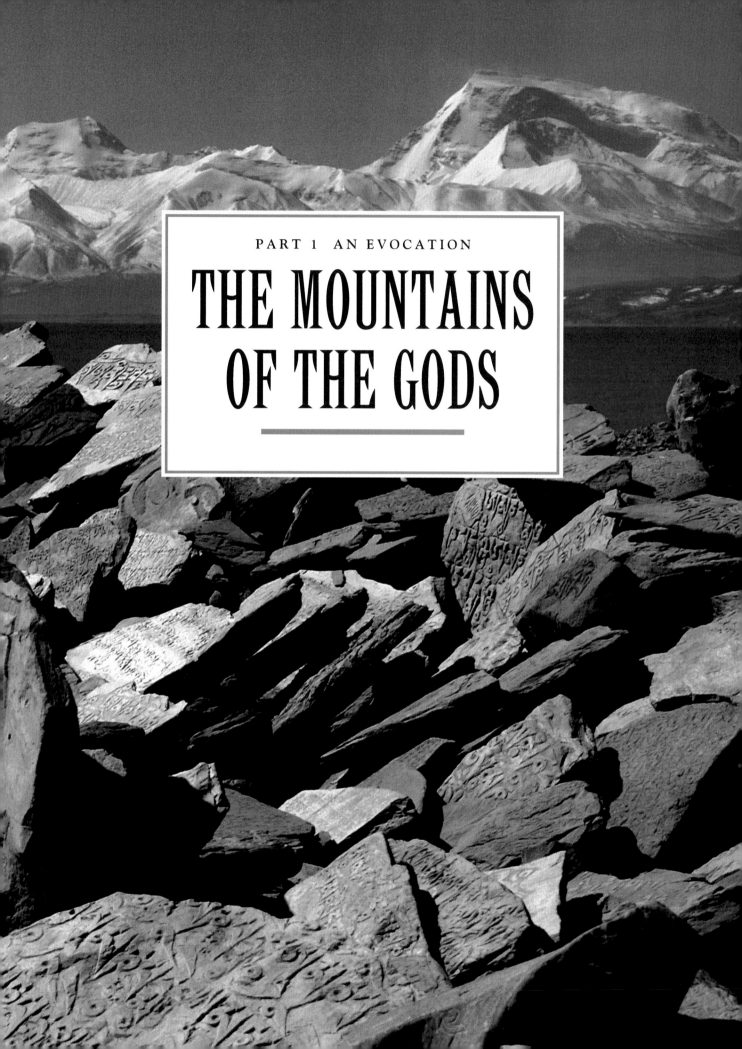

PART 1 AN EVOCATION

THE MOUNTAINS OF THE GODS

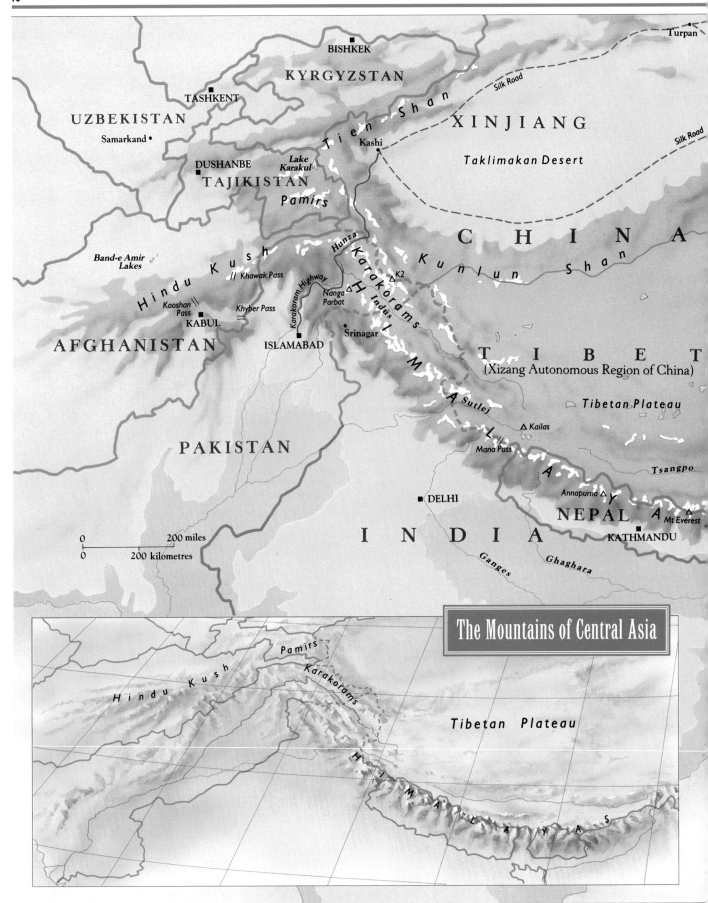

Turpan

BISHKEK

KYRGYZSTAN

TASHKENT

UZBEKISTAN

Silk Road

Tien Shan

XINJIANG

Samarkand •

Kashi

Silk Road

DUSHANBE

Lake Karakul

Taklimakan Desert

TAJIKISTAN

Pamirs

C H I N A

Band-e Amir Lakes

Hindu Kush

Hunza

Karakorams

Kunlun Shan

Khawak Pass

K2

Kaoshan Pass

KABUL

Khyber Pass

Karakoram Highway

Nanga Parbat

Nanga Parbat

H

Indus

ISLAMABAD

Srinagar

T I B E T

(Xizang Autonomous Region of China)

AFGHANISTAN

M

Tibetan Plateau

A

Sutlej

△ Kailas

PAKISTAN

L

Mana Pass

A

Tsangpo

DELHI

Y

Annapurna △

0   200 miles

NEPAL

A

△ Mt Everest

0   200 kilometres

I N D I A

KATHMANDU

Ganges

Ghaghara

The Mountains of Central Asia

Pamirs

Hindu Kush

Karakorams

Tibetan Plateau

H
I
M
A
L
A
Y
A
S

Dunhuang

Namcha Barwa

LHASA

THIMPHU

BHUTAN

Brahmaputra

BANGLADESH

DHAKA

BURMA

Bay of
Bengal

The Mountains of the Gods

IN THE HEART OF ASIA four great mountain ranges encircle the highest plateau on Earth. This is *Bai-i-Duniah*, the roof of the world: an area of mighty peaks, glaciated plateaux, barren deserts, deep valleys, spectacular beauty and surprising contrasts. Astronauts, looking down from space, have said that 'this vast mountain complex illuminates the heart of the continent like a circle of white fire'.

How was this colossal physical formation created?

Birth of the Mountains

According to a Hindu legend found in the *Mahabharata*, a pair of seagulls once lived on the shore of a great ocean. Each year the female gull laid her eggs far inland, but the sea always swept in and washed the eggs away. Eventually the gulls cried to the god Vishnu, the Preserver of Life, to help them. Vishnu took pity on them and swallowed the sea, which vanished as though it had never been, and in its place lay the newly created Mother Earth. Satisfied, Vishnu slept. But as he slept, the demon Hiranyanksha leapt on Mother Earth and raped her with such brutal violence that her bones were broken and levered high into the clouds to form the peaks of central Asia: mountains that are truly 'of the gods'.

Geomorphologists have another explanation. They say that about 120 million years ago the Earth consisted of two supercontinents, one in the northern and one in the southern hemisphere, with a great ocean between them. The southern continent broke up into five separate landmasses, four of which drifted slowly around the South Pole, working their way into the positions that South America, Africa, Australia and Antarctica occupy today. But the fifth, India, travelled much farther, moving up from the southern hemisphere into the northern, where it crashed into the landmass of Asia. The result was spectacular. On its voyage north India had passed over a hot spot in the crust of the Earth, where a sheet of basaltic magma had been fused into it; so by the time it collided with Asia it contained rocks which were volcanic and hard. Southern Asia, in contrast, consisted of rocks which were mainly sedimentary and soft—the original ocean bed which had been pushed up ahead of the advancing mass of India into folds of sandstone, limestone, coral and clay. As the continents came together, these folds of soft, sedimentary rock were squeezed upwards, forming the ranges of mountains which today make up the roof of the world. In evidence of this, fragments of coral and fossilised sea snails can be found on the upper slopes of Everest.

Although these two explanations *seem* very different, in fact they tell the same story: the story of a disappearing sea, and newly created mountains being violently levered up from seabed to over 29,000 feet.

Since these mountain ranges were formed at the same time and by the same cataclysmic collision, you might expect them to be alike. They do indeed have similarities. Their southern slopes tend to be wet and fertile, while their northern slopes are dry and barren. They are nearly all bisected by deep valleys: the rivers were there before the mountains, and as the mountains rose up around them these ancient rivers kept to their original course, cutting spectacular gorges through the soft, upthrusting rock. However, the mountains' similarities are not nearly as great as their differences. For over millions of years each range has evolved in quite a different way and each now has its own distinctive characteristics, people and history.

We can see how fundamental these differences are if we examine the four great ranges—the Hindu Kush, Pamirs, Karakorams and Himalayas—which, together with the Tibetan Plateau, make up the Mountains of the Gods.

The Hindu Kush: The Hindu Killer

The mountains of the Hindu Kush are the most westerly of the ranges: a fragmented mass of sandstone and limestone stretching for 650 miles across present-day Afghanistan. They are high and cold, with several peaks over 23,000 feet. A Berber traveller, Ibn Battutah, writing in 1334, explained how they got their name: '*Hindu Kush* means "Hindu killer". Many of the Hindu slaves brought to us from India perish while crossing these high mountains on account of the cold and the great quantities of snow.' As well as being high, these mountains are arid, for the monsoons which sweep in each year from the Bay of Bengal deposit less and less rain as they move northward and westward.

▲ At almost 10,000 feet, the spectacular Band-e Amir lakes create a superb splash of colour in an otherwise stark landscape.

The Kalash are a proud people who were converted to Islam by force, and still retain many distinctive traditions. ▶

▲ **Afghan tribesmen chatting with their boy children. In this part of the world, women and girls are largely excluded from male society.**

The Desolation of the Hindu Kush

THE MOUNTAINS OF THE HINDU KUSH form a barrier between the steppes of central Asia and the plains of Pakistan and India. They consist of desolate heights in which great escarpments of sandstone, limestone and schist stand like the remains of vast, shattered medieval castles.

The people who live here are as dramatic as their surroundings. Warlike, fiercely independent and forever feuding, they include many different groups: Turkomans, Hazara, and the intriguing Nuristanis or Kalash, who were forcibly converted to Islam by the Turks in the 1890s and who still follow many traditions of their pagan past. Most numerous and influential, however, are the Sunni Muslim Pathans who follow a code of behaviour known as *Paktunwali*. As well as forbidding violence against women, their code has three basic tenets: hospitality to strangers, sanctuary to those who seek it, and retribution for every wrong that has been suffered. There is no turning the other cheek, and memories are long. If a boy's father has been murdered, his mother will raise him to take revenge when he is old enough. In many ways, this is a man's world, as is clear from the Turkoman maxim: 'When a husband's guests are present, a wife must cover her mouth with her headcloth and not speak. She must sit in a place reserved for people of low status, and quickly obey orders given by the men.'

Hindu Kush means 'Hindu killer': it was along passes such as this that 14th-century Arab slave traders lost many of their valuable Hindu slaves. ▼

Few people would call the Hindu Kush beautiful, but it has an austere grandeur, which many come to admire. As a British ambassador to Kabul once wrote:

This is a wild, desolate country: a country of great peaks and deep valleys, of precipitous gorges and rushing grey-green rivers; a barren land of intense sunlight, clear sparkling air and wonderful colouring.

It is also a land in which warfare is virtually a way of life. For the Hindu Kush is the gateway out of central Asia: the only place through which it is possible for large numbers of people to cross from the barren steppe of the Asian heartland into the fertile plains of the Indian subcontinent. From time immemorial the people of the Hindu Kush have had to defend their mountain passes against would-be invaders—Darius, Alexander the Great, Genghis Khan, Tamerlane, 19th-century British mule trains and expeditionary forces, and 20th-century Soviet tanks. This is a dessicated land, a land with a history of violence, whose predominantly Muslim tribes have constantly fought among themselves when not united against an invader: a land of strong colours, strong passions and fierce independence.

The Pamirs: 'Where No Bird Flies'

The Pamirs lie to the north of the Hindu Kush: a huge block of domelike peaks covering an area of about 40,000 square miles, mostly within the former Soviet republic of Tajikistan. They are almost as high as the Hindu Kush, with several peaks of over 22,000 feet, and they are even drier. For as the subcontinent of India continues to grind into the soft underbelly of Asia, the range to the southeast of the Pamirs, the Karakorams, is being pushed up ever higher each year, and is blocking off more and more of the Pamirs' already inadequate rainfall. Lake Karakul (high on the north flank of the Pamirs) receives less than an inch of rain a year, and is surrounded not by ice and snow but by deserts and sand dunes.

Yet snow does fall here, and in the upper reaches of these mountains it never melts; instead, it accumulates and grows ever thicker (by about 2½ inches a year) to form the world's largest ice cap outside the polar circles.

Few animals can survive in such a harsh environment, but of those that do, many grow to an impressive size; for it is the creatures that have the smallest surface area in proportion to their bulk which lose their body heat least readily. So here are some of the world's largest wild cattle (the yak), as well as the endangered markhor, a mountain goat whose corkscrew horns are

▲ This characterful Kirghiz tribesman is well protected against the cold by his large fur hat.

A group of Kirghiz girls in the high Pamirs watch their menfolk on horseback playing the traditional, daylong game of *buzkashi*—a very violent sport played with the corpse of a goat. ▶

▲ The markhor with its impressive corkscrew horns. One of the few wild animals of the region, this noble beast is now in serious danger of extinction.

The Pamirs

ARCHED LIKE THE ROOF OF A HUGE cathedral, with 20,000-foot ridges for its flying buttresses, the Pamirs soar where Afghanistan meets the former Soviet republic of Tajikistan and the western-most Chinese province of Xinjiang. Here is the world's greatest accumulation of ice outside the polar circles, and each year the ice grows thicker.

Most mountain ranges grow higher because of seismic pressure or volcanic activity. The Pamirs, uniquely, grow higher because of a continuous accretion of snow. As the tops of these mountains are comparatively level and unfailingly cold, almost every snowflake freezes as it

settles, and is then compressed by the weight of further snowfalls into a solid, ever-thickening mass of ice. Recent research shows that this ice sheet is rising at an average of 2½ inches each year—over 2,000 feet in 10,000 years.

The people of this inhospitable land are Muslims: the Tajik and the Kirghiz. The Tajik live in the western foothills as subsistence farmers, growing wheat, barley, onions and turnips; while the nomadic Kirghiz inhabit the more barren uplands. They are forever driving

their flocks from one sparse pasture to another, their tents and children loaded onto camel-drawn wagons. Of all the peoples of the former Soviet Union, the Kirghiz resisted collectivisation most fiercely. They love their mountains—because, as one of them recently put it, 'they are clean and they are free'.

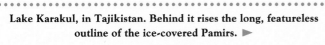
Lake Karakul, in Tajikistan. Behind it rises the long, featureless outline of the ice-covered Pamirs. ▶

The Towering Karakorams

THE KARAKORAM RANGE is a daunting
massif of rock and ice and is home to 30
of the world's 40 highest peaks—including
K2 which, at 28,253 feet, is second in height
only to Everest. These enormous, starkly
beautiful mountains are cut by only one
major road, the Karakoram Highway, which
links Pakistan and China. This road is a
magnificent feat of engineering, achieved
at enormous cost. 'Say a prayer,' reads a
plaque beside it, 'for the brave men of the Pakistan
army who gave their lives to realise a dream.'

The Karakoram Highway runs along the Hunza
valley, a green and fertile oasis in a barren wilderness.
This is the home of the enigmatic Hunzakut, a people
whose blue eyes have led to the folklore that they are
descendants of troops of Alexander the Great.
Whatever their origins, they have outstanding farming
and irrigation skills, and have turned their valley into a
rich haven of terraced fields among stark, rocky slopes.
In dramatic contrast with their lives are those of the
tenacious Baltis, the people who inhabit the high
Ladakh plateau, site of K2. These are poor Muslims of
Tibetan origin who eke out a meagre living growing
barley and fruits in remote valleys where the annual
rainfall seldom exceeds six inches, and who therefore
rely on melting snow and ice for irrigation.

▲ The dramatic peak of
K2, the world's second-
highest mountain, rises
behind the spiky, icy
back of the Godwin
Austen Glacier.

◀ A lean, hardy Balti
tribesman from Ladakh,
high in the Pakistani
section of Kashmir.

▲ Trucks and buses on the Karakoram Highway are often elaborately decorated with traditional Muslim designs.

◄ The rich colours of terraced wheat fields in the Hunza valley contrast dramatically with the barrenness that lies beyond them.

often over four feet long. However, in the upper reaches of these mountains there are few birds. You will find condors in the Andes and griffon vultures in the Himalayas—but among the high, arid peaks of the Pamirs, as Marco Polo recorded, 'no bird flies'.

The people of this desolate land are the Tajik, who farm wheat, barley and millet in the western foothills, and the nomadic Kirghiz of the barren uplands. The Kirghiz band together in groups of five or six extended families which are ever on the move, ever driving their horses, yaks, sheep and camels from one sparse pasture to the next, ever locked in combat with their harsh environment. They are a hospitable, proud, fiercely independent race. 'A Kirghiz,' wrote the climber Eric Shipton, 'is an enemy to fear, a friend to cherish.'

The Karakorams: World of Ice

The Karakorams, named from the Turkish for 'Black Rock Mountains', are like a hub from which the other ranges radiate—to the west the Hindu Kush, to the north the Pamirs, and to the southeast the Himalayas. They form a massif of mighty peaks crammed together into an area of about 50,000 square miles where China, India and Pakistan converge. Here lies Baltistan, a northern province of Ladakh, home of the hardy Balti tribe, a Muslim people of Tibetan origin who eke out a meagre living through farming the lower slopes.

In this spectacular wilderness of bare rock, blue and black ice, sheer cliff and foaming river, are three of the six highest mountains in the world (including K2, at 28,253 feet), 33 peaks of over 24,000 feet and 60 peaks of over 22,000 feet. Here too is one of the largest non-polar glaciers—the Hispar-Biafo, stretching 76 miles from snowfield to terminal moraine.

The first European to set eyes on this magnificent confusion of peaks was probably the British spy Godfrey Vine, who explored the area in 1835. A man well accustomed to the magnificence of the Alps, he wrote:

> I shall never forget the glorious view that presented itself. Mountain seemed piled upon mountain in a most stupendous confusion. If Mont Blanc had been placed here, it would have been disregarded on account of its insignificance.

This is a world mostly too rock-girt for cultivation, too precipitous for grazing, and too inhospitable for habitation save in a few remote villages. There is only one major road—the spectacular Karakoram Highway—and only one river, the Hunza, a tributary of the mighty Indus. But many of even the finest passes in the Karakorams are open for only five or six months of

the year, and are steep and rugged enough to deter all but the most dedicated travellers, even when the snows do clear.

The Himalayas: Abode of Snow

Of all the great Asian mountain ranges, the Himalayas are the youngest, largest, highest, most populous and, to many people, the most beautiful. They stretch in an unbroken curve for 1,500 miles from Nanga Parbat (26,661 feet) in the west to Namcha Barwa (25,445 feet) in the east, and consist of three parallel ranges: the Siwaliks, the Lesser Himalayas and the Great or Trans Himalayas. Towering above the permanent snow line, their glittering heights were named by early Indian pilgrims from the Sanskrit words *hima*, 'snow', and *alaya*, 'abode'.

The Siwaliks are gentle foothills, little more than 3,000 feet high. The rainfall here is heavy, and much of the range consists of a mixture of swamp, tropical forest and elephant grass that is known as Terai. A hundred years ago this Terai was a paradise for big game hunters; today it contains National Parks and Wildlife Reserves for many endangered species—chital deer, langurs, rhinos, Asian buffalo, gharial crocodiles and more than half the world's dwindling population of tigers.

North of the Siwaliks are the Lesser Himalayas: a chain of magnificent peaks which leap 20,000 feet out of the plains. No other mountains on Earth rise so high, so steeply. The writer Nigel Nicolson recalls camping one night at the foot of Annapurna and seeing a brilliant light apparently directly over-head. When he asked his Sherpa porters what star it could be, they laughed and told him it was a shepherd's bonfire.

Although they are so steep, the south-facing slopes of this range are well populated. Villages cling to the hillsides, their thatched-roof houses filled with barking dogs, crowing cocks and chattering people who adore these mountains and celebrate their beauty in song:

> High are the mountains,
> Siva lives in them.
> This is my homeland;
> It is more beautiful than heaven.

Beyond the Lesser Himalayas lie the even more spectacular Great or Trans Himalayas. Here are names familiar not only to

◀ **'Five thousand leagues around, with its range of eight-and-forty-thousand peaks, the source of five hundred rivers, the producer of manifold perfumes, enriched with hundreds of magical drugs, the Himalayas rise aloft, like a cloud from the centre of the earth.'**
—*Sage Nagasena, 5th-century Buddhist monk.*

mountaineers but to millions of armchair travellers throughout the world—Nanga Parbat, Kamet, Lhotse, Kangchenjunga and Everest (known to the Nepalese as Sagarmatha, and to the Tibetans as Chomolongma)—peaks which form a chain of huge massifs split by deep valleys. One of these valleys, the Kali Gandaki, has sides which rise almost vertically for more than 18,500 feet, making it the deepest valley on Earth. Yet in the Himalayas everything is on so majestic a scale that the stupendous seems commonplace. Avalanches rip away mountainsides, floods devastate whole valleys, earth tremors are continuously levering the peaks ever higher into the sky. As the 19th-century botanist Joseph Hooker put it, 'Upon what a gigantic scale does nature here operate!'

Tibet: Land of Mystery

Tibet is an enigma to the outside world. Some people still think of it as the sheltered, idyllic Shangri-la of James Hilton's *Lost Horizon*; in fact, the country which used to be Tibet and is now the Xizang Autonomous Region of China consists of a huge plateau of about 460,000 square miles. This plateau is ringed by high, almost impassable mountains—in the north the Kunlun Shan, in the west the Pamirs and Karakorams, in the south the Himalayas; in the east it merges into the highlands of central China. Apart from the *altiplano* of the Andes, this is the highest inhabited land on Earth with an average height above sea level of 16,500 feet (higher than Mont Blanc). In summer the average temperature is about 45°F; in winter about 10°F, but it can fall as low as –25°F. Rainfall is sparse, winds are strong, and climatic changes violent and unpredictable.

In spite of these harsh conditions, much of the north of the plateau is grassland, well suited to the nomadic grazing which for millennia has been the traditional method of farming for most Tibetans. The historian Swami Pranavananda sums up their characteristics:

> Both men and women are strong, sturdy and hard-working, with great powers of resistance to cold and hardship. They are cheerful, pleasure-loving, hospitable, peaceful and religious-minded.

This 'religious-mindedness' used to be the key to the lives of these people. Before the Chinese invasion of 1950, a third of the population of Tibet were monks, nuns or hermits; mantras (sacred texts) were painted on every wall; korlos (prayer wheels) were endlessly turning, and the country's many monasteries were centres of cultural life. This old Tibet was undoubtedly hierarchical and feudal; but it was spiritually free. The new

▲ Samye monastery, built on the north bank of the Tsangpo River in about AD 780, was where an Indian abbot ordained the first Tibetan monks.

▲ In a magnificent inner courtyard of the Jo-Kang temple, against a background of flickering butter lamps, monks offer a prayer before their day's main meal.

Tibet's Ancient Monasteries

Chanting monks draped with white khatas (scarves of salutation) parade at the start of a sacred ritual. ▶

FIFTY YEARS AGO there were around 7,000 monasteries and nunneries in Tibet. Today there are at most 11. The rest, bastions of a way of life that was already old at the time of the Battle of Hastings, were destroyed during the excesses of China's Cultural Revolution in the 1960s.

Many were unbelievably ancient. At least a dozen major Tibetan monasteries had been built before AD 1000, which made them older than most of the great cathedrals of Europe. And Tibet's oldest surviving religious building, dating back to the 1st century BC, is a palace–temple built on the banks of the Tsangpo River (the Brahmaputra).

There were a great many of them also: one for every 90 or so people in a population of which over 30% were monks or nuns. Some, especially on the bleak northern plateau, were tiny—no more than two or three rooms. Others were huge, like cities—the largest, the Drepung near Lhasa, accommodated over 8,000 inmates.

The larger monasteries were very rich, their wealth necessary to maintain the lavish trappings of Lamaism; for example, 80% of all the butter produced in Tibet was used to keep alight their eternal lamps. Many were magnificent beyond belief, with gilded roofs, huge, gold-plated statues and shrines; exquisite frescoes, and lavishly decorated rooms; 200,000 pearls ornament the Pearl Chamber in the Potala Palace.

Few Tibetans resented this opulence. Deeply religious, they saw no clear division between the monastic life and the secular. Most people lived within sight of a monastery and had daily contact with it; monks were their healers and their teachers. Even today, though the outward signs of Lamaism lie in ruins, the people's faith is still strong in their hearts.

• •

Detail of a monk's sumptuous robe and ornate trumpet. ▲

Ganden monastery, which once covered a hillside near Lhasa, was all but levelled by the Chinese during the 1960s. Now, with Chinese help, it is slowly being rebuilt, though mainly as a tourist attraction. ▶

Hinduism

HINDUISM—THE RELIGION practised by around 500 million people in India — is the oldest living world religion. Its earliest surviving sacred texts, the *Vedas*, are a collection of hymns dating from 1500 BC, centuries before the rise of other great faiths. Added later were scriptures such as the *Mahabharata*, an epic poem of the 4th century BC, and the *Upanishads*, a set of scholarly commentaries from about 800 BC.

At the heart of all these texts is the belief that every creature contains an immortal soul which is working out its own sacred destiny. This in turn underlies the central concept of reincarnation— the notion that the souls of all living creatures are reborn in new bodies after death. People who act virtuously in life are reborn in a higher social caste, while those whose actions (or *karma*) are evil return in a lower caste, or even as animals. Release from this endless cycle of death and rebirth is achieved through spiritual discipline and meditation leading to a state of enlightenment.

One consequence of this belief in immortal souls is a respect for all life; which is why many Hindus are vegetarian and practise nonviolence. One sect, the

▲ A Hindu holy man, or saddhu, seated beside a statue of the elephant god, Ganesh. The saddhu's trident, snakes and matted hair mark him as a worshipper of Siva.

Jains, takes nonviolence to its limits: a Jain monk wears a mask and sweeps his path as he walks, to avoid breathing in or stepping on any living creature.

The two major gods worshipped by Hindus are Siva, the creator and destroyer, and Vishnu, the bringer of order. Siva has many aspects, some benevolent, some terrifying. He is the god of creation, fertility and medicine, whose dancing symbolises the eternal cycle of creation and destruction.

Vishnu, on the other hand, is an

awesome but kindly god. He is often depicted asleep on a coiled serpent called Ranganatha, the lord of the stage. For Hindus, Vishnu's dreams are the world in which all humans live, and he has many incarnations or *avatars*, which come to help men in times of special need. The two best known of Vishnu's *avatars* are Rama and Krishna, the latter being an especially popular subject of Hindu folklore. The *Bhagavadgita* ('Song of the Lord'), one of the best-loved books of the *Mahabharata*, consists of a long dialogue

between the warrior Arjuna and the Lord Krishna, disguised as Arjuna's charioteer.

In fact, there are many other gods, but they are all seen as various forms of one supreme God or all-pervasive divine spirit called Brahman. This sentiment is expressed in the following wry passage in the *Upanishads*:

'How many gods are there?'
'Three thousand.'
'How many are there really?'
'Three.'
'How many are there *really*?'
'One.'

The religion of the average Hindu is one of devotion, ceremonial washings, and visits to the temple. Worship is often individual and private: prayers may be said alone, on a river bank, at home, or in a temple. Every Hindu home has a shrine with images of the gods, and throughout India there are elaborately carved temples where ritual washings and ceremonies take place. Sometimes these are great festivals in honour of a particular god, but people also gather at temples on pilgrimages or for daily prayer.

Religions are perhaps best talked of in terms of their ideals. The Hindu's ideal is to achieve enough stillness within to create order in the world outside.

▲ Siva, the dancing god, the creator and destroyer, appears here in one of his fiercer manifestations, with his trident in one of his six hands.

◄ Vishnu, the bringer of order, sleeping on the coiled serpent, Ranganatha. Vishnu's followers believe that all humans are figures in his dreams.

Chinese Tibet has better roads and sewers, but most of its 7,000 monasteries have been razed to the ground, the prayer wheels no longer turn, and the religious heartbeat of Tibetan life has been all but stilled.

For thousands of years this great plateau, encircled by defensive mountains, was virtually inaccessible to the outside world: it was a last redoubt of the unknown, and the Tibetans were keen to keep it that way. Tibet was known as 'the land of mystery', Lhasa was 'the forbidden city', and the snowcapped peaks surrounding it were 'the third Pole'. The recent Chinese invasion of Tibet has been, in a way, only the most recent act in a drama that has gone on for millennia: the outside world finally forcing its way into this mountain complex while its people struggle to keep outsiders at bay. Just how resistant the people of the mountains can be to the winds of change may be seen from their long and often violent history.

The Hindu Pilgrims

The first people to sight the mountains of central Asia about 400,000 years ago were probably migrating eastward from their African homeland. Some of these early travellers settled along the south-facing slopes of the mountains, and their descendants live there today.

In many parts of the world our ancestors were afraid of mountains; they thought of them as places to be avoided, the home of dragons and evil spirits. But the people of the Indian subcontinent realised that the great Himalayan snowfields gave them water, and the water gave them life. They therefore paid homage to the mountains, building shrines on the mountain paths. One peak both they and the Buddhists regarded as particularly sacred: Mount Kailas.

Mount Kailas is a symmetrically shaped but comparatively minor peak on the rim of the Tibetan Plateau, far to the north of the main Himalayan ranges. Yet according to the book of Hindu legends, the *Mahabharata*, Kailas is 'the monarch of all mountains, a never-tiring worker for the common good. Its rivers are covered with the golden lotus and near its summit is the hall of Brahma, full of fountains out of which are flowing the waters of life'. Those who visit Kailas today will find there is not a lotus in sight, let alone a fountain.

So why did the Hindus consider it so holy? The answer must be that they knew that Kailas is situated at a watershed, and that the four great rivers of the Indian subcontinent—the Indus, Sutlej, Ganges and Brahmaputra—all have their source within a few miles of this beautiful, but otherwise unremarkable peak.

Long before the birth of Christ, Hindu pilgrims must have crossed the main range of the Himalayas, skirted the Karakorams, penetrated deep into the Tibetan Plateau and traced the major rivers of India to their source.

Invaders Through the Snow

The first Europeans to set foot in the Mountains of the Gods were almost certainly the troops of Alexander the Great.

In the winter of 330–329 BC Alexander led his army into the Hindu Kush, hoping that if he crossed the range in winter, he would catch his adversaries, the Persians, unawares. It was a nightmare journey, especially in the 11,650-foot Khawak Pass where conditions were atrocious. The snow was deep, the cold beyond endurance, and food scarce; all the soldiers had to eat were the brittle leaves of turpentine bushes and the raw flesh of their mules—raw because they had no firewood. Alexander's troops died in their thousands, many of them frozen fast to the rocks during the night. But the mountains were crossed and the Persian army, taken by surprise, routed. Two years later, in 327 BC, Alexander recrossed the Hindu Kush, this time by the Kaoshan Pass, before descending on India via the Indus.

More than 1,500 years were to elapse before another, and more terrible, army was to force its way through the passes.

The 14th-century Mongol conqueror Tamerlane (known in Christopher Marlowe's play as Tamburlaine the Great) made no bones about his motives for invading India:

> I came to Hindustan to lead a campaign to the death against the infidel, to convert them to the true faith, to purify their land from the abomination of idolatry, to overthrow their temples, and to seize their riches.

After fighting several successful campaigns against rival Mongol rulers, Tamerlane led his army of 90,000 into the Hindu Kush, where he encountered the Nuristanis, a pagan, mountain people, said to be such formidable fighters that they had never been conquered. They were no match, however, for the Mongols, who stormed their mountain strongholds, massacred their men, and carried their women and children off as slaves.

Tamerlane proceeded to force his way over the Khawak Pass and, like Alexander before him, suffered heavy casualties here. In places, his entire army had to swing across ravines and be lowered down enormous cliffs by ropes. Over 20,000 are said to have died of exposure and exhaustion. But by summer 1398 the survivors stood on the banks of the Sutlej, and before them the rich cities of the plains lay ripe for plunder.

▲ Alexander, regarded by many as the greatest military genius of all time, seen here in a mosaic found at Pompeii.

A medieval Persian illustration of Tamerlane's Mongol horde rampaging through the city of Isfahan in 1387. ▼

Armies in the Mountain Passes

FOR THOUSANDS OF YEARS, great generals have recognised that the mountain passes of the Hindu Kush have enormous strategic importance. They have not always anticipated the dangers of these mountains.

In the 6th century BC, Darius the Great of Persia used the Khyber Pass to cross into India. Two centuries later, Alexander the Great and his generals twice rampaged through the Hindu Kush—in 329 and 327 BC—but lost thousands of men in midwinter snows. A similar fate awaited the 14th-century Mongol conqueror Tamerlane (Turkish for 'Timur-the-Lame'). For three decades he led his army of mounted archers on a triumphant series of campaigns from the Mediterranean to Mongolia, and up to Russia. Then, in 1398, he inflicted horrifying carnage on India, but only after suffering enormous casualties in the Khawak Pass.

In the 1520s, India was again successfully invaded from the north, this time by King Babur, a descendant of both Tamerlane and Genghis Khan. Because of his ancestry, Babur was known as 'the Mughal'—meaning 'Mongol'—and the dynasty he founded in northern India became known as the Mogul Empire, famous for the culture and talent of its rulers.

The 19th century saw Britain also sending unwelcome armies across the great mountain passes—this time from the south into Afghanistan, where they suffered some appalling massacres. And the mountains, once again, showed their perilous nature. The Khyber Pass, in particular, has ever since been notorious for the high risks it held for troops entering it.

◀ **The Moguls were responsible for some of northern India's most magnificent buildings. This is the Agra Gate of Fatehpur Sikri, the city built in the 16th century by King Akbar, grandson of Babur.**

The dangers of the passes: in this 19th-century watercolour, the rearguard of a column of redcoats is ambushed by tribesmen in the Bolan Pass. ▼

On the Historic Silk Road

DURING THE PERIOD OF RELATIVE peace in central Asia that followed the succession of ravaging invasions by Genghis Khan and his rapacious family in the 12th century, regular travel became possible between East and West. In medieval times there were only two reasons for Europeans to travel great distances: trade and religion. Christianity proved to have little appeal east of Turkey. Western gold, on the other hand, along with fine paper and other fancy European items, could readily be traded for goods from the East, in particular exotic luxuries such as spices, precious stones, carpets and silk.

The Silk Road is our name today for the 7,000-mile caravan routes, first described by Marco Polo, which once existed between silk-producing areas in China and major Mediterranean trading centres such as Constantinople and Venice. Used also for local trade, the Silk Road was in fact a complex web of highways, often hardly more than faint desert tracks between villages, along which each merchant followed his own commercial interests, buying and selling as he went.

Travelling east from Turkey, the trader's route might well have taken him through Syria, across northern Iran, to Samarkand in Uzbekistan, and then on to Kashi in western China. From there he might proceed southwest, across the foothills of the Kunlun Shan mountains, or northwest, across the top of the great Taklimakan Desert. His journey was always dangerous, and its outcome often depended on such factors as the weather, the honesty of innkeepers, and local politics: which regional chieftains were at war that week, and with whom.

◀ **Fine silks were among the treasures brought overland from China in medieval times.**

What followed was a holocaust. One by one India's northern cities were captured, burned to the ground and their inhabitants massacred. The Indians' defending army made a last desperate stand outside Delhi; but in spite of its phalanxes of elephants it was defeated, and for three months the Mongols indulged in an orgy of destruction. Then, as suddenly as they had come, they disappeared to the north up the Afghan valleys, leaving behind them burned crops, towns reduced to rubble and ash, and upwards of five million dead: a legacy of chaos from which the people of India took more than a century to recover.

From that day to this, those who live to the south of the mountains have regarded the passes through the Hindu Kush and the Himalayas as the key to their survival. And that is why Indian troops today are manning the highest human habitation on Earth: Fort Basisi, altitude 19,700 feet, overlooking the Mana Pass on the Indian–Chinese border.

The Travels of Marco Polo

Fortunately, war and plunder were not the only incentives that drove men to cross the mountains of central Asia. In 1271 Marco Polo, aged 17, set out from Venice with his father, uncle and two Dominican friars, to travel to Shangdu in China. The friars gave up while still within sight of the Mediterranean; but the Polos, made of sterner stuff, headed east on what was to prove an epic journey.

After crossing the deserts of Persia, they entered present-day Afghanistan, which they found to be a devastated land; for the great Muslim trading centres had been pillaged by the Mongol Golden Horde. Of Balkh, once described as the mother of cities, Marco wrote: 'Here there used to be many fine palaces and mansions of marble, but these now lie in ruins. Grass grows in the streets and wild goats graze in the deserted fields.'

Northeast of Balkh they came to a major obstacle—the Pamirs, which Marco describes as follows:

> On top of these ranges are broad plains with a great abundance of grass, few trees and springs of the purest water. This is said to be the highest place in the world. It is so high, fire burns with a pale flame and gives off so little heat you may put your hand in it, and there are huge sheep with horns six palms in length.

Descending into the plains of central Asia, the Polos crossed the Taklimakan Desert via a skein of oases at the foot of the Tien Shan mountains; and eventually, after a four-year journey, they reached China and were escorted to the Kublai Khan's summer palace at Shangdu.

▲ Typical Silk Road terrain. Here the ancient trade route passes along the western edge of China's Taklimakan Desert.

◄ The first Westerners to travel the Silk Road to China and return to tell the tale were Marco Polo and his father and uncle. In this medieval illustration, they are honoured with the gift of a golden seal from Kublai Khan, the mighty Mongol emperor of China.

▲ Vividly coloured spices from the Far East (here on sale in Nepal) are still traded all along the Silk Road.

◄ Twin-humped Bactrian camels still carry merchandise along the Silk Road, pictured here in the eastern Pamirs.

The Venetians were well received, and the 21-year-old Marco soon made a deep impression on the Khan, who employed him as his personal ambassador. As a result, Marco spent the next 17 years travelling all over China, where he found a civilization in many ways more advanced than his own. He saw 1,000-ton five-masted ships, paper currency and printing presses, among other wonders, and recounted these in great detail in his *Travels* when he and his family at last returned to Venice in 1295. His contemporaries were amazed, and Marco's book soon became a best seller of his age. More importantly, he reminded medieval Europeans that the world extended far beyond the shores of the Mediterranean and the Atlantic.

In Search of the Forbidden City

One result of Marco Polo's travels was an increase in trade between Europe and China. Nearly all this trade was by camel-caravan via the Silk Road, a section of which lay along the north edge of the Taklimakan Desert; and it was from merchants using this road that Europeans first heard rumours of Lhasa, a remote and mysterious city said to be encircled by impassable mountains. Rumour also had it that there were Christians in the city—'who wear white robes, sing ritual songs, use incense, take communion and worship one God'. In 1661 two priests, Albert D'Orville and Johann Grueber, set out from the Jesuit mission in Peking to see if these rumours were true.

Passing through the Great Wall of China—'very high and so broad that six horsemen may ride abreast on it'—D'Orville and Grueber crossed the great Taklimakan Desert by a little-used southerly track which brought them to the edge of the Tibetan Plateau. 'This,' wrote Grueber, 'is an impossibly barren land, the bleak hillsides broken only by the occasional cluster of yurts, home of the predatory Mongols.' All Grueber has to say about the next part of their journey is that they 'suffered much': probably an understatement, as the two priests struggled for weeks across the vastness of Tibet, a territory unknown to Europeans.

At last they reached Lhasa, where Grueber found that there were no Christians; only Buddhist monks, whose ceremonies seemed remarkably familiar to him. He wrote:

It is amazing how the Buddhist religion agrees with the Romish. For they too celebrate Mass with bread and wine, give extreme unction, bless those about to be married, say prayers for the sick, sing in choirs and build monasteries and nunneries.

Observers mistaking Buddhist rituals for Christian must have started the rumours about there being Christians in Lhasa.

Himalayan Buddhism

BUDDHISM IS THE RELIGION of those who try to practise the way of life of the Buddha, the 'Awakened One', in order to achieve enlightenment and mystical awareness. There is no worship of a supreme god in Buddhism; and the Buddha himself is not worshipped: he is imitated.

According to tradition, the Buddha was a prince who lived in northern India between about 563 and 483 BC. His name was Siddhartha Gautama, and he was brought up in a luxurious palace, where he was protected from all unpleasant sights. But one day he encountered in succession an old man, a sick man and a corpse. He realised with a shock that life was not just about enjoying oneself; it was full of suffering and led ultimately to death.

Siddhartha then met a wandering holy man, whose serene expression showed that he had somehow come to terms with the unpleasant reality of life and had transcended it. So for the next few years he became a wandering ascetic, subjecting himself to extreme hardships in his search for the truth. Eventually he realised that if he continued in this way he would probably die of starvation before finding the answers he sought. He took a little food, and spent the night in deep meditation beneath a bo or peepul tree (also called the Bodhi tree—'the Tree of Wisdom') in the place now called Bodh Gaya in modern Bihar. There he finally gained a deep insight into the way things truly are; he saw into his past lives and

The ornate main altar of a monastery in Lhasa. Yak-butter lamps burn brightly in front of gilded effigies of the Buddha. ▼

▲ Followers of the Buddha prostrate themselves before his image in the grounds of the great Swayambunath temple near Kathmandu.

perceived the cause of suffering and how to vanquish it; he realised how to overcome both hatred and attachment. He had now become the 'Awakened One'.

The state of mystical awareness and blessedness which the Buddha reached is known as Nirvana. It is reached through enlightenment, and is the ultimate goal of the Buddhist faith. The Buddha himself spent the rest of his life teaching his followers how to achieve Nirvana, essentially by means of the 'Four Noble Truths'. These are that the world is full of suffering; that suffering is caused by human desires; that suffering stops when desires are renounced; and that the way to achieve this is through the 'Eightfold Path'. This consists of eight principles of behaviour: right understanding, right resolve, right speech, right action, right livelihood, right effort, right mindfulness, and right meditation.

The Buddha's teachings spread south to Sri Lanka, Burma, Thailand and Indochina, where they became known as the *Theravada* tradition. Later, what became known as the *Mahayana* tradition spread north to Sikkim, Bhutan, Nepal, Tibet, Mongolia, China, Korea and Japan. The *Theravada* school regards Nirvana as the means by which the individual is

liberated from earthly existence. The *Mahayana* school, on the other hand, asserts that the disciple who gains enlightenment willingly remains in the world as a *Bodhisattva* to help others along the path.

In Tibet and the other Himalayan countries, there is a branch of the *Mahayana* school known as *Vajrayana* or Tantrism. The practice of Tantra involves meditations and visualisations of Buddha images, with special incantations and rituals. The purpose of this is to take the 'quick path' to Buddhahood by visualising oneself as a Buddha *now*, and constantly acting in a compassionate and caring way as if one were already enlightened. The extensive use of symbolism in Tantric meditations has resulted in the beautiful and complex iconography which adorns the interiors of all the temples of the Tibetan tradition.

One typical representation is of the Wheel of Life, depicting the central Buddhist belief in reincarnation and the need to escape it. Within the Wheel are six realms into which, depending on one's past actions (*karma*), one may be reborn:

gods, demigods, humans, animals, hungry ghosts and hell. In the centre of the Wheel, a pig (ignorance), a cockerel (attachment) and a snake (hatred) pursue each other round in never-ending circles, perpetuating rebirth in the lower realms. However, there is also a Buddha in each realm, doing his best to teach the resident beings how to transcend this constant cycle and leave the Wheel for ever.

The Wheel of Life, held in the claws of Yama, the snarling god of death. ▶

Sadly, however, the amazing journey of these intrepid priests did little to increase the outside world's knowledge about either Lhasa or Tibet. D'Orville died on the way home, and Grueber's report lay in the archives of the Vatican for 250 years before being published.

During the next century several priests, explorers and traders tried to get through to Lhasa, but only one, the Jesuit Desideri, succeeded; for it soon became clear that not only was the city inaccessible, outsiders were not welcome in it and were dubbed 'foreign devils'. This was because the priestly hierarchy of Tibet realised that contact with the outside world would pose a threat to their traditional (and privileged) way of life. When representatives of the East India Company tried to reach the Dalai Lama and negotiate a trade and military alliance, they were rebuffed. It was 1811 before an Englishman, Thomas Manning, got through to the Tibetan capital, and he succeeded where abler explorers had failed, largely because he had no inhibitions about grovelling. 'I was always seeking,' he wrote, 'to kowtow or kneel; and if there was an option between making one curtsey or three, I invariably made three.' Manning, however, was so eccentric a character that when he got back to India, few people believed his account of his adventures.

The aura of mystery surrounding Lhasa was temporarily lifted in 1904, when a British diplomatic mission ended up as a full-scale military invasion, in which troops with fixed bayonets surrounded the Potala Palace of the Dalai Lama. 'At last,' wrote the mission's leader Francis Younghusband, 'the sacred city, for so long hidden behind the ramparts of the Himalayas and guarded from strangers, lay before our eyes.' The victory, however, proved short-lived for the British, who were not prepared to garrison the country they had invaded. They negotiated a treaty which dashed Russian hopes of expanding into the area, and effectively left the country self-governing. The veil of secrecy fell back into place, and for most of the present century visitors from the West have been as unwelcome as ever.

The Great Game

Younghusband's diplomatic mission to Lhasa in 1904 had been a move in 'The Great Game': the name coined by the British spy Arthur Conolly, and used by 19th-century commentators to

◄ **Lhasa's spectacular Potala Palace overlooks the city from a great outcrop of rock known as the 'Red Hill'. The present building was constructed between 1645 and 1694, but is said to contain two rooms dating back to the 7th century. Until 1959, it was the winter residence of Tibet's ruler, the Dalai Lama.**

describe the power struggle between Great Britain, Russia and China (then known as the Lion, the Bear and the Dragon). By the middle of the 19th century Imperial Russia was pushing her frontier relentlessly south-eastward; in 1800 the Russian and British (Indian) empires had been 3,000 miles apart, but by 1860 they were virtually touching. British policy was to defend India from the threat of the Bear by advancing her frontier to the north to gain control of the mountain passes—the potential invasion routes—through the Hindu Kush and the Himalayas. This meant either conquering the mountain people or making alliances with them. Conquest was not easy—even though in those days the cream of the British army was stationed in India, reinforced by those formidable indigenous warriors, the Gurkhas—while the people of the mountains proved reluctant allies. So the order of the day was clandestine diplomacy, with every other northbound trader a spy intent on locating and mapping the passes, and every other soldier a diplomat with a secret treaty sealed into his orders. It was a recipe for disaster.

Players in The Great Game

Most of the players of The Great Game who ventured into the mountain complex from the south met violent deaths. William Moorecroft, the first (and possibly greatest) British agent, spent ten years in present-day Afghanistan, ostensibly looking for horses for his East India Company stud farm. In 1825 he was found dead in the desert. In the 1830s two army officers, Stoddart and Conolly, arrived in Bukhara to offer the Amir help in case he was attacked by the Russians. They were thrown into the Siah Chah (or 'black well'), a 20-foot-deep pit stocked with ticks, snakes and carnivorous reptiles. For several years they were hauled in and out of the pit and mocked; finally they were publicly executed. The itinerant clergyman Joseph Wolff was tied to a horse's tail and flogged, stripped naked and left in waist-deep snow; while Colonel Alexander Gardiner was stabbed 14 times and left for dead, but not before he had seen his young wife and son hacked to death. A few survived: John Wood, a tough, laconic naval officer, the first European to reach the source of the Oxus; the enigmatic Ney Elias, largely disregarded by his fellow countrymen, but hailed by the Russians and Chinese as 'greatest of all the explorers of central Asia'; and an unknown number of Pundits—Indians trained by the British army to make secret journeys into the mountains to collect data for map-making.

To the north the Russians were playing the same game. In the 1850s Peter Semyonov explored the Tien Shan mountains,

▲ A trade mission with a difference: in 1904 (having defeated the Tibetans in battle at Gyangzê), Colonel Younghusband's soldiers entered Lhasa in an attempt to 'persuade' the Dalai Lama to sign a trade agreement with Britain.

"SAVE ME FROM MY FRIENDS!"

▲ A Punch cartoon of 1878 that sympathises with the plight of Afghanistan, which was sandwiched at that time between two 'friendly' powers, Russia and Britain, each eager to 'protect' it from the other.

Playing The Great Game

ONLY A VICTORIAN ROMANTIC, and a British ex-public schoolboy at that, could have coined the phrase *The Great Game,* in one of his letters home, to describe the murderous political shenanigans that Russia, China and Britain got up to during the 19th century in the mountainous area north of India where their empires met and might conceivably be enlarged. Arthur Conolly was the man. A British army officer, he spent much of his short military career (he was executed as a spy by the Amir of Bukhara when only 35) travelling in the disputed territory, often in native disguise, gathering information for Whitehall.

Other brave men followed Conolly. Often the data they brought back provoked open warfare. In 1878, for example, learning of possible Russian plans to invade Afghanistan, the British got in first, sending a substantial army to 'protect' the Amir, the ruler of Afghanistan.

As late as 1904 Britain was still an active player in The Great Game, and chose military invasion over peaceful negotiation when it wanted a trade agreement with Tibet. Ultimately, though, it was a game nobody won. Afghanistan, Nepal and Tibet remained sovereign states, a buffer separating the three players. Then, in 1950, possibly the most dramatic move was made by China when it invaded and occupied Tibet.

▲ A much-decorated Gurkha veteran and his wife. Comrades-in-arms of the British since 1818, soldiers from Nepal's Gurkha villages played a vital role in British military operations during The Great Game.

◄ A painting of Captain Arthur Conolly (1807–42), a famous and enthusiastic British player in The Great Game, wearing the native-style clothes he often assumed as a disguise.

Wildlife of the Himalayas

THE HIMALAYAS ARE HOME to a great variety of animals. In the Terai, or jungle, at the base of the mountains (about 600 feet), live crocodiles, elephants, rhinoceroses, tigers, leopards and monkeys. Higher up, in the foothills, are bears—both black and brown—jackals, and rare red pandas, also known as cat bears. Above the level of the tree line (13,000 feet), are wild goats and sheep—many bearing enormous horns—wild asses and also wild yaks, the world's highest-dwelling mammal. At all three levels there are deer, the favourite prey of carnivores.

In most areas, local people observe religious taboos against killing, but this does not mean that the animals of the mountains face no threat from man. Virgin forests are constantly being cleared for firewood or for agricultural land, leaving many animals without any habitat. Others have been hunted to the edge of extinction by Westerners for some trophy they bear: the markhor goat for its four-foot-long corkscrew horns; the fanged musk deer for its musk gland, used in the manufacture of high-grade perfumes; and the magnificent snow leopard, for its beautiful, dense pelt.

The red panda, or cat bear, is about the size of a fox. ▶

▲ This mild-looking snow leopard can kill animals three times its own size. It rarely descends below 6,000 feet, and has been seen as high as 18,000 feet.

▲ The Himalayan monal pheasant, Nepal's national symbol, is found principally on open scrubland high in the Nepalese mountains.

▲ The musk deer, highly prized for its musk gland, also has long canine teeth, which it uses for territorial combat.

The Bengal tiger was once common in the Himalayan foothills, but is now found mostly in lower, jungle regions. ▼

which lie north of the Taklimakan Desert. The announced purpose of his visit was to collect scientific data but he nevertheless took with him a troop of Cossack cavalry, 'to show the flag'. In the 1860s a husband-and-wife team, Alexis and Olga Fedchenko, explored the huge, ice-choked valleys of the northern Pamirs, discovering not only some of the world's largest glaciers, but also attractive deposits of coal, iron, marble and gold. In the 1870s and '80s Nicholas Przhevalski explored the Taklimakan and the northern reaches of Tibet. As he saw it:

> The scientific attractiveness of central Asia is counterbalanced by the appalling difficulty of the terrain—wind-lashed deserts devoid of water, temperatures alternating between burning heat and searing cold—and a suspicious and barbarous population.

Few expeditions have ever had to endure such hardships as Przhevalski's; nonetheless he collected a wealth of information, noting 1,000 specimens of birds, 3,000 insects and 4,000 plants, as well as discovering the wild horse now named after him.

Ironically, it was the third of the players, the patient and experienced Dragon, who did best out of The Great Game. The Chinese acquired more influence in the area by diplomacy than the Russians and British ever acquired by force or stealth.

The Naturalists

The second half of the 19th century was a great age for fact collecting. All over the world scientists of every discipline were amassing data, and for botanists the Himalayas were a particularly exciting field: the mountains rose so steeply that an enormous variety of plants could be found in a comparatively small area. In 1847 Joseph Hooker arrived in India. Only 31, he had already spent three years as James Clark Ross's botanist in Antarctica and was utterly devoted to his work.

His botanising began in the Terai—a belt of swamp, dense undergrowth and bamboo at the foot of the Himalayas—where he classified 850 different species of trees and plants. His journeys were often extremely arduous, as he records:

> We were wading much of the time through deep mud. Leeches were everywhere. They got into my hair, hung onto my eyelids, and crawled up my legs and my back; the sores they produced were not healed for five months, and I retain the scars to this day.

It must have been a relief to ascend from Terai to rain forest, where he identified 400 orchids and 280 ferns, and then to the more open woodland above 5,000 feet. This, as Hooker recorded, is a world of deep gorges, fast-flowing rivers, and a cornucopia of flowering trees and shrubs. Here he classified 430 species, including many that are now established favourites in English gardens—buddleia, clematis, hydrangea, magnolia and rhododendron. Above this mainly deciduous woodland are the pine forests: juniper, larch and the monumental chir pines, often clinging to slopes so steep that the roots of one are level with the topmost branches of its neighbour. Higher still, above the tree line, are aconite and edelweiss, saxifrage and gentian, and the highest plants in the world, ermania and ranunculus. Hooker climbed to 18,000 feet (and few people in those days had ever climbed higher) to classify them.

It is now reckoned that there are about 6,500 known species of trees, shrubs and wild flowers in Nepal and Sikkim. Hooker identified over 4,000 of them. This was a feat of rare endurance and erudition: sometimes he was hacking his way through the Terai, at other times reeling with nausea and snow blindness among the great peaks. His monumental work, *Flora of British India*, is a remarkable and highly readable compendium.

The Mountaineers

Climbing is a modern pastime. It is only in the last 100 years that people have pitted their skill and strength against the mountains of central Asia for pleasure—although before that a number of peaks had been climbed in the course of duty during the Great Trigonometrical Survey of India.

The first person to climb in the Himalayas 'purely for my own enjoyment' was the Englishman W.W. Graham, who in 1883 reached the summit of Forked Peak (20,340 feet). A few years later, in 1892, the first major expedition 'to explore and survey the glacial area of the Karakoram' was sponsored by the Royal Geographical Society and led by the experienced alpinist Martin Conway. Conway and his team pioneered a technique of mountaineering which was followed for the next 75 years: first the long trek, with columns of porters, through the foothills; then the setting up of a base camp at the foot of the mountain to be climbed; then the laying siege to that mountain, with a succession of camps being pushed ever higher up its slopes; and finally the assault on the summit. Conway climbed higher than anyone had ever climbed before—to the top of Pioneer Peak (22,600 feet); but his greatest achievement was that, with the help of his Gurkha officer, Lieutenant Bruce, he established a rapport with his porters. Hitherto the people of the mountains had been reluctant climbers, regarding the Europeans' obsession with 'conquering' their gods as blasphemy. But Conway got them on his side. Time has proved his wisdom; for virtually all

▲ A long line of porters carrying the supplies of a large Everest expedition.

Aluminium ladders, roped together, bridge a crevasse that would have been a major obstacle 50 years ago. ▶

Today's Himalayan mountaineer: a Sherpa guide wearing high-tech clothing, with nylon rope, plastic boots, steel crampons and ice axe, and Polaroid glacier-glasses. By contrast, George Mallory and Edward Norton in 1922 (inset) wore tweeds and leather fell-climbing boots.

The Intrepid Mountaineers

MOUNTAINEERS HAVE ALWAYS challenged the frontiers of what people believe to be possible. In the early 1920s, when the first assaults on Everest were being planned, doctors were not even sure that men could survive on the mountain's summit. Those who decided to find out were clad in tweeds, woolly pullovers, and nailed boots; they used primitive ice axes, frail manila ropes, cumbersome primus stoves, fragile tents and inadequate maps. They were remarkably brave men: the astronauts of their time.

Since then there have been dramatic improvements in equipment, and in the medical and psychological understanding of what mountaineers face at the highest altitudes on Earth. Today's Everesters, equipped with the best that modern technology can provide, supported by sophisticated medical research and familiar with the route, are also courageous; but they are no better mountaineers than the early pioneers. They are simply challenging new frontiers.

Nevertheless, a new humility is present. Mountains may be climbed, but they are no longer 'conquered'; and their environments are now being respected. The siege tactics of the huge, costly expeditions of a few years ago are generally frowned on, although still sometimes mounted by countries or groups concerned more with glory than with ethics.

the great peaks of central Asia were first climbed by expeditions which owed their success to their native porters.

The early years of this century witnessed many big nationalistic expeditions intent on laying siege to the mountains. In 1909 the Duke of Abruzzi tackled K2 with a team of 350, in 1924 Norton tackled Everest with 400, in 1934 Merkl took 500 to Nanga Parbat. Today small, mobile groups of three or four world-class climbers sometimes achieve in days more than their predecessors achieved in months. Everest, for example, defied the big battalions for half a century; yet in recent years it has been climbed solo, by women, by a father-and-son team, and by more than a dozen different routes; it has even been climbed in midwinter and without oxygen. Package tours now regularly take trekkers to Everest's Base Camp, while those willing to pay can arrange to have themselves guided to the summit itself.

Mountaineering is still a hazardous pastime, and those who take the Himalayas lightly are liable to end up buried in them. Nonetheless almost anyone who is fit and careful can now go on the sort of treks which 50 years ago would have been classed as climbs.

Tourists and Trekkers

For the many tourists who now visit the south-facing slopes of the mountains, the most popular centres are Srinagar in the Vale of Kashmir and Kathmandu in Nepal.

The Vale of Kashmir is renowned for its rich palaces, beautiful scenery and magnificent lakes, the best known of which is Lake Dal. This is the site of Srinagar, 'the Venice of India': a city with as many canals as streets, and almost as many houseboats as houses—numerous because the Maharajah of Kashmir prohibited Europeans from owning land. In the mountains to the northeast is the Amanurth Cave, where a huge column of permanent ice has been formed by water welling up from a natural spring and freezing solid in the cold air. This column is sacred to Siva, the Hindu god of creation, and is visited each year by thousands of pilgrims.

Kathmandu, the capital of Nepal, is every bit as beautiful as Srinagar, though in a more rumbustious way. The city is old—it was founded in AD 732—a maze of narrow streets with overhanging balconies, and squares jam-packed with markets, monuments and temples, all filled with bustling, good-humoured people. In recent years Kathmandu has become an immensely popular centre for trekkers.

Because there are virtually no roads in the mountain areas of Nepal, walking has always been the local people's main method

▲ Early-morning quiet in Kathmandu's Durbar Square, the site of more than 50 impressive temples and monuments.

Kathmandu—Gateway to the Mountains

THE COLOURFUL CAPITAL of Nepal, Kathmandu, lies at an altitude of over 4,300 feet at the crossroads of two major ancient trade routes. It nestles between several great mountain ranges in a large, flat, fertile valley—the Kathmandu Valley—along with two other magnificent medieval cities: Patan and Bhaktapur.

Kathmandu supposedly takes its name from a wooden temple—the Kasthamandap, or 'House of Wood'—that stands in Durbar Square, in the very centre of the old city. Numerous other temples and shrines crowd this square, bearing witness to the depth of religious devotion that pervades the area. In fact, the whole Kathmandu Valley has so many holy places that it is said to be inhabited by more gods than people. Some of the world's most imposing religious buildings are situated here—among them the Hindu temple of Changdu Narayan and the glorious Buddhist stupas of Swayambunath and Bodnath.

Kathmandu itself has two distinct aspects—to the west, the old city, characterised by red-brick buildings with intricately carved wooden façades; and to the east a sprawling, modern industrial city, which is expanding at an alarming rate into the precious arable lands of the valley. Yet even the modern quarter retains a strong traditional ambience, as sacred cows wander amiably among sophisticated businessmen.

▲ A shop in the city centre with a not unusual visitor: a cow, sacred to Hindus, decked with festive garlands.

◄ Vegetables for sale from farms close to the city, watched over by the Buddha's all-seeing eyes.

Foresting the Mountains

DEFORESTATION IS ONE OF THE MOST serious problems confronting the people of the Himalayas.

Down the centuries, the natural forests growing on the south-facing slopes of the mountains have been vital to the ecology of the region. In addition to providing a habitat for many wild birds and animals, their shade and, in particular, their roots have enabled the soil on steep slopes to act as a giant sponge, holding in the heavy monsoon rains that fall in this region and then releasing the water gradually. Where there are no trees, there is no wildlife; instead, there is flooding and catastrophic soil erosion.

Yet the people of the mountains have also needed the trees for firewood, consuming them at an average rate of a ton-and-a-half per family, per year. Until recently, the forests have made up this loss, but now, with an increasing local population and large numbers of tourists, the balance has broken down. In some parts of the Himalayas, wooded hillsides have already become barren deserts.

Two men in particular have spent much of their lives working on this problem: an Indian, Chand Saklani, and the New Zealander, Sir Edmund Hillary, perhaps better known in the West for being the first man to climb Mount Everest. Chand started a campaign in a remote corner of northern India, persuading the women to 'plant a little forest round every home'. The idea caught on and the women's hillsides are now some of the most densely wooded areas in the Himalayas.

Sir Edmund's work is on a larger scale. Since 1960, his Himalayan Trusts have planted 100,000 trees a year and have helped to create and maintain the Sagarmatha National Park, in which Mount Everest is situated. They have also founded schools for the Sherpas, as well as hospitals and medical centres. The Sherpas, who welcome him as a luminary, say, 'He is mother and father to us all.'

▲ **Nepalese firewood-sellers carry their wares through an area that has already been cleared of most vegetation.**

◀ **Sir Edmund and Lady Hillary, with Sherpa friends, outside a Nepalese hospital funded through Sir Edmund's tireless campaigning.**

Soil erosion can here be seen destroying the terraces on these steep, deforested slopes in the Kathmandu Valley. ▶

▲ An early stage in the process of
reforestation: a Sherpa forester tends pine
seedlings in a nursery in the Everest region.

of travel. Well-worn trails connect village to village and reach northward to form ancient trade routes into Tibet. Today's trekkers who follow these trails not only see some of the most spectacular and beautiful scenery in the world, they also come into contact with an outgoing, friendly people.

The Mountains Today

The mountain stronghold has been breached, and its people have probably seen more changes in the last generation than in the previous thousand years.

In the mountains of the northwest, Soviet engineers have siphoned off so much water from the Amudarya River for irrigation that the desert wells below are drying up and the desert people are being forced to give up their nomadic way of life.

In the central plateau, Chinese Red Guards and Tibetan malcontents have torn the monasteries apart and looted their treasures, while in the mountains of the south whole areas have been deforested and mountaineers' and trekkers' discarded rubbish is turning the slopes into a garbage tip.

But modern ways have brought benefits also. Across the Tien Shan, forestry workers are planting more than a million trees a year in the world's most ambitious forestry programme. In Tibet the Chinese are bringing into production the country's vast mineral resources. And for the Sherpas of Nepal, whose lives have been particularly hard hit—they have had to meet the needs both of the trekkers and of large numbers of Tibetan refugees and their herds of domestic animals—international charitable foundations have come to the rescue with aid for reforestation. Sir Edmund Hillary, too, has given his support, helping the Sherpas to build bridges, schools and hospitals. The winds of change have not always been ill winds.

It was into this beautiful, changing, troubled land that Peter Somerville-Large ventured, with his writer's eye and his Irish wit, and returned triumphantly to tell the tale.

Introducing *To Everest and Beyond*

It was a crazy idea, two Europeans travelling from Kathmandu to Everest and the holy places of Nepal and Tibet on yakback, and in fact Peter Somerville-Large and his companion had to fall back eventually on transport of a more motorised sort. They pressed on, though, through remarkable lands to mysterious places on a journey that was an exciting, moving, sometimes hilarious experience—both for them and now for the reader.

PART 2 · AN ADVENTURE

TO EVEREST
AND BEYOND

by Peter Somerville-Large

Condensed from the author's book TO THE NAVEL OF THE WORLD,
published by Hamish Hamilton

CHAPTER 1
Spring in Kathmandu

'IF A YAK WAS OFFERED to me as a present, I would not accept it,' said my old friend Nhuche. 'Their karma is not good.'

It was March 1985, and Nhuche had just met me at Kathmandu airport with his Volkswagen and chauffeur. I had first stayed at Nhuche's school in Swayambunath, a suburb of Kathmandu, in 1955 and had always hoped to return. Now, in my sixty-second year, after rereading Stevenson's *Travels with a Donkey*, I was planning a journey through Nepal to Everest with a yak.

The yak is the highest-dwelling mammal in the world. Wild yaks, which are the size of large bison, with immense horns and tongues so harsh that they can scrape the flesh off bones, have sadly been slaughtered to the edge of extinction, but the numbers of the domesticated yak, a beast of burden in Nepal and Tibet since ancient times, are increasing.

Everyone at home in Dublin had thought 'Travels with a Yak' a charming idea. My wife Gillian had been beguiled by the thought of a shaggy little yak as my travelling companion, though she had been less thrilled when she learnt that I also planned to be accompanied by a tall, handsome, Anglo-Irish girl called Caroline. I had to explain that Caroline would be there just because she could take photographs and speak Chinese and—yaks or no yaks—the frontier between Nepal and Tibet now being open for the first time, I wished very much also to go to Tibet.

Gillian studied the lists Caroline sent: '… thermal underwear, lipsalves, ice crampons, flea powder, snow glasses, foot alcohol, nylon rope'—that was for tethering yaks.

'She won't approve of your boots,' said Gillian. I had bought an Irish brand that had been used in the Falklands. Afterwards someone told me that water had seeped into the soles of theirs on the spongy bogs of Goose Green. Port Stanley was recaptured in spite of them.

▲ The calm, wise eyes of the Buddha look out from the tower above the temple at Swayambunath.

I hadn't visited Kathmandu for thirty years—the average lifespan of a Nepali—and then I had been one of just two tourists. Now I steeled myself for changes, and as Nhuche's chauffeur drove us, I tried to identify all the places that had been fields when I was last here. The new buildings spread down the valley towards Swayambunath, where Nhuche's school was situated beneath the sacred hill crowned by the famous temple with the four pairs of wavy eyes.

Nhuche is a Newar, a member of the race which has always inhabited the Kathmandu Valley. As a young man he went to Tibet to study Buddhism, staying

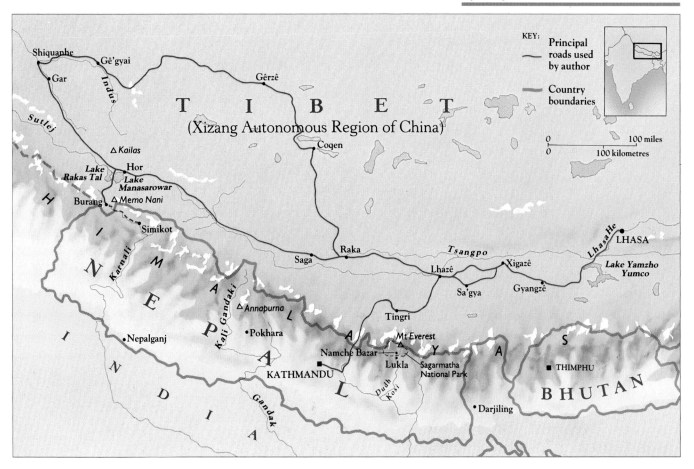

▲ The territory the author travelled through after flying to Kathmandu. After exploring the Everest region by yak, he and his companion journeyed across the vast emptiness of Tibet.

in a house where a woman was married to five brothers. He could tell which brother was in her bedroom by the shoes placed outside the door. When he returned to Nepal, he started a school which became well known. This year, 1985, his sixty-fifth, he had opened a sister establishment for orphans on the principle that one school would pay for the other. The rich would help the poor. The new school below the village consisted of three buildings, a courtyard and a garden. Above the classrooms the small, community prayer room contained a wooden statue of Buddha, a picture of Christ and an altar covered with flowers.

In the evening I walked up the flight of stone steps to the temple through trees shivering with monkeys. There were just as many as there had been thirty years ago, but now there were beggars as well who waited for prey. A thin arm stretched from a sheet, a boy with a gashed mouth followed me up the steps, two at a time. 'Hello, hello, what is your name?' shouted a wild man, running out of a shrine rattling a bowl. From the centre of the temple's plinth rose a spire composed of thirteen gilded discs, graded in size, symbolising the thirteen stages of Nirvana, topped by an umbrella-like canopy. Giant blue eyes beneath the golden top-knot gazed out complacently in four directions above the question marks that represented stylised noses. The four faces may have shown cynicism rather than the all-seeing power of the godhead, as they looked down on the antique dealers among the shrines and the foreigners twirling prayer wheels. Dirt, stench, monkeys, beggars, tourists—it was still a place where religion was practised among the cares of life. An evening wind stirred the trees as sunset glowed over city and valley. Above the huddle of shrines and buildings, the strings of circus-coloured prayer flags crackled and the buildings became alive with movement.

In the village at the foot of the steps, the hippies came out like crepuscular animals attracted by the last glow of the evening sun. The small colony living here had found the combination of squalor and beauty irresistible, particularly when it could also enjoy the Nepalis' tolerance and lack of curiosity. They were subdued, almost with an air of somnambulance: the dusty-haired woman carrying a baby on her back; the American saddhu in saffron robes, his hair pulled back in a bun; another man, also with long hair, but worn loose as a fairy princess's, complemented by an equally vigorous frosted beard. The hairy men sat on their haunches swallowing little pastries dipped in yellow sauce. They were gaunt compared with the confident Tibetans walking past arrayed in cloaks that fell down to coloured felt boots.

All night dogs yapped and howled, a sound known locally as Kathmandu music. At daybreak Swayambunath was wrapped in haze but, as the sun rose,

fields and houses gradually emerged into view and sharp colours took hold—the gold of the spire towering above the trees, the glare of blue eyes painted on white, the dark green of the valley, the shining wall of distant snow mountains, and the tiny children who rushed out into the garden under the statue of Buddha, where lessons would be held among the flowers. Around the gateway leading up to the temple, among the monkeys cavorting in and out of sacred stones, some Tibetans were praying and prostrating themselves beside a line of taxis. A group was straining to turn an enormous prayer wheel. From here it was a short walk down to the river and across the bridge to the centre of the city.

Festive Kathmandu

Much was as I remembered in the small area where Kathmandu retains its market squares and temples and manages to preserve a world which tourism has not changed. The rose-brick houses, with their blackened, intricately carved doors and windows and jutting eaves almost touching each other across the

◄ The vivid, tumultuous street bazaars of Kathmandu, largely free of motor traffic, are crowded with traders and their customers from all over Nepal.

lanes and gateways, were ancient buildings which had survived the earthquake of 1934. Everything that was wood was carved with robust detail. Below the steps of a temple a pile of fruit and vegetables showed a similar obsession for pattern—an hour must have been spent arraying the onions and brinjals and oranges like a knot garden. A cow snatched at salad heads. Behind latticework the dark interiors of shops and houses swarmed convivially with people like a beehive on a summer's day. Out in the street were other swarms—flies homing in across the sacks of rice and dhal to the trays of sticky cakes.

Here was the same rich mixture of people: Newaris, Rais and Tamang from nearby villages, porters loaded down with burdens that would crush a pony, a file of Sherpa women each with a conical basket roped across her head. Past a circle of pedicabs with brightly coloured hoods, an elephant strode down to the river with two boys perched on its back.

The traffic clashed with my memories. I could recall precisely the special, ancient hubbub of a city without motor traffic, but now cars pushed their way through the crowds down dark little lanes never meant to accommodate them. A policeman vainly blew his whistle above the infuriated noise of horns, as two Australian girls dressed in little more than bikinis argued with a taxi driver about their fare.

It would have been a grand day for sightseeing, except that it was the festival of Holi and the air was full of flying plastic bags filled with coloured dye. Every child in the city seemed to be armed with powder and lying in wait. The little plastic missiles came plummeting down from rooftop and window or darted straight out of a doorway. Soon my hair was blue and my trousers and jacket were smeared red, as if I had been wounded. All day the flying reds, blues, greens and yellows slapped many a tourist so that he resembled something out of a very young child's colouring book. A Hawaiian shirt received a red sunset as the podgy wearer was photographing a woman kneeling beside a small metal shrine with her tray of offerings. Not only tourists—by evening almost everyone in the city had become a painted victim of carnival. The wandering cows were battered with splodges.

▲ The woodwork in traditional Nepalese homes is exuberantly carved, often with figures derived from Hindu as well as Buddhist legend, in a country where both religions are important in the people's lives.

I went to the Kathmandu Guest House, a place that makes an instant rapport with any traveller who leaves the crowded streets and finds himself a few minutes later in a lush garden full of flowers, nursing a glass of beer. I have met people who, hearing the name, wince with great pleasure. The food was good and clean, service efficient, terms cheap. The atmosphere evoked a stately past. I sat with my glass surrounded by cannas, arums, ferns and the Corinthian pillars built for the old nobility. Here I could learn the best route to a mountain top, find out about permits, pack animals and porters, where to meet a male or female partner, acquire cheap tickets or dispose of surplus equipment.

A group of overlanders came in on their way from Australia to London looking like people who had braved desperate odds, after crossing India pinioned in two sweaty rows in the back of a truck. The Guest House offered a short respite, and then on to Karachi. They collected in a corner of the garden, gulping beer and listening to their group leader lecturing them predictably. 'Always buy two toilet rolls at a time if you have the chance ... Respect the driver, we're all one big family ... See you later at the bar ...'

I went over to the notice board. Meningitis shots available from Tek hospital, free and painless. Deutschbus to Europe, some seats available.

'My dear fellow. How nice to see you after all this time.'

Here was my old friend, Promode, looking encouragingly unchanged. We talked briefly about the vanished medieval past. I praised the Guest House and mentioned that I understood it had once been a Rana palace.

'Only C-class Ranas lived here, I can assure you.' Promode was a former member of that ruling elite, excusing its fall from grace in a coup some years ago. 'Come. My car is outside.' He escorted me to an ancient-looking Volkswagen. When I had known him before he had owned one of the dozen or so serviceable vehicles in the capital, all of which had been carried up in pieces from India on the backs of porters. His had stood out from the other little Model T Fords, a long, low-slung monster with a fish-head exhaust and a curving, brass horn in the shape of a snake with ruby eyes.

We drove past the Tunde Kehl, the open space in the city centre where, last

Colourful Holi Festival

HOLI IS CARNIVAL TIME all over India and Nepal. Celebrated at the time of full moon in late February or early March, Holi is a Hindu festival heralding the spring. In many areas, it is enjoyed as a five-day-long feast culminating in an outburst of revels, fireworks and parades: a day on which the world is turned upside-down.

Holi is marked by the burning of effigies, the singing of bawdy songs and mock fights between men and women. Its most important characteristics, however, are laughter and the enjoyment of colour. People throw coloured powders at one another, smear coloured pastes and squirt coloured liquids; and today, with the coming of Western technology, they often spray coloured aerosols.

This sort of response to the end of winter is common among men and women the world over, but it is particularly extravagant in societies such as Nepal's, which are normally very decorous and

▲ Fortunately most of the coloured pastes and powders happily thrown around during Nepalese religious festivals can be washed off fairly easily!

rule-bound. During Holi, for just a few days, all the rules are ignored, respectability is unimportant, youth is celebrated, and reverence for age and experience is forgotten. It is a time, literally, to tweak old men's beards, or make them do foolish things. Holi is rebellion made safe: life and laughter asserting themselves within agreed limits against God or the gods, and against custom, law and commandments.

One of Kathmandu's
many old palaces,
here decked out for
a royal visit. ▶

time I was here, a whole lot of animals were having their heads chopped off as part of some ceremony. Promode pointed out the statue of Jung Bahadur, who seized power in 1846.

'His statue survives only because he was a relative of the king.'

Since the political changes which caused the Ranas to lose their power and privileges, a good many of the Rana statues have been discreetly removed; in one provincial city an ex-prime minister presides over the local garbage dump. Meanwhile, King Birendra has asserted his position as divine monarch of Nepal by pulling down his palace and building a glossy new white model that stands behind wrought-iron railings and evokes Hollywood and soap operas.

Promode showed me some of the remaining Rana palaces scattered in a dowdy group in the old compound. They had been fairly down-at-heel thirty years ago, a number of them half-ruined in the earthquake of 1934. Their owners had tended to spend their time visiting their other palaces in Benares or moving on to Calcutta to dispose of vast sums of rupees on wine, women and song. Now they had been demolished, or taken over by the government, or let out. The American Club rented most of the buildings owned by Promode's cousin, Dermode. Where was the one owned by the cousin who was a field-marshal? The baroque extravaganza run by another cousin as a private zoo?

Promode waved a dismissive hand: 'Rented or ruined.'

His own palace, the Hitty Durbar, was one of the few to remain in private hands, but not without a struggle. In 1955 his chief worry had been how to dismiss his sixty remaining servants and ensure that they would not starve. Now it was how to collect his rents.

The Hitty Durbar was a white-stuccoed, three-storeyed building, which had been designed in the early years of the century by a Japanese architect who had been an admirer of the Graeco-Roman style. Massive balconies, whose wrought-iron balustrades alternated with empty niches which had never contained statues, were supported by a forest of Corinthian pillars. The exterior retained the air of a Riviera casino. But inside—all utterly changed. All offices and shops.

I indulged in nostalgia, recalling the old decor: the drawing room with its heavy gilt chairs and pink chandeliers; the walls covered with hunting trophies and family portraits of kings and great-uncles among splayed tiger skins and elephant tusks; the lines and lines of sepia photographs of solar topi'd figures squatting beside dead tigers, attended by elephants and beaters and soldiers and bearers; how we sat under the dusty chandelier nibbling sugar rice and flicking cigarette ash into silver-mounted elephants' feet, looked down on by maharajas displaying blazing decorations on golden jackets and maharanis in prim Victorian black.

All were gone; the tigers snarling to reveal plaster tongues between finger-length eyeteeth, the silver equestrian statue presented to Promode's grandfather by Edward VII, the bird-of-paradise crown with its plumes and pearls and fringe of emeralds. At least, almost all gone—the flat that he retained on the top floor contained a few relics of old decency, ormolu furniture and a Venetian mirror. Promode and myself were just recognisable.

'Say that we have become elderly persons, Peter, though not old.'

He was horrified by my plans. Like most Nepalese living in Kathmandu, he found the idea of moving outside the valley appalling. At one time he had been governor of a remote hill station and had never forgotten the awful experience. All his sacrifices were so that he could stay in the city.

'In those primitive areas there are no modern amenities. It will be such a hard life. I pity you with all my heart.'

Nevertheless he helped me in my search for permits. I went round the tourist agencies which have proliferated in the boom years of international travel: Tiger Tops, Mountain Travel, Yak and Yeti, and numerous others. You might ski down Everest, float by raft down a river, observe tigers in a game park, study Buddhism or join a queue to climb a mountain. It was all big business. But no one sought adventures with yaks, so no company supplied them, not even Yak and Yeti.

'You want to ride one of these dirty animals? I would not advise such a foolish enterprise.'

I would have to find my own yak.

Onwards to Namche Bazar

As Caroline was not yet ready to join me—she was off to Lhasa for a quick trip with a friend—I would take a flight to Lukla on my own and trek ahead up to Namche Bazar, good acclimatisation experience before tackling higher elevations.

Outside Lukla I paid to enter the huge Mount Sagarmatha National Park, which stretches to the Tibetan border on the far side of Everest. Sagarmatha, 'Goddess Mother of the Mountain Snow', is what Nepalis call Everest. In return, I received a leaflet which exhorted the trekker to keep Everest tidy.

The park is one of six created since 1973 by the Nepalese government in an attempt to lessen the destruction of the primary forest, which has traditionally provided fuel and building materials. In the past thirty years the cut-and-come-again custom that controlled the gathering of wood has been put under fatal pressure by a huge increase in population. Nor have the forests been helped by the arrival of visitors from outside Nepal.

During the 1960s big mountain expeditions began invading the Khumbu area with armies of non-Sherpa porters who, unaware of local tradition, cut down trees along the trail. Porters, retained for months at the foot of the big peaks, made devastating raids on the juniper forests for firewood. The Sherpas in their turn discarded age-old restrictions on collecting firewood. Then after 1950 thousands of land-hungry Tibetan refugees arrived, also needing fuel and space.

The National Park is intended to benefit the Sherpas by preserving what little forest remains, restricting the activities of tourists and carrying out some reafforestation. But the people still largely rely on wood for fuel and old men grumble because of the prohibitions on livestock. Cattle and zopkioks (yaks crossbred with cattle) are forbidden to graze among newly planted saplings, while goats, the great changers of landscape, formerly a mainstay of village economy, are not allowed in the park at all. The upper forest teems with pheasants, which are a protected species, and these birds dart out of the greenery onto the terraced fields looking for potato shoots. There are places where Sherpas have given up cultivation altogether. While the need for preserving the forest is recognised, the hacking away at green timber and removal of forest cover continue inexorably. Looking at denuded hillsides it is hard to remember that Buddhism holds it a sin to cut down trees, except in unavoidable circumstances.

I walked towards Namche in drizzle among oaks, whitebeam and hemlock buttressed by ivy-dark rhododendrons yet to flower. Further up were Himalayan pines. They had been salvaged in the nick of time. Outside the park the hills were shaved like lamas' heads, with here and there the stubble of felled trunks left as a reminder of where the forest had stood.

For a time I was in the company of a couple of Englishmen who had completed a quickie course in Buddhism in a gompa near Kathmandu and were hoping to enlarge their religious experience. Then an Australian, Ted, came along.

'I'm buggered. But I wouldn't miss it for worlds.' Above us were the famous snow peaks dotted with mountaineers. Below the trail rushed the milk-white waters of the Dudh Kosi River.

'Where are you going?'

'Base Camp.' His panting was horrible. Each winded visitor contributed to grotesque changes. At present around five thousand trekkers come this way annually, and there are times of the year when there are more visitors than Sherpas in Namche Bazar.

As elsewhere in the Himalayas, trekkers divided between those in groups and independent travellers. The guidebooks unhesitatingly recommended group trekking through agencies which kept people all together under control. But the independents persisted in great numbers, trying to be wild and free. Most carried

their own rucksacks, provisions and lavatory paper, and were mean. They drank black tea because it was a rupee less than white, shamelessly badgered the Sherpas for bargains, and tended to discuss prices among themselves rather than great thoughts.

'I'd hate to be reincarnated into a baggage coolie,' said my companion, watching another weary tour group plod up followed by the long line of porters steadying the orange and blue luggage with the aid of straps across their fore-heads. This was no way to experience the forest.

I passed an Englishwoman with a huge pack on her back, tears streaming down her face. Her husband was far ahead. 'He wouldn't allow me a porter. He said he couldn't bear to see the little fellows carrying so much. He wouldn't listen when I told him he was depriving them of money.'

A Sherpa Welcome

Arriving in Namche Bazar I put up in a lodge where I experienced for the first time the rich, enveloping hospitality of a Sherpa household. To the father, mother, two sons, two daughters and the odd friend or stray servant were added the trekkers who called in throughout the season, stayed a night or two and moved on. Father, whose name was Passang, was a sick man who rarely got out of bed. Between helping their mother with the housework, the daughters spent their leisure with their schoolbooks or brushing their long black hair. From time to time an old man would appear with a puppy thrust into his trousers, the woolly head peering out above his waistband.

▲ Nepal's beautiful forests have been completely destroyed in certain areas; in others, they are seriously threatened by the firewood needs of a rapidly growing population and the country's many foreign visitors.

The children did their homework for the Hillary School. I helped the youngest with his English. He had written his name in Roman script in the front of his exercise book, Ang Noma Sherpa. Ang was passionately learning English, the key to prosperity. 'What is a tortoise? What is a dictator, please? How do you spell aeroplane?' He planned to become a guide.

The lodge was a long, two-storey building with a stone terrace in front. The bottom rooms were used for animals. On the second floor the household lived in the main room, which ran across the top of the house under a high wooden ceiling. Everything was wooden: floorboards, dresser, beds, benches and shutters cut from the forest. Glazed windows, the glass carried in by plane and up by porter, were an innovation of the last fifteen years.

The first task of the morning was to light the fire around which life revolved. Guests lay in their sleeping-bags watching one of the daughters bring in bundles of sticks and pats of dung, and then kneel down and blow, head on one side, coaxing the first cigarette-end spark into a fierce little fire that would burn all day. There was no chimney and the smoke made its way upwards, nudging the ceiling which, after decades of smoky caresses, had acquired the sheen of black enamel.

The other daughter was carrying up the first of the day's relay of water in two plastic containers once used for petrol, and pouring it into a line of shining copper cauldrons. Apart from the altar set between shelves of religious knick-knacks, these cauldrons were the most precious things in the house. The menu card hanging on the wall, written in neat, Hillary School script with prices marked against each item, offered yak steak, momos (Sherpa dumplings), fried

Namche Bazar, the main town of Khumbu, the region around Mount Everest, and home of the Sherpa people. Sherpas are an ancient tribe who crossed into Nepal from Tibet centuries ago. They are famous now for their bravery and knowledge of the mountains. ▼

potatoes, eggs, porridge, rice and Mustang coffee laced with rakshi, a powerful alcoholic spirit.

As the sun rose, a deep braying came from next door, where two young lamas in saffron robes sat on a rooftop bellowing through collapsible Tibetan trumpets. To sound the long wavering notes that rose or fell according to lung power, they rested the nine-foot-long silver-painted horns on an oil drum. Sometimes the noise was a sigh and a whisper; then one of them would blow hard and a note snorted all over the town, a vast raspberry, a piece of grass between giant thumbs, a magnified corncrake.

'Namaste.'—'I salute the god within you.'

The fire-lighting daughter bent over my sleeping-bag with tea and the smile that was part of her, like a limb. In the smoke and soot the sleeping-bags moved like pupae about to reveal insects. A bearded head poked out, another, a third that had no beard and could have been a woman. Men and women were mixed up. Ted, for instance, was mixed up with his porters, two smiling Sherpa girls. He sat and glared at the other guests, a pretty moon-faced porter at each shoulder, looking like a Moghul prince dallying with court ladies.

Mine host and hostess (smiling) watched without curiosity as the talk began about Bali, Singapore, Bangkok, Tamil Nadu, Kashmir, Burma—a brief stay in Burma since you are only allowed six days and the Burmese make everything expensive. Sri Lanka was cheap, so was the commune in Kerala. You could last on a hundred dollars a month. The Gilgit trail took you up to Hunza, full of old men who lived to be a hundred on a diet of apricots. Hunza was quite cheap, but during the summer the bazaar tended to run out of soft drinks like Coca-Cola. Nepal was cheap. Langtang, Manang, Muktinath, Jomosom, Annapurna …

The other topic was sickness, although the only person here who was actually supine and would lie in his sleeping-bag all day was another Australian, who had dislocated his knee on a piece of Khumbu ice while returning from Base Camp. He seemed quite content to spend his time practising Nepali swear words he had learned from his porter.

The little room off the passage could not have been worse for people so obsessed with the state of their health. In the gloom they peered to see if their urine was cloudy or green. Slits in the wooden floor gave a glimpse of dark regions where what went down was mixed with leaves and straw and carried away by yak to fertilise tiny fields.

In surroundings like this, medieval Europeans must have lain and waited in dread for the coming of the Black Death. Now the menace was AMS: 'How's your head?' was the constant question in between the talk of travel and bargains, and the checking of pulses. Acute Mountain Sickness is said to affect one person in five. Symptoms to watch for at altitude include wet or dry coughs, abdominal cramps, large amounts of gas after eating, breathlessness and periodic breathing:

In a land so rugged that the wheel is often useless, the immense loads that porters carry require both strength and a remarkable sense of balance.

Prayer Wheels—Sowing Hope in the World

PRAYER WHEELS AND PRAYER FLAGS are used throughout Nepal and Tibet as a means of spreading prayers and religious messages across the world. Both have holy texts written on them, and these are believed to be blown far and wide on the wind.

Prayer wheels come in many sizes, and are usually rotated by hand. Small wheels, made of wood or horn, and mounted on handles, are turned by being swung like football rattles. Larger wheels are set in walls to be spun by passers-by; or they may be placed in streams to be turned, like millstones, by running water.

Some temples and monasteries have giant, 20-foot-high prayer wheels. Most are rotated simply by being pushed on their leather-covered rims, while others are more technologically advanced, having metal gears at the base; these allow one person to sit quietly for hours, turning the wheel. The biggest wheels are tightly packed with thousands upon thousands of printed prayers. Some Buddhists have even taken to cramming their prayer wheels with microfilmed texts so as to send forth as many prayers as possible.

◀ **Prayer wheels, to be turned always clockwise, line the walls of many Buddhist temples and holy places. A row of colourful prayer flags (inset) flutter in front of Ama Dablam, a significant landmark in the Everest region.**

four or five breaths, and then a frightening period of no breathing at all for as long as ten or fifteen seconds, a pattern that can go on for hours at a time.

So far I had no symptoms apart from spasms of bad temper.

In Search of a Good Yak

Namche Bazar put me in mind of Babar the Elephant's Celesteville with its rows of simple little houses placed one above the other up the slope, connected by lanes as steep as ladders. Most buildings were new and presented themselves as hotels and shops. They had signboards freshly painted each season, many saying WELCOME. One advertised a new Sherpa mail service. Nearly all the houses had prayer flags stuck on poles on the roof, and just below the town God was also receiving messages from the series of prayer wheels turned by the river, which kept them spinning away in their little stone huts.

The unending visitors dribbled up and down, followed by porters who had given up farming years ago and left the planting of crops to their womenfolk. A party of American children was arriving, a group on a tour arranged by an agency called Family Trekking. How could they possibly be enjoying themselves? The tiny children were being carried up in traditional baskets on porters' backs to the dusty slopes where their mothers were looking round for proper lavatories. Another chain of porters unloaded in a dirty lane with an air of achievement, while their Japanese employers took photographs. The people of Namche are remarkably tolerant about cameras. They don't ask for money, but smile and smile, the old man with one long tooth waving a plastic prayer wheel, the child in the long dress and bonnet like an Elizabethan baby—oh, how cute!—the Tibetan woman holding up the kukri, or curved Gurkha knife, which will be purchased and added to the load.

I visited the yaks under the living room of Passang's lodge and peered through the gloom at large, scowling creatures with thick black hair and plumed tails. Winter had passed in the dark stable, but now there were springtime excursions carrying the muesli of dung and leaves from the lavatory out to Passang's fields to be dumped in smelly brown heaps. Soon there would be ploughing. I made the mistake of trying to stroke the biggest animal, who was called Roko, meaning black, and received my first demonstration of yak temperament when, to the accompaniment of orange saliva fountaining from a gaping mouth, curved horns flashed at me in the darkness.

There were not many other yaks around Namche, which stands at 11,000 feet, just about the lowest limit of their habitat.

'Too low here for good yak,' I was told. So next day I went up to the livestock farm outside Shyangboche (pronounced '… bo-chay') to see more. I set off to the sound of lamas' horns accompanied by Passang's children on their way to the Hillary School at Khumjung. Having already done a morning's work attending to trekkers' needs, they rushed ahead of me, *Good morning, sar*, meeting a stream of other children all wearing Western clothes and carrying leather satchels, who bounded up the steep hill at the beginning of a journey that would take them an hour. It would take me two.

Most of the early morning movement in Namche was centred around the little crossroads leading to the post office and bank. An old woman settled in a doorway, preening herself in the first rays of sun. Crows squawked and danced among trekkers' garbage, piled behind the ladders that linked the houses and strewn in front of a turnip-shaped chorten, or shrine. A Sherpa in a track suit collected a bit of precious dung off the street. Dung-collecting is part of the daily round, and at any encampment you can watch people moving slowly about, looking for argols (a much prettier word than turds). In a country without trees, a large yak-dropping is important for making a fire, and the very survival of many nomads would be in doubt without the yak standing by.

The day was fine with streamers of cloud that drifted up from the lowlands looking like white prayer scarves. At the top of the town, near a mani wall carved with sacred lettering, figures of Buddha and wheels of life, stood a dilapidated little gompa, a monastery, with an empty courtyard and empty rooms. Above the rooftops were a scattering of small, terraced

fields, thin ledges of ochre-coloured earth scraped clean of rocks and stones. Three girls in long black dresses were planting potatoes, two digging the earth towards them with mattocks, the third carrying a basin of seed potatoes which she deftly threw into each hole made for them. When they caught sight of me, their laughter was uproarious. Even after two decades of tourism each reeling, gasping foreigner was still a good joke. Or was my appearance particularly comical? Children continued to run past, *Good morning, sar*. I followed an old woman bearing an immense load in a basket who was putting increased distance between us.

Down in the bowl of the Dudh Kosi valley leading back to Lukla, the preserved forest rose and fell in dense different greens, an undulating ridge which reproached the bare brown slopes above and formed a plush foreground for a cold circle of giant mountains—Khumbulyullha, Taweche, Lhotse, Ama Dablam, Tramserku, Kusum Kang. And the biggest of the lot, Sagarmatha: Everest. I climbed to Shyangboche airstrip, another dusty field a little longer than usual gouged out of the side of a hill. A sign beside the highest airfield in the world said ALTITUDE 3800 M. There was only one approach and if the pilot fluffed the landing, he hit rock. A decade ago this had happened to a plane belonging to the Royal Nepalese Airways—which was one of the reasons why the airfield was so moribund, with its control tower half-finished and a woman herding yaks on the deserted runway.

▲ A typical mani wall, made up of stones carved with prayers and religious texts and images. No matter how tumble-down these walls may become, their messages never lose their power.

Shyangboche airstrip was constructed to provide access to the Everest View Hotel, a vainglorious idea developed by a consortium of Japanese and Nepalese entrepreneurs in 1971. Five-star luxury would look out on the highest mountain. And everything—carpets, curtains, taps, saucepans—had to be brought in by porter or flown in. Guests were flown in too, an hour's flight from Kathmandu, and then they were carried by yak from Shyangboche along a track leading above a gorge on an almost perpendicular descent. They were all rich and some were old; clinging to coarse yak hair, they hardly had a moment to look up at the peaks overhead. They hadn't time to become acclimatised during the flight, and when they reached the comfortable hotel with the fine view, they tended to get ill and even die. That was in spite of the oxygen-breathing apparatus supplied in each room instead of television and Gideon Bibles.

The royal Shyangboche yak farm, just up the trail through an arched wooden gateway, consisted of a few austere buildings and a long, walled enclosure surrounded by trees. There was no sign of any yaks, only a cow. This was a Swiss cow.

'She will be mated to a yak and no doubt will give birth to a satisfactory calf. Swiss cows give better milk,' declared Mr Charad Chandra Nenpane, the chief livestock officer. We sat in his office with its picture of the royal family and a tapestried cushion on my chair on which was embroidered an ideal yak—noble, handsome, its horns and fur worked in gold thread.

Mr Nenpane, a graduate of Kathmandu University, told me that, although tourism had generally supplanted farming as the main source of income throughout Sherpa territory, nevertheless the yak and its hybrid offspring were still essential for the well-being of small communities.

The domesticated yak is less than half the size of a wild yak. Yak is strictly the name for the male of the species. The females are naks. For many thousands of years yaks have been crossed with other cattle such as the Tibetan *bosaunus typicus*, whose bulls are known as lang. The results are zopkiok and zhum. So far no name has been devised for the offspring of a Nepalese yak and a Swiss cow.

'What do they eat … grass?'

Mr Nenpane threw up his hands. 'And where do you find grass?' We looked out of the window at mountains and shrivelled vegetation. 'At this time of year, before the rains, there is nothing for these beasts. We give them hay and potatoes and maize flour mixed with water twice a week.' When yaks went trekking on the bare mountain, a good proportion of the load they carried had to be their own personal provisions. They got lonely and liked to travel in pairs. A lonely yak was a bad-tempered yak.

'What about riding them?'

'Indeed, Mr Peter, riding yak bridles are very hard to come by. A riding yak must be especially trained. Tell me, in Europe do you go around riding bulls?'

An assistant rushed in, looking worried. Mr Nenpane listened anxiously.

'My friend here tells me some very bad news. A yak has been killed by a wolf.'

'I'm sorry. Do wolves often attack?'

'Sometimes at this time of year. And we can do nothing. In a national park no wild animal can be trapped or killed. Not even damned wolf.'

'How can you protect your yaks?'

'It is very difficult, let me assure you. Now we have fifty-six animals. This morning when I awoke we had fifty-seven.'

'Where are they?'

'Most of them are high up on the mountain in a yersa.'

I elicited that a yersa was a stone mountain hut. The ownership of land in yersa settlements used to be very important among livestock breeders, and until the advent of tourists whole families would move up to higher pastures during the monsoon months. Since the keeping of large herds of yaks by Sherpas has declined in the face of tourism, many yersas have fallen into disuse or have been turned into tourist lodges. The few that are occupied by herdsmen during the summer months have become rarities.

Mr Nenpane said, 'I think it would be better if you learn more about yaks.'

But the mountains beckoned me. 'I want a yak to go to Gokyo.' It was a beacon for trekkers.

He threw up his hands again.

The Indomitable Yak

FOR THE MOUNTAIN VILLAGERS of Nepal and Tibet, life depends to a great extent on the hairy mountain cattle known as 'yaks'—a name that in local usage often refers specifically to the males of the species; the females are variously called *naks* or *dri*. The yak's enormous lungs make it immune to altitude sickness, which can be fatal to horses and most other cattle, and it can live on the sparsest vegetation. In fact, yaks prefer high altitudes, and are unable to survive much below 10,000 feet.

For centuries these hardy beasts have been domesticated (often only partially) for ploughing and for use as pack animals. They also supply a variety of invaluable products: their meat is tough but edible; their milk provides butter for burning in lamps; their wool is woven into blankets; their hair is braided into ropes; their hide is used for all manner of leather goods (including boats); and their dung, in a land with little or no firewood, is invaluable when dried for fuel. The great strength of these animals can, however, be a drawback, for they have huge horns and are often obstinate and ill-tempered. Consequently yaks are often crossed with other, meeker cattle to produce a smaller, more manageable animal known as a zopkiok, which has the extra advantage of being able to live and work at lower altitudes.

▲ **This magnificent Tibetan yak, tastefully decorated by his proud owner, is clearly unperturbed by the precipitous drop he is standing beside.**

Two large slabs of yak butter on sale in a market in Tibet. They are wrapped, in the traditional manner, in yak skins. ▶

◀ **A line of heavily laden yaks plods through the snow on the approach to Mount Everest. These animals are vital for bringing in some of the heavier equipment for today's climbers.**

▲ Yaks wait patiently with their burdens outside the Nepalese customs post at Thame after their long journey over the steep Khumbu La Pass from Tibet. The long, furry coats of these animals suggest that they are probably Tibetan yaks.

◄ A Tibetan and his yakskin boat. Made from skins stretched tightly over a square wooden frame, these craft are lightweight and surprisingly waterproof.

A pair of placid zopkioks—crossbreeds of yaks and cows. They are more amenable than yaks and, though skinnier in appearance, make strong and hardy pack animals. ►

CHAPTER 2

Trial Run by Zopkiok

BACK IN NAMCHE I WAS ADVISED to seek out Pemba, who lived in Jarkot, the cluster of houses planted between vast rocks overlooking the town. It appeared that Pemba knew all about yaks and would bring one along tomorrow. He would take it from his brother's field.

Pemba was a Tibetan who had escaped to Nepal as a child. His family had settled in the Khumbu area, and when photographs of refugee Tibetans were circulated among individuals and charitable organisations throughout the world, a Belgian priest took on the responsibility for his education. Every month they exchanged letters, and then one month nothing arrived.

'He was an old man and he die.'

Although Pemba was by then in the tenth class, he had to leave school. Having learned English there, he found work for a trekking company at 35 rupees a day, the same wage as a porter, and tried to see a future for himself. 'In Europe I might have been a pop star.'

He wore the smart, blue-jean suit sent to him from Belgium by his adoptive father. His baseball cap was scarlet and white.

The yak, whose name was Nangpa, was a scrawny, piebald animal. I had my rucksack and tent, together with a few provisions. Pemba brought his own small bag and a large burlap sack of hay and started the business of loading up, balancing everything around the small, wooden pack saddle and tying the bundles down with ropes. The hay sack in particular was big and slippery, and kept sliding off. At each delay Nangpa showed increasing signs of impatience, snorting and shying. The operation was watched by jeering trekkers.

'You cannot seriously propose to take that beast to Gokyo,' said a Dutchman from Passang's lodge. 'The place is so cold your urine freezes solid.'

'It looks real hungry to me,' said an American, 'and you intend to feed it all that distance on one teensy bag of hay?'

The lady of the house got Nangpa going by picking up a stick and belting him.

The day was hot with only a few clouds rolling up the valley. The Namche shopkeepers were arranging their goods on the pavement outside: jewellery, bags of biscuits and sweets, a Tibetan lama's skull trimmed with silver. There were yak blankets, yakskin shoes, yakskin coats, toy yaks. On the wall of one house was a stuffed yak's head. An old woman politely stuck out her tongue.

The market in Namche Bazar. Contact with Westerners has brought prosperity to the Sherpa capital, not to mention the ubiquitous blue jeans. ▼

The track went past the police checkpoint where theoretically every tourist was supposed to produce his trekking permits. The three men sitting outside the hut were bored. 'You want to sign the book?' One of them got up stiffly and brought me into the office, yawning. I signed the ledger which keeps everyone satisfied: officials in Kathmandu, the trekkers who have paid for permits. This year 25,000 would be allowed to wander over Nepal.

Nangpa was slothful, stopping on the track every few yards, moving on reluctantly when urged by Pemba's enraged screams and thumps. He would go on for a very short distance and stop again, kicking up dust. He stopped for the tenth time and refused to budge.

'Why don't you lead him?'

'It is done this way, Boss.'

I looked at Nangpa critically for the first time. His horns were formidable enough, his tail was reasonably bushy, but he lacked substance. His little legs scarcely came up to my knees, and he had hardly more hair than a cow.

'Yak?'

'Zopkiok,' Pemba said casually.

'We agreed a yak.'

He looked away at a mountain and there was a long, pained silence. 'Zopkiok good as yak. My mother need yak for ploughing.'

The real thing approached from the opposite direction along the trail, a line of proper yaks bearing big loads and hurrying, hurrying. Nangpa was a flawed

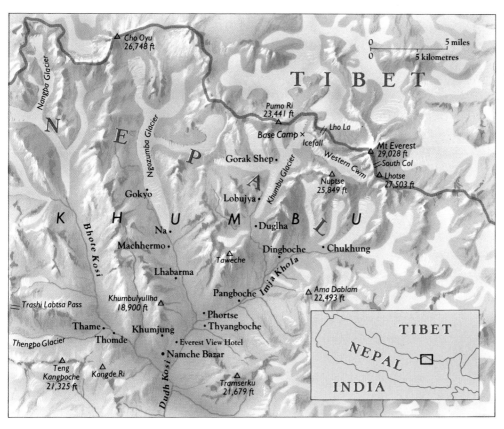

◄ The area around Namche Bazar, including Mount Everest, through which the author travelled with the help of a zopkiok and two yaks.

The Dudh Kosi River, here at relatively low level, drains from the Ngozumba Glacier and flows past Namche Bazar through some of the most spectacular mountain scenery in the world.

imitation. You could see the difference as they swept by with their hovercraft gait, how much hairier they were, altogether bigger, their bison humps distinctive, their massive figures somehow majestic. In comparison Nangpa looked seedy. Sluggish, his head constantly hanging down, he did not even seem to be a good example of a zopkiok.

We continued on the trail in sulky silence, punctuated by Nangpa's spurts of movement and awful grunting combined with a grinding of teeth. The noise was distressing, with a perpetual suggestion of effort about it and a tinge of pain. The name 'yak' is onomatopoeic.

Below the village the potato fields thinned out, and soon we were descending into a narrow, boulder-filled valley covered with birch and fir trees. Then we came out above the main gorge of the Dudh Kosi, facing ranges of mountains that were so high the mind did not fit them in with the rocks and ice below and the places where the forest still clawed up their lower slopes. They were like clouds.

A Refuelling Stop for Nangpa

The small village of Phunki Thanghka lay at the bottom of the valley, reached by a long skinny bridge. Nangpa stopped at the bridge with an air of long practice and began chewing leaves while he observed how the whole valley sparkled with the approach of spring. Light shone on the budding trees, on the cascading stream and the distant water wheels for quite a long time before he could be persuaded to trot across. Birds were singing. Behind the teahouses half-naked Germans were sunning themselves outside their tents, while a group of French were shrilly objecting to the price the teahouse charged for tea and fried bread.

We stayed for half an hour so that Nangpa could be fed on potatoes to give him strength for the climb up to Thyangboche, en route for Gokyo. We plodded uphill, glimpsing through the fir trees a bright blue sky and a snow-caked mountain looming across the valley, its crevices and serrated edge shining like glass. Ahead charged another convoy of yaks weighed down with large boxes of tea and pyramids of eggs. We met people coming down, Sherpas moving at an easy trot under their loads, trekkers looking jaded. An elderly Englishman, his leg bandaged, hobbled down with the aid of a ski stick. He had been to Base Camp.

'It's like Piccadilly Circus. There's a glut of Norwegian and American climbers. What's the weather like in Lukla?'

'Misty, when I last heard. People have been waiting for the plane for two days.'

'I have to be back in London by Monday for a directors' meeting.'

Just a little higher up, Thyangboche monastery was waiting for us. From the small tower built over the main courtyard a line of lamas sounded horns while another rang a bell. I read the notice board.

Welcome to Thyangboche. Please Step in the Land of Trekkers Paradise for Remote Shelter. We ask Your Help to Keep our Place Clean.

Not so long ago Thyangboche was remote as well as holy. The monastery traces back to Lama Sanga Dorje, the fifth of the reincarnate lamas of the Rongbuk monastery in Tibet. Towards the end of the seventeenth century he brought Buddhism to Khumbu by flying over the high mountains from Tibet and landing at Thyangboche, and later at Pangboche, leaving his sacred footprints at both places. When he died his body evaporated into a rainbow, and his eyes, tongue and heart remained to be placed in a silver casket.

More recently Thyangboche has had its ups and downs. After the monastery was destroyed in the 1934 earthquake, rebuilding took many years. In the 1960s the arrival of mountaineers had a devastating effect on the numbers of monks, many of whom were induced to leave because of the large wages offered to anyone capable of carrying a load at high altitudes. Today the monastery has been enriched by gifts; every Everest expedition includes in its budget a large donation to be offered to the current Rimpoche or abbot. The establishment is flourishing, but it is a different place from the holy spot of forty years ago when nothing disturbed the lamas' meditation except the rustle of wind. It is bedlam.

Tourist lodges are scattered around the compound beneath the little knoll on which the main gompa stood, and there is a Gompa Inn, run on behalf of the monastery by a holy man released from his ritual duties. Here trekkers were reading books, eating, complaining or boasting, like the Dane who had been up to the

The players of these collapsible, eight-foot-long trumpets often blow in carefully timed sequence, so that the deep, melancholy sound may appear continuous for many minutes. ▼

▲ The monastery of Thyangboche. The golden spire on the chorten (shrine) in the foreground has 13 gilded rings that represent the Buddhists' 13 steps to enlightenment.

Khumbu Icefall a dozen times. A haunted-looking German woman had sickened above Pheriche and had been forced to turn back; another German wearing scratched spectacles hoped to study the ecology of Base Camp.

'You could save yourself the trouble by inspecting any old municipal garbage dump,' said one of three fierce Australian girls. A plump American in a T-shirt saying 'When the Going gets Tough the Tough get Going' carried a copy of the *New York Times* not much out-of-date. His companion's head was bad.

'I'm sorry, Margaret, you're not handling altitude too well. Everyone going up to Kala Pattar is psychopathic. Try some Diamox …'

'I have, I have …'

An English girl was dying to meet the Rimpoche. 'Don't we need khatas?' White greeting scarves are as essential a part of the serious trekker's equipment as stomach pills. Her friend, who was as hairy as a yak, said, 'I've got the bloody khatas. Anyway it's not that wonderful meeting him. Reincarnated lamas are two a penny in Nepal since they cut down on them in Tibet.'

The German with the scratched spectacles gulped a mugful of chang, the local beer. 'You can time the effects of chang to the exact hour. In thirty-three hours you will get diarrhoea, then severe vomiting. A pity they do not distil the water … it is a good drink.' The holy man brought him more.

When he brought chang for us, together with chapattis and fried potatoes, Pemba became happier.

'I think it will be a good trip, Boss.'

The central gompa stood on a little hill. Upstairs was the main room with religious pictures and images of Buddha; lamas' cells huddled round it, together with a newly finished library intended to be a major literary source for those wishing to study Mahayana Buddhism—and there were plenty of them around. Nearby were some of the highest latrines in the world; you peed over a drop of a thousand feet.

A New Day

Pemba, Nangpa and I set off when the morning air was still crisp. The light is more intense then and the mountains have a sheen which they lose as the sun gets higher. Nangpa had been given potatoes, but he looked disgruntled.

'It is the weather, Boss,' Pemba volunteered. 'You hear thunderstorm last night? Zopkiok and yak not like thunder. Too much noise.' He shook his head, as if I were to blame.

We plunged down on the far side of the hill through a wood which was under the care of the monastery. There was no discernible track, just a thick slice of woodland falling down to a river where tendrils of lichen and moss fell over our heads in silver curtains. The other side of the valley was just about bare of trees; once I heard a woodman's axe ringing out another death note. It took holiness to preserve trees in these parts, and the monastery was doing a better job than the park people.

Soon I was experiencing Sherpa's First Law—in the Himalayas a short run down is invariably followed by a much more difficult ascent. Ahead of me Nangpa was busily demonstrating Yak's First Law: the most lacklustre yak hybrid will occasionally show a frantic burst of speed as if it is being pursued by hornets. While Pemba ran after him whistling in vain, the zopkiok had disappeared upwards and out of sight.

I abandoned any idea of keeping up with them; the day was hot and cloudless and I sat on a ledge looking across the river back to Thyangboche on its wooded hill. The sun shone on the gold toren and caught the wings of a flight of snow pigeons so that they glinted like tinfoil. Far below, the river fell in a deep blue line; I slept and woke, walked on and got lost. Here the smaller tracks were nothing more than the imprint of dust between stones, with nothing to indicate where zopkiok and attendant had vanished. By the time I found them, panicking about my tent and provisions, there had been plenty of time for the two of them to sink back into listlessness.

We reached Phortse, a lovely little place standing facing Thyangboche on a high shelf of sloping land above the confluence of two major river valleys—those of the Dudh Kosi, which rises from Cho Oyu, and the Imja Khola, which comes down from Everest. There were chortens (shrines), houses and some small fields starred with flowers. Pemba stopped outside a house and began unloading with great haste.

▲ **Tibetan-style books in a temple library. Their pages are wrapped in sumptuous silk and then enclosed between carved wooden backs.**

'Good place for camping, Boss. I stay in house. You put up tent.'

In the months to come my tent would be a valued friend, but this was only the second time I had erected it. On the last occasion I had been watched by my applauding family in the garden at home.

Most of Phortse watched me and Pemba struggle. Then Nangpa stirred into life and walked through the maze of equipment, his sharp little hoofs treading on nylon ropes. Two husky girls digging in a field lay down their mattocks and ran over to help, chortling and laughing.

Then the primus would not light.

Pemba stood outside the tent watching. 'Very difficult stove. Over ten thousand feet no pressure.'

I joined him in the house near which the tent was perched. Upstairs above the hearth fire the Dalai Lama was placed beside a coloured cut-out of Everest, an ice axe and a rucksack, with a certificate dated 1980 from the Eastern Sierra Himalayan Expedition; the usual glass-fronted wooden frame holding precious family photographs. A couple posed resolutely in their best clothes, the man in a Western-style suit a little too big so that the trousers made waves around his ankles, the woman wearing a wonderful patchwork silk apron in scarlet and yellow and a pair of gilded earmuffs that had kinship to a Celtic torque. Other photos showed the man in snow goggles and a balaclava, the king and queen and a couple of small children.

Here were the children, rather bigger, together with a baby and a whiskery old grandfather. The man of the house, like so many heads of Sherpa families, was away. 'He porter.' After a supper of potatoes taken from the embers and eaten in their skins, I watched the young wife mush a piece of potato in her mouth like a pigeon and give it to the baby. The children drank glasses of chang, the baby cried, a mouse ran across the floor. Then the woman put the baby in a basket on her back and gently rocked it from side to side. From the stable downstairs came the sound of yak bells. My tent waited below.

After I had shivered all night on stony ground, in the morning I could see in the dim light that the flysheet was frosted over. Up in the house Pemba had slept by the fire near the old man, and while I munched dry muesli he cajoled the woman into cooking him a Sherpa breakfast. It was time to strike camp.

'I don't think we reach Gokyo today, Boss. Nangpa still tired.'

Nangpa was not showing immediate signs of fatigue. He twisted like a rodeo horse as Pemba struggled to tie down bags and sacks.

'Eh!' He gave him a clout and another bag fell to the ground.

'Why don't you let him calm down?' I was holding the nose rope as if I had a swordfish on the end of a line.

'Zopkiok must learn obedience. Must learn I am master.'

A long time later, Nangpa surrendered to Pemba's blows and returned to his apathetic movement. We were on our way at last, and I felt once again the exhilaration of the Himalayan spring morning, watching the sun hit the mountain tops, touching the high peaks and glaciers, then slowly descending into the valleys towards the dark thumb of land on which Phortse sat. Suddenly the grey stone walls and fields where women were already working became suffused with golden streams of light. Smoke poured out through shingled rooftops as we left the village and walked through another patch of woodland that the axe had spared. As we moved among black velvet shadows, a small deer watched us walk past from a thicket of bushes and trees, which blended perfectly with the spotted brown skin. Chital, Pemba told me, bored. Very common deer.

All day we walked among cruel white peaks and screes of navy-blue rock. Then the track squeezed its way downward through a maze of rocks that had spilled from a glacier towards Na. As Nangpa kept slipping, his hoofs ringing on stone, threatening to go over, he appeared to be contemplating a demonstration of why yak steak was readily available in a country where taking life is discouraged. Then, in a moment, he recognised where he was and sensed a release from his labours. As if a brake had been released, he put on a burst of speed like a horse on the way back to its stables, as usual taking Pemba by surprise and leaving him whistling and screaming.

Chital, or spotted deer, are common in the forests of the Himalayas at heights of up to 9,000 feet. Since they are not hunted by the local tribespeople, they are unafraid of humans. ▼

Tea and Potatoes

Na was situated below the snout of the great Ngozumba Glacier at the head of a valley which syphoned wind through wretched little houses indistinguishable from the stones around them. I sat shivering in a small stone

enclosure above the river while Pemba went off whistling to himself, returning with two popeyed men wearing shaggy coats and identical baseball caps.

'Very good men, Boss.'

Their hut consisted of two black rooms. Everything was black: the sacks of potatoes, the potatoes themselves, the baskets heaped with wood and dung, the earth floor, the porous walls and the roof through which the wind howled. For once the fire was inadequate to keep up the usual Sherpa fug and as usual, when I tried to light the primus to cook instant soup, the white magic failed.

'You eat with us, Boss.'

Potatoes were served in a tin basin on the floor. There were sacks of potatoes stacked against a wall, there was a loose pile of them on which we sat and, after eating a dozen or so sprinkled with salt, our hosts used potatoes for gambling with a dice and board. Hour after hour, while my eyes smarted and stung with smoke, a man would toss up the dice and bang down a handful of raw potato chips, each worth so many rupees. Then the other would raise his call and count out another pile. Bang, shout, bang, shout. Bedtime loomed.

A simple test for accommodation is to be able to lie down and curl up without hitting anyone. You may put your feet in another man's face or be conscious of his heartbeat or garlic breath, but there are limits, and the hut was far too small. Pemba had retired to the stable, where he shared a pile of wood and dung with the popeyed men's yaks. I envied him. Inside the tent, inside the sleeping-bag, I was chilled in my kapok trousers, thermal underwear, two sweaters, Gore-Tex jacket, balaclava and scarf.

I could not feel my feet and the tent was stiff, frozen solid as an igloo. There came a prolonged crackling as someone outside struggled to unzip the flap, and a wild head and a dirty hand with bitten nails appeared with a tin cup of smoky tea. When I peered out the two men were there waiting, together with Pemba.

'He say you owe money for potatoes and tea.'

'Tell him to come back later.' The time was half-past five.

'They want money now. They go to Namche to buy food at market.' Pemba shivered in his cotton shirt. 'They go now.'

Thirty rupees put the tea and potatoes in the champagne and caviar class. The two men skipped away with their yaks, while Pemba took a ration of frozen potatoes over to Nangpa, who had spent the night in a small enclosed field and may have been as cold as I was.

We went off from Na in the grey light of early dawn in silence, except for the wind and the clattering of stones under Nangpa's feet. Just below the settlement a few planks had been pushed over the baby Dudh Kosi, a brook that would gather strength from glaciers and melting snow so that in only a few miles it would become the familiar white torrent. All around was the roar of cataracts falling over rocks. Beyond the river the track ascended another moraine, where Nangpa halted. I had a good rest while Pemba twisted his tail; he was nearly badly hurt by a swipe of horns followed by a vicious kick.

'Whaa … whaa …' Nangpa bellowed before moving on, climbing out onto a stretch of level land above the narrow funnel of the valley. Like the mongrel

◀ Porters and yaks carry supplies for a trekking party on the Everest trail above the Imja Khola valley. The distinctive peak on the right is Ama Dablam (22,493 feet), a landmark observed several times by the author.

offspring of a Siamese cat, he had inherited the distinctive voice of his fore-bears—the moaning, grunting note that almost more than anything else evokes Himalayan travel. The sun had come out. An hour ago I had felt like a preserved mammoth, but now it was as warm as a Mediterranean beach in summer. I stripped off extra clothes and then took a photograph of Nangpa and Pemba standing together in the wilderness. Nangpa went galloping away, scattering baggage over rocks and snow.

'You shouldn't have done that, Boss. Zopkiok not like cameras.'

Number One View of Everest

Gokyo comprised half-a-dozen yersas—stone mountain huts converted into tourist lodges—standing on the shores of a frozen lake with a background of mountains, the same old friends. Colours were sharp, aquamarine and white blending with the rubble of grey rocks. Directly facing the little settlement was a steep, golden-brown hill called Gokyo Ri ('Gokyo Peak'), which every trekker who comes here must climb if he is to have Number One view of Everest. Nangpa, given temporary freedom, spent his time gazing at his reflection in the lake. Dull eyes, shaggy mottled head. I still felt disgruntled to be wandering through the Himalayas with a bullock.

Above the doorway of one of the rough stone yersas was the usual sign; there cannot be a Sherpa in Khumbu who does not know the meaning of WELCOME. Half the interior was taken up with tiers of bunks, and at the other end was a kitchen and an open fire around which a dozen people were being served food by

▲ The village of Gokyo consists of a group of scattered stone huts (yersas), their stonewalled fields stretching down to a magnificent lake. The low hill behind the village is the lateral moraine of the Ngozumba Glacier, which can be seen stretching away to the south, while Cholatse (21,129 feet) towers in the background.

a lovely Sherpa girl. Within a few minutes I was enjoying an omelette with chapattis and chips. She offered tinned porridge, powdered milk and beer at 50 rupees a bottle. There were potatoes.

'Yak food,' said an irritable Israeli beside me, peering into his bowl. Like me, he had lived on potatoes for days, and we owed a mutual debt of gratitude to the common spud.

All day trekkers sat in the lodge around the fire as the girl cooked a continuous supply of meals. There was rice and dhal, yak steak and stew, and all the eggs carried up on yak back. For variety she offered mountaineers' leftovers: Japanese octopus, Polish chocolate, ravioli in tomato sauce.

'The stuff accumulates, especially when someone dies climbing.'

At 15,500 feet Gokyo, located at the last stage before the mountain barrier with Tibet, appeals to the more experienced trekker. Here the riffraff had been weeded out; it was no place for softies. The talk was of lateral moraines, Schneider's map and difficult passes.

In between cooking, the Sherpa girl fed the baby that Pemba held on his knee. I had noticed that Sherpas and Tibetans have an instant rapport and, while her husband was away on his weekly descent to Namche to buy provisions, any visiting porters had a duty to help her.

People turned in around nine. Many were kept awake because they had headaches or were rendered sleepless by the coughs and wheezes and the voices droning away about prices and travel destinations. In the morning I could see a line of bright anoraks, yellow, orange and blue, moving up the coffee-coloured hill. Everyone was going up. Here was another test of fitness and adaptability to altitude, a two-hour climb over slippery rocks and gravelly spills of loose stone.

'We do it for the training,' said the German scrambling up in front of me. 'Ya … two times each day…ya…is good.' He patted his bulging biceps. He wore corduroy trousers buttoned down over his knees, thick woollen stockings tucked into massive boots and an Austrian hat with a feather. He was full of advice. 'Take plenty of rest…A man your age … You must wear those glasses so … The sun will scorch your eyeballs …'

All around Gokyo Ri, against the background of the mountains and chill blue sky, were sounds of wheezing and gasps for breath. A party of Americans was perched all round the summit like a flock of brightly coloured parrots. They had pushed their way to the best position right at the top, and they scarcely had room to move.

'Oh God, isn't it wonderful!'

'Wow! If I stand up here on this rock I'm over eighteen thousand feet high.'

'Where the hell is it?' They were on the lookout for Everest.

Clouds were dancing in front of the whole range.

'That must be Makalu.'

'What about the one two-along?'

'I think that's Lhotse.'

'She's gone too.'

'Not a sign of the big one. Curse it, anyway.'

Pemba enjoyed sitting by the fire eating at my expense, but I wanted to travel up the valley as far as I could towards Cho Oyu.

'Zopkiok tired, Boss, after climbing.'

'He's had two days' rest.'

'He need plenty potato and grass. Here very little.'

I said my mind was made up. Grumbling, he packed up the various bags together with two sacks of hay, taking longer than usual doing the balancing acts with ropes and pulleys on the zopkiok's back. We set off walking up the valley to many complaints, stumping over rocks and boulders towards Cho Oyu which loomed ahead, blocking out the horizon and sending an icy wind down on us as we arrived at another lake, frozen among rocks and snow.

'I think we stop here.' Pemba settled in a small field dotted with cushions of moss that Sherpas use for burning. It was being grazed by some yaks, proper yaks, smothered in long black hair. Just ahead was the dusty grey moraine and glacier sweeping up to the mountain.

After putting up the tent, I set off walking alone.

'I tell you, Boss, it is better we stay in Gokyo.'

'I want to see the glacier.'

'No good glacier.'

The greyish, convoluted fringe of ice reaching into the heart of the mountain among great spills of ice and rubble proclaimed desolation. Every detail was on such a gigantic scale; Cho Oyu, a daunting, steel-grey pyramid dappled white, and the peaks to left and right forming a ferocious line of crests. I had been told that at one time yaks crossed this barrier into Tibet; they must have had wings.

When I returned to camp, Pemba was lying on the far side of the tent under his old blanket—he had no sleeping-bag—his cap pushed over his eyes. He was shivering. Gusts of snow began falling out of an ash-coloured sky.

We sat in the tent while, ever optimistic, I encouraged Pemba to work on the primus. Outside, the snow fell more thickly. When he managed to get a little spurt of flame going, we had a lozenge of tepid soup and two cold chapattis.

Later I said, 'I can't see much point in staying here.'

'We go back, Boss?'

'I think so.'

He leapt up. 'I think that good decision.'

No camp was ever struck more quickly. Even Nangpa cooperated. Gusts of snow had begun falling. Down came the tent, and in a few minutes all our bags were roped together on the zopkiok's docile back. We left that unimaginably beautiful site like an express train.

The return to Namche was pleasant and easy. We spent the next night at Machhermo on the dusty brown tableland overlooking a valley filled with

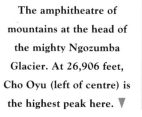

The amphitheatre of mountains at the head of the mighty Ngozumba Glacier. At 26,906 feet, Cho Oyu (left of centre) is the highest peak here. ▼

grazing yaks. This was the place where in 1974 a yeti was reported to have killed three yaks and attacked a woman. Next day we trotted through Lhabarma and Dole, and seven hours later the familiar rooftops of Namche appeared. Nangpa broke into a gallop and nothing would stop him until he pulled up beside the lodge.

'He very happy,' Pemba said, throwing off the bags. 'Gokyo bad for zopkiok.'

A Side Trip to Thame

Next I planned to make a leisurely reconnaissance towards Thame, birthplace of the legendary Sherpa Tenzing, and the Trashi Labtsa Pass, taking Pemba and Nangpa. (Mother still needed the yak.)

'Not to cross. Too dangerous. Zopkiok and I go with you only to look.'

In Passang's lodge was a party of Americans who had crossed the Trashi Labtsa Pass roped together.

Jake, their leader, was small, lean as a pencil and wore a wispy red beard. He sat drinking a lot of chang. 'Yaks? You must be out of your mind. The only way to get them across the Trashi Labtsa is by carrying them in baskets.'

We set off on the day of the Namche market, a weekly event that tied the area together. People came down from the most distant villages and yersas to buy and sell provisions. I recognised one of the wild men from Na, while Pemba waved to the husband of the woman of Gokyo. By the grey light of dawn the dusty terraces were filled with a multitude, while on the rock above weary

porters squatted with their empty bags. Already tourists were making their way towards the antiques and yakskin blankets.

The track followed the course of the Bhote Kosi, a tributary of the Dudh Kosi, through another high valley full of waterfalls and precipitous slopes, closed off by the mountains.

In front of us a team of four yaks carrying potatoes was being urged along with piercing whistles by two fat girls. Pemba tried to keep up with them, prodding Nangpa ceaselessly, at the same time giving me an idea of the remarks being shouted back at him.

'She say why don't I visit her in Thame. Do you think her pretty, Boss? Sherpa girl very free to lovemaking, not like Indians. I like foreign girls best. Last year I meet Australian lady. After trek she say why you not come home with me? She say she get ticket and look after me.'

At Thomde we came to the headquarters of the Hydel Project, which planned to bring electricity to the area. In the little office of the chief engineer, Mr Ganesh Bahadur Shortse, were a number of uplifting texts: 'Any Man who Rules Himself is an Emperor'; 'Where there is no Sound in the Mind God's Voice can be Heard'. Seven years working with the scheme had inclined Mr Shortse towards natural philosophy, if not resignation.

'Please listen to me,' he said, offering a cup of tea. 'Is there any other country

The Mysterious Yeti

THE YETI—OR ABOMINABLE SNOWMAN—is a creature that refuses to fade away, despite being repeatedly debunked by scientists. Supposedly a monstrous ape-man some seven or eight feet tall, it lives, if anywhere, in the mountain fastnesses of Nepal and Tibet. Local monasteries display pictures and relics of the yeti, which is taken so seriously by today's Nepalese government that it is even protected by law.

The evidence is inconclusive. The fossilised remains of a giant hominid, *Gigantopithicus*, some eight million years old, have been found in northern China. Instead of becoming extinct, *Gigantopithicus* may simply have been driven back by *Homo sapiens* into the remote mountains where it has lived ever since. Recent 'sightings', however, have been limited to mysterious footprints in the snow, and a blurred view through binoculars of a large, apelike creature bounding along on all fours. Although several well-organised yeti hunts have taken place, no specimen has yet been killed or captured.

Even so, yeti incidents continue to be reported.

Nepalese village women recount terrifying experiences with ape-men, and yaks are found with their necks inexplicably broken. Sceptics offer rational explanations for such events, but it is also fair to point out that until quite recently both China's giant panda and Africa's mountain gorilla were themselves mere legends.

▲ A boy shows off what the monks at Pangboche monastery claim is the scalp of a yeti. Scientists who have examined it are mystified, but remain unconvinced.

in the world where all goods must be carried by porter for fifteen days?' Bags of cement, nails, steel rods, electrical conductors had to come up on porters' backs. Each man or woman could only carry fifty or sixty pounds on a track which often vanished under a landslide or met a river whose bridge had been washed away.

'I need help with God and also with man.' Mr Shortse gazed out of the window at the mountains. 'Please guess how many months in the year men can work up here.'

'Eight? Seven?'

'Five months only. That is all they can manage because of the snow. Years must pass before the Sherpa people may switch on.' He smiled wearily. 'You love Nepal?'

'It is a beautiful country.'

▲ Porters such as these have only five months each year in which to carry up building materials from the valleys below for the Thomde Dam and other projects.

'I wouldn't say that. We respect the guest as the god, but there have been very many bad changes. I tell you, when you have no money you are very honest and innocent, but when you make money you become materialistic. I see it coming. The East goes to the West and the West to the East. Do you approve?'

I said something about possible benefits.

He raised his hand wearily to his head. 'I tell you another thing. Tourism brings disease. When you have all this free sex it soon loses its charm, I assure you. The day is coming very soon when Sherpas will have AIDS.'

Later he gave me directions to Laondo Gompa, a popular monastery among the young.

'You are a tourist. No doubt you wish to study Buddhism. Many tourists like Buddhism. Many hippies visit Laondo.'

'Why go up there?' Pemba asked, pointing to the gompa, a mere speck over our heads. 'Much better keep to main path.'

As usual, he was right. The track gyrated straight up in a series of skinny ribbon loops, past a few juniper bushes which were having trouble with gravity; a climb like scaling the side of a building, a sense of overpowering inertia and a long, gasping struggle to reach a cluster of trees and some prayer flags fluttering on outstretched poles.

The World's Most Beautiful Nun

The gompa was a small red building balanced on the edge of a crag, poised for meditation. It was like Thyangboche, only second-best. The main gompa building contained a large room with four big, seated Buddhas facing the door. Placed in front of them was a photograph of Lama Subha who had founded Laondo fifteen years ago; he also established a school for local children and an international centre for Buddhism in Kathmandu. At present he was in Los Angeles.

A charming girl in lama's clothes greeted me with a smile. She must have been the world's most beautiful nun. She was the product of two different cultures, her father being Asian, her mother European. After attending a short course on Buddhism in Kathmandu and finding the experience deeply spiritual, she had come here. Others besides myself must have wondered impertinently why she should hide herself away. Dark eyes flashed. 'Why not? In Christianity there is a strong tradition of women seeking peace and enlightenment in this way. You must know this.'

I was shown a small cave where Lama Subha had meditated and one of his books lay open, translated into English: 'The world has a red sky, reflected from the jewel "ruby"... Its size is two thousand pak-tse wide and the name means cow enjoyments...'

We gathered in a small dining room, eating momos, the local dumplings, as the sun filtered through the windows and outside prayer flags flapped and dipped in the wind. How peaceful everything seemed. An elderly nun, the Lama Subha's sister, sat with an equally elderly Nepalese follower and the tall, beautiful girl in yellow robes. Perhaps, if she came down from this Shangri-la, she too would turn into an old, old woman.

Clouds boiled up from the valley and the sudden cold was accompanied by a rumble of thunder. It was time to leave. Pemba and Nangpa waited impatiently outside the gate. Snowflakes drifted down from the overcast sky as we hurried down from the gompa to the trail. A woman filling her pannier with pieces of dung smiled at us, but Pemba did not have time to stop and banter when Nangpa changed gear and his pace became a miraculously quickened trot. Pemba ran after him yelling and in a minute they were out of sight. The wind freshened, the falling snow blotted out the mountains as the vanished gompa assumed a dreamlike aspect, a legend of holiness. Once again I was in the predicament of finding myself alone, this time in dense cloud accompanied by wind. Occasionally the wind would blow the cloud apart, revealing a flash of light on a distant mountain before everything returned to cotton wool. I walked for two hours in white darkness before reaching a stringy little bridge slung over a torrent. In a field beyond, a dog barked beside two women pounding the earth with mattocks.

'Thame? Trashi Labtsa?'

'Ah.' They held up their arms vertically and one of them nodded and clicked her tongue. For the second time that day I was subjected to a lonely, painful, gasping climb. Poor feeble body. I clambered to a grove of stunted trees looming out of the mist and a

At heights above 10,000 feet, and in atrocious weather conditions such as these, yaks and zopkioks are the only animals that can carry burdens up the steep mountain slopes. ▼

sign saying WELCOME with an arrow pointing out the track.

The wind blew the cloud away, revealing dusty fields laced by thin stone walls with mountains looking down. Two women were unloading yaks watched by an old lady sitting in a sunny doorway spinning a prayer wheel. A chained mastiff burst out barking at the sight of me and beyond, tethered outside a door, stood Nangpa. Inside, Pemba was installed in the upper room eating potatoes from an enormous tin can.

Firelight made highlights on the copper cauldrons and Thermos flasks, lit the Dalai Lama and the king and queen, but failed to reach the dark and smoke of the roof. The hearth fire is sacred; it has taken time for trekkers to learn not to spit, pee or throw rubbish into the flames. An old man peeled a bowl of potatoes, adding a touch of salt and popping them into his mouth with as much relish as if they were grapes. I watched the woman of the house cooking in her elaborate costume: long grey dress with a red jacket, striped apron, fringed scarf and pounds of jewellery. It was like bending over the pot in evening dress.

▲ The home at Thame of Tenzing Norgay, who accompanied Edmund Hillary to the top of Everest in 1953. The northern flanks of Teng Kangpoche can be seen in the background.

At daybreak the big mountains of these parts revealed themselves. Teng Kangpoche and Kongde Ri, both over 20,000 feet, but not big enough to attract the trekkers the way the giants did. Pemba agreed to bring Nangpa on a cautious reconnoitre of the route along the valley leading to the Trashi Labtsa Pass. A snow-topped wall closed off the end of the valley. We first came to the gompa, one of the largest monasteries in the area, famous for a rumbustious and colourful spring festival. The lama who showed us round produced a donation box and a book filled with donors' names and the sums they had given. On the prayer wheel outside the gate, someone had written the single word NO. Thame would never do as well out of trekkers as Thyangboche, but not for want of trying. Another lama ran to spread a piece of red cloth on the ground and laid out a selection of antiques from a bamboo basket.

Beyond the gompa the valley narrowed and the mountains closed in. It was time to turn round. Back at Thame two soldiers sat outside a hut, knitting. It was a checkpoint; the valley branching northwards was a restricted area.

'Tibet?' I pointed up the valley. One of them finished a row, looked up and nodded. On this clear sparkling day when distances seemed to shrink, I thought how easy it would be to keep going. Even Nangpa could cross into Tibet, past the last lonely gompa in Nepal with its small courtyard and a line of gilded Buddhas gazing through an open doorway. Instead we ambled back to Namche, ending what the guidebooks describe as a 'side trip'.

Nangpa galloped down the final stretch as if longing to see the last of me. Payment was made. 'Goodbye, Boss.' The denim track suit and baseball cap, together with the piebald bullock, vanished out of my life.

▲ Sowing and ploughing in the time-honoured fashion on a terraced hill in Nepal.

◀ Harvest-time in the medieval town of Kirtipur, west of Kathmandu. The elaborately carved window frames of the building in the background are typical of this area.

Newar villagers returning from work at sundown. Unlike other castes, who carry goods in a single, large conical basket suspended from a strap across their foreheads, the Newars employ two circular baskets hanging from a pole. ▶

The remote, barren desert of Mustang in northern Nepal is home to about 8,000 people who live in oasis villages. They fight a constant battle against wind and weather to farm grain and potatoes in sheltered plots. ▶

A retired Gurkha soldier in eastern Nepal. Jutting out of his waistband is his kukri knife, the fearsome trademark of Gurkha regiments. ▼

Nepal and its People

THE KINGDOM OF NEPAL is made up of over 30 different ethnic groups with their own unique cultures and languages. They include the Sherpas, who live among the central and eastern mountains and are famous as high-altitude guides; the soldierly people of the middle hills from whom the British and Indian armies draw their Gurkha regiments; the Newars of the Kathmandu Valley, responsible for some of the country's finest art and architecture; and the isolated, amazingly hardy inhabitants of Mustang in the far north. The population is 90 per cent Hindu, and 9 per cent Buddhist. In spite of this diversity, Nepal has a tradition of harmony and tolerance, rather than conflict.

Historically, however, Nepal was closed to foreigners for many years. The country's landlocked, mountainous terrain made it easy for its kings—first of the Malla dynasty, and then, after 1769, of the Shah dynasty—to maintain a self-imposed isolation. This was intensified after 1846, when an army officer named Jung Bahadur seized power to establish the powerful Rana dynasty. By 1928, no more than 130 Westerners are estimated to have entered the Kathmandu Valley.

Things are very different today. The country is now a multi-party democracy, headed by a constitutional monarch, King Birendra; while tourists, trekkers and climbers are welcomed in large numbers for the revenue they bring to one of the world's least developed nations.

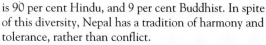

Playtime on a swing made from living bamboo. ▲

CHAPTER 3

To Everest and Back

At Namche I enquired about riding yaks while waiting for Caroline, who arrived from Kathmandu precisely at the time she had indicated. Items in her luggage included Tiger Balm and tapes of Beethoven, Edith Piaf and Count McCormack to play on her Walkman.

'I must have two days' rest and solitude.' She avoided Passang's lodge with its restless trekkers. 'I've been lent a house. A friend has given me the code numbers of the lock on the door.'

She sought out a small, traditional Sherpa building which had been rented by her friend Brock. Brock was a celebrity in Namche, a blond American with Viking moustache known as the God of Light. He had been responsible for installing the first turbine and bringing electricity to the town. While Mr Shortse struggled with the Hydel Project at Thomde, Brock had succeeded. The first night no one had believed that anything would happen, in spite of the parade that preceded the big event. People stood outside waiting for the miracle, which came suddenly as all the windows in the rows of little houses were lit up simultaneously. Now electricity was a commonplace in Namche, where the video film playing twice weekly at the cinema helped to change attitudes as much as the incoming tourists.

After Caroline had recuperated with the aid of Beethoven's symphonies, we left Namche for Thyangboche in search of a riding yak.

'Of course I can ride. I've ridden in Ireland for years.'

I told her about my experiences with Pemba and Nangpa.

'Surely, Peter, the difference between a yak and a zopkiok is obvious?'

We employed two little boys to carry our baggage. They climbed ahead under their loads. 'You don't know how strong these Sherpas are. Why do you suppose they are used on Everest?'

We followed the familiar route up the Dudh Kosi valley among the trekking groups, the biggest mountains in the world floating high above us. She walked much more slowly than I did, moving with a non-stop plod, always keeping going even up the steepest hill.

'You should breathe through your nose. It's no use just running on and then gasping.'

'I feel fine.'

▲ The immaculate terraces of Namche Bazar, which lies in a natural curve on a steep hillside.

'There's a lot of dust about, which is why I always wear a face mask. And look at your nose and hands—no protection at all from ultraviolet rays. Of course, it's your own decision if you want to wreck your skin.'

At Thyangboche there had been an epidemic of gastroenteritis. Caroline said, 'I think it's important that even boiled water should be filtered. The first rule when travelling abroad is never to trust the local water. If you don't believe me, look around.'

In the big room at the lodge, inert shapes were lying in sleeping-bags one above another in tier bunks. The groans were continual, while every now and then an invalid would struggle out of his bag and make a dash for the door, carrying the precious roll of paper.

Possibly because of our precautions we escaped infection and spent two healthy days at the monastery. Some fine yaks had been recommended and a message had been sent up for them to come down to us. Meanwhile time passed pleasantly. I talked with Janbu, a guide who acted as chauffeur-nanny to endless trekking groups. I mentioned the changes I had observed since my previous visit.

'If you ask me about the benefits to Sherpa people, I tell you that tourism only brings cheating and pimping and carnal arrangements.'

'How do local people feel about foreigners climbing onto the summits of their mountains?'

'The whole world knows the picture of Tenzing Norgay standing a few feet below the top of Everest in order to keep her untouched. That does not matter any more. Now mountains are big business and you have to book them.'

High-Altitude Hazards

THE ROOF OF THE WORLD is a hazardous place. Precipices abound, as do less visible dangers such as hunger, thirst, the cold, and two particular consequences of the thin, oxygen-poor air: altitude sickness and the harsh effects of the sun's unfiltered ultraviolet rays. Europeans use elaborate barrier creams and face masks to protect themselves against these rays. Locals do not bother, and their skin eventually becomes amazingly seamed and wrinkled.

Mountain people are, however, much better adapted than visitors to the low levels of oxygen of their environment. Over many generations they have developed superefficient lungs to cope with the thin air that can be such a serious danger to outsiders. Oxygen starvation causes altitude sickness (also called acute mountain sickness or AMS), the symptoms of which are headaches, shortness of breath, poor coordination and vomiting. In acute cases fluid accumulates on the brain or in the lungs, a condition that can prove fatal within six hours. Youth and fitness are no guarantee of immunity to AMS. The best way to avoid it is to gain altitude slowly, climbing the first 8,000 feet over several days and limiting further climbs to 1,000 feet in any 24-hour period. Anyone suffering from this condition must be returned promptly to a lower altitude—on the back of a porter or yak if necessary.

▲ **The wind in the Himalayas, and the unfiltered rays of the sun, do not treat complexions kindly. This woman may well be much younger than she looks.**

I was stopped by a young lama with shining, pop eyes like blackberries. I think he waylaid a lot of people.

'Can I help you, please? I want to practise English.'

He was twenty-three years old and had been educated at the Hillary School at Khumjung. He brought me to his small, mudwalled house overlooking the compound. In his room containing a couple of benches and an open fireplace he cooked his meals, read and made his devotions. It seemed a limited life.

'I am happy.' He smiled as we sat drinking tea over the fire. His brother, who had climbed Everest, visited him regularly, and every now and again he was allowed to go to Namche and see his family. Coming here was his own choice, one that he did not regret.

We sat translating his lists of English words. The day before an American woman had given him a romantic magazine ('What is ardour, please?'), but most of his books were about Buddhism and meditation.

▲ The author in Thyangboche monastery examining a young lama's stylised painting of the monastery and its surrounding mountains.

Another young lama, Phurba Sonam, was a painter. He had turned his cell into a studio where, in addition to images on silk of seated Buddhas and Bodhisattvas, he painted pictures for tourists of mountain peaks, lamas in furry hats, yaks and the gompa itself. I bought a spidery little view of Thyangboche, showing the gompa, the chorten with a golden barber's pole and umbrella, a tourist lodge with a tin roof, Everest topped by a pink cloud painted to look like a plume of feathers, and three yaks.

'I would like to go to the west coast of America,' Phurba said, as we drank tea surrounded by rolled-up paintings. A passing trekker had promised him an exhibition in Los Angeles and he was looking forward to the adventure.

'Is it difficult for you to leave?'

He shook his head. The monastery did not mind, there were no special permissions to be obtained, and all he had to get was the American visa.

Sod and Mucker

I returned to the lodge to find the yaks had arrived.

I couldn't get over how much bigger and hairier they were than Nangpa. Their long furry tails reminded me of the fox furs worn by women in the 1930s. It appeared that only one could be ridden, the black one with the white tail which had been specially trained as a riding yak and was extremely valuable. Its name was Sod. The other, which was called Mucker, could only be used to carry baggage. Mucker had an alarming white face and was much cheaper to hire. He cost 60 rupees a day; Sod was 200.

Their owner, Ang Tenzing, wore the usual track suit and baseball cap and a grim expression, which never softened. His frown came from the worries of looking after difficult and valuable beasts.

Loading the yaks was a long process accomplished with the usual display of temperament. Mucker twitched, groaned, ground his teeth, stamped his little feet, lashed his tail. In addition to our baggage he carried two sacks of hay which towered above his back, so that he had the proportions of a galleon. Sod had a small leather saddle and a rope through a ring in his nose; there was no question of a bridle or reins.

I agreed to ride Sod first. Ang held the ringed nose and Caroline watched from a distance.

My legs almost touched the ground. In spite of my low seat I was surprisingly comfortable, as if I were sitting astride a furry blanket. In front of me jutted a massive head and cabriole horns framing a view of a snowy mountain. These horns were polished and black with pointed tips.

'If he turns his head, put your leg up across the saddle so that he can't gore you.' The voice evoked a moment of the past when Miss Duggan was putting my class of small boys through our first riding lesson. Walk on!

But after twenty yards Sod came to a halt.

Ang shrieked. 'Peter weigh too much! He too big! Caroline better!'

I protested, thinking of the 200 rupees, but he was insistent. Caroline jumped up with effortless grace, giving the impression of having ridden yaks all her life. Sod took the lead with Mucker and Ang following, while I trailed in the rear.

The track passed the main gompa compound where trekkers emerged to cheer Caroline, who was stylishly turned out. She wore a bright ethnic sweater made by Tibetans in Kathmandu, lightweight boots and baggy trousers. Over the pink scarf tied tightly around her head was a bush hat, from the side of which jingled the bunch of keys that locked her bags. A white, Chinese face mask covered her nose and mouth and a pair of black silk gloves covered her hands. There was plenty of time during our slow progress for whistles and catcalls.

'Give it to her, cowboy!'

'She's a beaut!'

Caroline waved back politely, and our passage continued, peaceful and slow. A yak goes at a steady three miles an hour.

The only problem was of control. The rider could turn the animal only in one direction by pulling the single rope tied to the ring in its nose. Kicking or urging it in another direction with the knees brought an erratic response that made me wonder if yaks were really as sure-footed as books describe them.

As we descended towards Pangboche and the inviting prospect of a teahouse, I was walking in front, and thinking of nothing more important than a cup of white tea and an omelette, when I heard a crash behind me. Looking back, I saw that Caroline and Sod had vanished. My first thought was that they must have fallen into the river, to be carried by the current back along the way we had come. But there was a yell from some bushes high over my head.

Without warning Sod had veered off the path and galloped up the cliff at an angle of about eighty degrees. Without any means of control beyond the useless rope, Caroline had been carried to the heights until she came into contact with a branch which had knocked her off cleanly.

Ang dropped Mucker's rein for me to retrieve and ran up the vertical slope almost as fast as his precious animal to find the miscreant somewhere near the clouds, peacefully licking some succulent grasses. In due course we trooped down to the teahouse, everyone on foot.

We continued on our way, taking turns in spite of the danger to ride our expensive yak. We were following the Imja Khola towards Dingboche and a whole cluster of mountains, pushed together like impacted dragon's teeth. Here were Lhotse, Ama Dablam and the rest curtained with serrated ice cliffs. For a time, as we plodded along beside minarets of snow and ice by a silver moraine, we were alone, a feeling that was unnerving.

Yaks can stand high altitudes, but they will not tolerate long periods of work or cover too great a distance in one go. Traditionally they travel about ten or twelve miles a day, but Sod was aiming for a lot less. Mucker had some excuse— his ship-of-war appearance was enhanced by his erratic gait as if he was tacking against the wind. His burdens were huge, and I was quite sure that I did not weigh anything like the load that wavered on his back. But Mucker was not to be treated with the same reverence as the riding yak.

Eventually, I grew tired of listening to Ang's complaints and allowed Caroline to take over the riding altogether, as we proceeded in what became an accustomed marching order: Peter walking ahead, Caroline behind sitting on Sod, who moved well for her when he was not trying to get her off his back, and Ang and Mucker walking in the rear. Mucker looked calm; his tranquil white face blinking ahead of the luggage on his back belonged to a patient beast of burden, but he possessed a wicked yak's heart.

Every now and again a little drama would take place. Caroline would wave her arms like a windmill. 'I want to take a photograph. Hold the rein, please.'

With mutters of 'No good!' Ang would drop Mucker's rope for a moment and come forward to seize Sod's. Sometimes this worked well, as Caroline clicked her camera in peace. But very often Mucker would stray. He would wait until attention was diverted and then slide off on his own, leaving the trail with an absent-minded air that suddenly changed to determination as he galloped up a mountainside, bearing his burden towards some overhang with a drop of several hundred feet. Ang would go off in pursuit yelling and throwing stones. A good many of these would miss and come clattering back down the slope. If we were really unlucky, one would hit us or, worse, Sod.

We Try Out the Tent

We moved in fits and starts until the evening, when we reached Dingboche, a place of stones, small stone houses, stonewalled terraces and stony fields beside the roaring river under the mountains. The first little stone building we came to, consisting of a kitchen–living room and a back room full of bunks, greeted us with the notice SHORTSE VIEW LODGE. This establishment had just been set up by a young Sherpa who had retired from working as a porter with mountain expeditions. This was his first year as hotelkeeper. He did all the cooking, while his brother, who was deaf and mute, carried endless supplies up from Namche. The menu card, written out in fastidious English, offered special milk potatoes, dhal, yak steak and the things his brother had brought up that day. Apart from the potatoes, everything had been laboriously carried up.

We sat eating with an American and his Japanese girlfriend. From the moment that Ang had finished feeding the yaks and released them to graze, he began devouring quantities of food. A three-egg omelette vanished in seconds, followed by a Sherpa fry. Then a pot of chang and some tea. Then another omelette. Then more chang.

Occasionally the Sherpa host would throw another precious log or handful of dung on the fire, and there would be a short blaze of light to answer the gusts of wind outside, pummelling the little door and window. The American and his girl held hands and crooned. It seemed indelicate not to let them have the small back room to themselves. Ang had already curled up by the fire, so I suggested to Caroline that we should try out the tent.

▲ Pangboche village, sheltering in its high valley, is the site of the oldest monastery in the Khumbu region. Towering behind it is the dramatic peak of Ama Dablam.

Before it got quite dark, I pitched the little green globe in a small enclosure behind the lodge. Back home Gillian, who knew about sleeping-bag romances like the one in *For Whom the Bell Tolls*, had been nervous of moments like these. I had tried to reassure her.

Caroline had a good many zip-bags carried up on Mucker, each one with an essential part of her equipment, hand and face cream, lotions, medicines, tapes,

▲ The arduous task of preparing recently frozen ground for potatoes. Not all villagers have yaks to help them with ploughing.

meticulously folded clothes. Her sleeping-bag was warm and luxurious; the rubber cushion used on Sod's back became a pillow.

'Do you have to have all this baggage—it takes up so much room?'

'I need it. Please don't disturb me. Can't you see I'm reading?' In addition to her torch, which she hung from the apex of the tent, she wore a special reading lamp strapped around her head like a miner's lamp. The batteries in my own torch had already grown weak. As I shivered on my side of the tent—Dingboche is over 14,000 feet—I watched her huge shadow on the green tent wall looking like a praying mantis.

Next morning I swore that nothing would induce me to sleep in the tent again. 'Please yourself,' Caroline said. 'I was very comfortable.' The American and the Japanese had had a good night. Ang was on his second breakfast.

We did not travel that day. The yaks were off-colour and Caroline stayed in the lodge. I left her beside the fire and went off along a track leading up to the end of the valley and a small settlement called Chukhung.

A pair of yaks was pulling a plough, preparing the ground for potatoes. Ploughing with yoked animals is a relatively recent innovation in these parts, and until the 1930s all ploughing was done by men.

Potatoes came into Nepal during the last century. No one knows exactly when and how. The two most likely sources are bungalow gardens in Darjiling and the garden of the British Embassy in Kathmandu. They spread quickly.

A hundred years ago the population of the Khumbu area was a fraction of its present size, and the potato has been held largely responsible for the fourfold increase. Something similar happened in Ireland before the famine. The new food supply not only reduced mortality among Sherpas, but encouraged immigration from Tibet.

I was reminded of the west of Ireland, seeing little fields surrounded by stone walls and cottages with smoke pouring through the roofs similar to Connemara cabins a century ago. A few differences—the big mountains, the stench of latrine manure.

I reached a scattering of houses surrounded by a wasteland of stones, where a bitter wind ruffled the hair of grazing yaks and blew through the cabins. Mountains glowered, the formidable south face of Lhotse to the north, Ama Dablam flanked by fluted ice walls blocking the horizon to the south, the east face of Taweche to the southwest. Sheer, rocky spines and tough-looking glaciers loomed a few yards away. I climbed a moraine up a buttress and then went horizontally along a razorback ridge. All around it was a dolorous, frozen realm of tumbling ridges and glaciers blocking off most of the sky. Dante's *eterno rezzo*, eternal shade. For once I felt myself with the real old-timers, who would think a view like this was a place of horror.

Down at Dingboche snow was falling on two yaks tied to a plough stirring up a patch of frozen earth. In another field men and women dug away with their hoes as the blizzard swept over them. Thick, dark woollen dresses and cloaks, old felt boots, crazy fur hats, smiling faces. Rasping wind and driving snow.

The lodge was crammed to the roof with trekkers: Israelis, Americans, Germans, English and a French girl incessantly playing a guitar. It was as if a bus had driven up and deposited them.

Paradoxically the search for grandeur and solitude results in communal living of a kind that would never occur domestically. An Israeli had the end of his sleeping-bag in my mouth, a talkative American placed his head on my knee, beside me the French girl protected her virtue with her guitar. The big problem was getting up and going outside.

'For God's sake ... some people are trying to sleep.'

'The Irishman has the runs.'

The wind had dropped. In the distance a bar of dawn light shone behind a

◄ **Trekkers and Sherpas enjoy an impromptu party in a typical trekkers' lodge—despite the sign prohibiting dancing!**

mountain, making it glow, and all around were stars. There was no sound from the little tent where Caroline slept aloof.

By seven o'clock the French girl was consulting her Schneider map, the Israelis were eating tinned porridge in between picking dirt out of their nails. By eight o'clock it was quite warm and the sky was clear. The best time of day. Caroline emerged from the tent legs first. Sod and Mucker were given hay and potatoes and Ang's face showed a meagre contentment as he settled down to breakfast. The bill was calculated on the honour system, guests writing down what they had eaten. I never saw a Sherpa query a bill.

▲ A typical Sherpa kitchen with Thermos flasks on the shelves, tea-kettle ready and steaming above the fire, and a cake of dried yak-dung fuel waiting on the hearth.

As we left the main track and climbed past a lone chorten above the village, a helicopter flew past in the direction of Everest. Climbing Everest was a seasonal occupation like planting potatoes. This year the government had raised the peak fee, but still there was a queue of international teams prepared to pay the price. Everest was millionaire country.

Caroline rode Sod, whose pace was infinitely slow. His gloom was bottomless; at the slightest excuse he would drop his head towards the ground. If Caroline wished to turn left, he went right, or backwards, or forwards, or just stopped. The yak always knew better.

We were entering what is generally regarded as the final and most dramatic sequence of the Everest trail. Far below the ridge on which we were travelling so slowly, we could see the hospital at Pheriche which treated AMS sufferers. The tin roof shone in the empty brown valley like a star.

At midday we stopped at the end of the Khumbu Glacier at Duglha, which consisted of two small tea-houses. A Sherpa sat darning his trousers on a wall on which was painted in futile white letters KEEP THE EVEREST TRAIL CLEAN. Caroline dismounted and the yaks were led across a small wooden bridge. 'Milk or black tea?' asked the woman who came out of the View Hotel restaurant, as matter-of-fact as if it was on a motorway. We sipped white tea, Ang ate some bowls of dhal and rice and the yaks were given a bucketful of slops.

The trail went straight up, and soon the View Hotel restaurant was reduced to a dot. There was nothing easy about this climb; every few yards I stopped, gasping, with thoughts of the shining tin roof of Pheriche. Behind me the two yaks followed step by step, showing more sense than usual, while above us circled a couple of choughs.

We came to a sad place, a line of chortens commemorating Sherpas killed in accidents on mountains. The casualty rate among Sherpas is high, as it is among all climbers on the highest mountains. Porters have to negotiate icefalls and glaciers a number of times during one expedition, lugging up supplies, while in many cases the foreigner who is paying them only has to do the same route twice, up and then down again. Often it is the most enterprising and promising young men from villages in the area who are victims of the lust to put a flag on a mountain top. And because there are so few of them, because they are all interrelated and their communities are small, the effect on Sherpa society can be terrible. The first attempt on Everest in 1922 brought about the death of seven Sherpas in an avalanche below the North Col, and since 1953 over a hundred have perished in mountaineering accidents.

Mucker's Fall

Beyond these first chortens we came out into another stark view of rocks and boulders, where a bluff of land below us fell into a plain of red shale with mountains beyond. It was not the best place to decide to take a turn on Sod's back, but the climb had been exhausting. The yaks stopped, Caroline dismounted, Ang complained and Mucker disappeared. One moment he was there with Ang beside him spluttering as usual, 'I tell you, Peter too heavy …' The next moment …

We went to the edge of the path and peered over where Mucker had rolled down the slope. Far below a forlorn white face gazed up amid luggage and scattered bags of hay. He may have been bruised, but he had bounced like rubber. A long time passed in the midst of desolation while he was caught and dragged back to the trail and the luggage was retrieved, reloaded and retied.

We trooped into Lobujya, Caroline back on Sod, Ang leading Mucker by the nose, the wretched animal showing not even the trace of a limp. Back in 1953

Heavily laden yaks and zopkioks bringing supplies to far-flung settlements, teahouses and travellers along the Everest trail. ▼

when Sir John Hunt had established a rest camp during the first ascent of Everest, Lobujya had been almost at the world's end, a couple of yersas in the trough between the glacial moraine and the mountains. Now the yersas had multiplied to become tourist lodges and guesthouses, while all over the moraine tents had been pitched full of weary travellers suffering from headaches and racking coughs.

We paid a visit to a Norwegian team which happened to be climbing Everest, a tough-looking lot of Vikings with golden beards and skin the colour of chestnut conkers.

Arne, the leader, told us that there might be an attempt on the summit during the next few days, and during that time trekkers who visited Base Camp would not be permitted to stay and put up their tents. But an exception would be made for us.

This was another night of dithering communal sleeping, when even Caroline rejected the tent and came into the heaving warren where sleep was snatched amid coughs and the sound of yak bells outside. In the morning, Everest fever gripped everyone. Except for the Canadian couple who crouched near a large

The great 'slag heap' of the Khumbu Glacier. It has been compressed into peaks and is scattered with boulders and grey shingle from the surrounding mountains. ▼

rock with another painted notice: KEEP THE AREA CLEAN. PLEASE BURN AND BURY ALL GARBAGE. The woman was diligently lighting a little fire only a few yards from a great pile of refuse left by other visitors.

Many trekkers had moved on, but some remained to watch Caroline prepare to mount Sod in a moment of grand theatre. Today he nearly killed her. Hardly had she mounted when he was off with a violent lurch, breaking into a gallop. One moment she was mistress of her fate, the next she was being bucketed along by a bolting yak. When he threw her, she found herself in the classic lethal hunting situation, with her boot caught in the noose of rope which acted as a stirrup. With her leg and foot stretched upwards and her head and body rumbling along the ground in Sod's wake, it looked as if she was going to be killed. Then he stopped.

I had the eyes of a dozen gaping trekkers on me as I ran up. 'Are you all right?'

'Don't be so bloody stupid. Get my leg out of the rope.'

Whether God was watching over her, or whether Sod had just run out of steam, was immaterial. Apart from a few scratches and a swelling round her ankle, she was uninjured.

'Stupid ass!' She had plenty of energy left to berate Ang, who had been lighting up a cigarette instead of holding the rein. Then she gamely insisted on remounting. There was no more trouble, and Sod walked on slowly and imperturbably through the rocks as if he was trying to make up for his awful crime.

Around him the grey shingle of the Khumbu Glacier looked like a giant slag heap. Here in this particular stretch of wilderness there was no trail, and the only method of finding the way was to follow the little heaps of stones put up as markers. At one of them we came across the body of a man; a small, well-built Sherpa wearing windproof jacket, jogging trousers and heavy boots was lying stretched on the ground, his eyes tightly shut, his mouth open.

'He take rest,' Ang said, peering closer. 'He famous climber. He climb Everest three time.'

We looked at the celebrity with more interest. He opened his eyes and gazed round blankly.

'Too much chang. People give me too much chang. Ooh … Aah …' He clutched his head. He was fêted wherever he went. Other Everest heroes have had a similar problem.

'Are you staying here?'

'No, no. Today I must go to second camp to join other team.'

As he walked along with us, he would sit down every few minutes and groan. Finally, we went ahead to Gorak Shep, leaving him holding his head in his

A yersa near Everest Base Camp, humorously signposted as a hotel, provides shelter for weary climbers and trekkers, especially in bad weather.

hands. Somehow, before the day was out, he was expected to climb the Khumbu Icefall and Glacier.

Gorak Shep was the end of the line—all change for Everest. Beyond the meagre converted yersa huts—one called Yeti·Lodge—were screes of rock heralding the Khumbu Glacier, and somewhere behind them we would find Base Camp.

After reviving with tea I spent the day under a boulder engaged in the familiar Himalayan pastime of admiring the view. The whole world of the Himalayas reached a crescendo here, with Nuptse and Lhotse pleated like ruffs, not to mention the grand old lady herself with wisps of cloud around her dark triangular summit. Occasionally I heard the rumble of an avalanche and saw white smoke flaring down a mountainside.

We slept in a Sherpa version of the Great Bed of Ware, a wooden platform at the end of a hut which managed to accommodate a couple of dozen bodies. Late at night I woke among the snoring sleeping-bags and saw the stars through a gap in the roof, nearer and brighter than I had ever seen them before. In the morning the first thing I laid my eyes on after waking was Mucker's white head framed in the doorway. He was hungry, Sod was hungry, Ang was hungry, and their meals, together with our porridge and expedition tinned pears, came to 60 rupees. Prices rose with altitude.

A large memorial slab inscribed with the names of dead Everest climbers marked where the final leg of the route dropped down onto the Khumbu Glacier. The hills of gravel were sooty grey and everywhere frozen needles of ice stuck out from the moraine.

The yaks were behaving like angels. Crunch, crunch went their footsteps across the glassy ice with its bands of light, pale green, arctic white, sapphire and winking ruby mixed together with kaleidoscopic changes. The ice curtain shrouding the glacier shifts constantly with the seasons and the movement of the glacier itself. We were conscious only of the perpetual, jewelled changes of light as we followed a track into the heart of the glacier, past hidden streams and pools of ice between the fingers of the moraine that had to be negotiated.

The yaks did not seem perturbed by the idea of vanishing down a gaping hole, and even appeared to be enjoying the walk. The worse the terrain became, the more flamboyant their manner, as if they wished to demonstrate their skill in movement. We rode and walked alternately until after a couple of hours we came to a frozen patch of water, which could have been a stream or lake. It had to be crossed. The distance was only about fifty yards, but there was no way of telling the thickness of the ice or the depth of the water.

If I had been Ang I would have turned straight back to Gorak Shep, but he meekly lined them up to face the crossing as we sat down to watch. Generally the two animals followed each other nose to tail, but now Ang's technique was to give them each an encouraging wallop and set them racing across the ice. Sod went ahead, and there was a nasty crunch as ice splintered. I covered my eyes.

'They're off!' shouted Caroline, like a racing commentator.

'What about Mucker?'

'He's after him!'

Even if yaks' manners and temperament are to be deplored, there is something endearing about them that makes people smile. The two comical furry animals hoarsely grunting to each other were skidding across the green surface, Mucker with his load, Sod's bushy tail held up behind his back like a cat's. Yaks are best. We gently tiptoed after them.

Base Camp

On the far side the glacier turned sharp right, and the final part of the route to Everest opened up to a vista put up by a grand master of theatrical design. All the rocks and silted debris of the moraine vanished, and in its place were glistening spires of ice that stretched ahead as thick as a forest. Once we were in among them, the light changed to a pale, ghostly green. For a long time two yaks and three people stumbled through this forest of huge green stalagmites until we reached a short escarpment. When we were at the top we could see the tents of Base Camp enclosed in ice; the Khumbu Icefall tumbled above our heads in white frills.

Base Camp is not actually a specific site, just a location among the moraines at the foot of the Khumbu Icefall where different expeditions have chosen to erect a series of shanty towns. The atmosphere was like a miners' camp without the saloon bar.

Glaciers—Vast Stores of Fresh Water

▲ An ice-table on the Khumbu Glacier. A column of ice supports a large stone, which shades it from the heat of the sun. All around the ice-table the glacier is rapidly melting.

IN THE COLDEST AREAS OF THE GLOBE, snow that falls heavily without melting is gradually compressed by its own weight into ice, which eventually forms into glaciers. This is a slow process, taking many millions of years and producing enormous volumes of ice. In Antarctica, for example, the continental glacier (or ice cap) is up to 6,500 feet deep—so deep that entire mountain ranges are buried beneath it. In fact, scientists calculate that roughly three-quarters of the Earth's fresh water is stored as glacial ice; enough to cause sea levels worldwide to rise by some 197 feet if it were all to melt.

Glaciers that form high on mountainsides (alpine glaciers) cannot grow to such great depths, as they are being pulled steadily downwards by gravity; for a large mass of ice under pressure is not brittle, but behaves like tar, flowing steadily at about six feet per day. Sometimes, however, for reasons that are not well understood, a glacier will surge forward at up to 192 feet per day and destroy everything in its path.

Himalayan glaciers usually carry vast quantities of rock and other debris on their upper surface, which they deposit in great heaps known as moraines. Strange sights can be seen here—not least the 'glacial tables' where a rock weighing many tons perches on top of a column of ice that has yet to melt.

Caroline went off to find our Norwegian friends. A few yards away was an American camp with its Stars and Stripes, for the Americans, too, were about to climb Everest by a different route. From a tent labelled COOKHOUSE came an appetising smell of Western food, something like hamburgers—why did it smell so different from yak steak? Up here in the sharp cold I felt a sudden longing for a change in diet, for something other than instant soup or potatoes or the massive choice of Sherpa menus. Various big men in climbing gear were drinking coffee and munching biscuits in the sun. The tents were interspersed with lines of prayer flags and little chortens, while here and there stone corrals containing stacks of folding plastic chairs had been built so that men could sit and sunbathe, protected from the wind.

Caroline returned with the Nepalese liaison officer.

'Please put your tent anywhere.' He pointed to rocks and boulders thrown up by a gigantic geological upheaval.

Leaving Ang with the yaks we skirmished around, and soon concluded that anything in the nature of a good place to pitch our tent had already been taken. What was left was a wedge of ice overhanging a garbage heap.

I nudged some sacks of trash and rusting tins. A number of choughs were hopping about, checking for discarded food. Choughs are amazing birds who think nothing of soaring with the climbers; Sir John Hunt noticed one strutting about on the South Col at 26,000 feet. At Base Camp there was plenty of food

Bright strings of prayer flags flutter over the tents and supplies of several international expeditions at Everest Base Camp. ▼

for them to search out among forty years' accumulation of rubbish. A lot of people have visited—if you take an average of three porters to every mountaineer—and everyone has left bits and pieces. The average tin can takes a hundred years to disintegrate; a plastic six-pack cover, four hundred and fifty years. That is at sea level; up here they are indestructible, unless sometime the glacier comes down and covers everything.

There was excitement in the Norwegian camp since two of their people were perched on the big mountain and hoped to reach the top next day.

'The weather prospects are not so good.' One of the support team looked up at the icefall. From down here you could not actually see Everest at all, and it was a strange feeling to sit drinking coffee, aware of the men above our heads in their icy starting positions. The blue cross of Norway wavered on its red background in the dusk. Whatever money could provide and human ingenuity could produce was being used for the national ego trip.

▲ A corner of Base Camp lies at the foot of the treacherous Khumbu Icefall—a constantly shifting 'waterfall' of glacial ice. Here, prayer flags fail to conceal the growing piles of rubbish.

We sat in our little tent, so much smaller than the rest, fiddling with the primus, watching the gushes of flame go up to sear the green roof. When the water refused to boil, we consumed half-cold noodles just before a climber from a large neighbouring tent came our way with the gift of some cookies and a warning. It seemed that the water we had scooped up from the crystal glacial stream bubbling out of ice and rock contained plenty of nasties which were difficult to boil to death. Pollution had come to Everest years ago with the early climbers and their attendants—people at Base Camp have been suffering attacks of stomach trouble for three decades.

The night spent beside the detritus of dirty mountaineers was made excruciating by sharp stones rising beneath the ground sheet, and the roar of avalanches. Caroline slept adequately in her cocoon. By eight o'clock the cold had gone and the sun had begun to heat up the rock. From our lowly position looking up the icefall, the distant peaks were like unattainable celestial abodes. Down here Base Camp, like Dante's Hell, was too hot or too cold.

Caroline managed to get some water from the Sherpa cookhouse which had been well boiled, and we had the luxury of tea. We lay among the rocks watching the Norwegians and Sherpas pass another day in the warmth. A group of Sherpas played cards; a Norwegian shaved outside his tent, one of the few to do so; and from the radio tent came a burst of anxious static to remind us that this was not an ordinary day. Among the half-naked figures lounging in the sun, you could feel the tension of waiting.

Things were a lot more relaxed in the American camp a few yards away, where an assault on the summit still lay in the future. Another acreage of tents, enclosures and prayer flags was surrounded by ice axes, air bottles, coils of nylon rope, canned food stacked in the snow. Someone had contrived to make a solar shower out of a plastic bag.

'Hold it there!' A photographer was taking pictures for the expedition book of a Sherpa pretending to play a shining steel ice shovel like a guitar. The shovel manufacturers were among the sponsors of the team. It was hard to find a place to pose without a backdrop of garbage.

The Americans were trying the more difficult route by the Lho La, while the Norwegians hacked their way up the more familiar Khumbu Icefall towards Hillary's 'impressive but not disheartening' (his words) approach to the summit. The two routes, almost beside each other, seemed equally dangerous: the precipice below the Lho La up which the Americans had to climb and winch their gear before making the final assault, and the glacier already studded with the Norwegians' sixty steel ladders. The climbers would have to pass by a corpse, someone who had perished up there a few expeditions ago, and could not be retrieved. Frozen, inaccessible, but not invisible, the cadaver remained there, a spectral sentinel, and anyone going by would see it.

In the afternoon we learned that the current attempt on the summit had failed because of bad weather. 'Second team have chance,' said the liaison officer.

The First Harp on Everest

Next day we set off on the way down. I looked back at the mountains, the four giants, Pumo Ri, Lhotse, Nuptse and Everest in its cloud, and decided that the difference in their heights was meaningless.

Coming back to Lobujya we could see with fresh eyes how we all tarnished the great landscape. Here was another group setting out for Pumo Ri. We were told of a surfboard enthusiast set to skim down Everest's side. Outside Lobujya we came upon a small Sherpa porter bending under the weight of a harp. Behind him strode a woman wearing an embroidered jacket on which was stitched in large gold letters FIRST HARP ON EVEREST. Without a word they passed on their way.

▲ Discarded oxygen cylinders litter the South Col (25,938 feet) of Mount Everest. They represent only a tiny part of the rubbish now polluting the mountain.

Next evening we reached Pangboche, the oldest village in the Khumbu area, settled around four hundred years ago from Tibet. We found Ang's house, a two-storey building set in a nest of fields. Ang's mother made us welcome, greeting us as honoured guests and sitting us in the long narrow principal room while she prepared a lavish meal over the fire. Everywhere around the house you came across reminders of climbing expeditions, since the family, like so many in this region, was closely involved in mountaineering.

In the morning we set out towards Namche. Ahead was Thyangboche crowning its wooded hill. In the short time we had been up to Base Camp spring had come. The slopes were sprinkled with pink primula and blue iris; the buds on the plants we had seen on the way up had opened, and as we climbed the hill to the gompa, azaleas and rhododendrons bloomed on either side. The yaks seemed even more disgruntled than usual, sniffing suspiciously at the flowers; they were

leaving their natural habitat of snow and ice to travel down into a decadent flowering forest made for other beasts.

We followed the familiar trail where trees had turned a bright green in the warm, spring light. A haze covered the mountains, the air smelt of resin and everything in nature seemed a harmonious whole.

From Khumjung, set in layers of potato fields, we followed the road up through the trees to the Everest View Hotel. In the big, cold, empty dining room we ate tinned soup and omelette.

The hotel manager, huddled in an anorak, a woolly hat pulled over his ears, came bustling up to tell us that the big mountain had just been climbed by the second team of Norwegians.

'Mr Bonington, he also top out.' We knew that Chris Bonington had been at Base Camp. We toasted him in Coca-Cola, feeling satisfaction at the achievements of old men.

Back in Namche, Ang was paid off, and the relationship between the hirer and the hired, so long, so intense, so full of emotion, drama and tension, came to an abrupt end. You could not call it friendship, but there was some sort of mutual respect and satisfaction.

Goodbye, Sod, goodbye, Mucker. Going to the airfield at Lukla, we hired a reliable old zopkiok to carry our baggage down along the Dudh Kosi valley.

▲ Spring in a valley in the Khumbu region. Only a few miles from Everest Base Camp, azaleas and rhododendrons bloom on the hillsides.

The Ascent of Mount Everest

IN 1852 THE SURVEY OF INDIA calculated that Peak XV, hitherto merely a distant summit in Nepal, was 29,002 feet high, and therefore the highest mountain on Earth. The Survey renamed it after Sir George Everest, the brilliant Surveyor-General of India from 1830 to 1843.

Early efforts to reach Everest were frustrated by its position on the border between the closed kingdoms of Nepal and Tibet, but in 1921 a British reconnaissance party was allowed to approach through Tibet. A full-scale expedition followed in 1922, when a British team, using primitive oxygen equipment, reached 27,300 feet on the Northeast Ridge. In 1924 Colonel Edward Norton climbed to over 28,100 feet without oxygen, and during the same expedition George Mallory and Andrew Irvine disappeared while 'going for the top'. Some people believe they may well have reached the summit.

By 1951 Tibet had closed and Nepal had opened, and in that year a British reconnaissance team climbed the hazardous Khumbu Icefall into Everest's secluded Western Cwm at 20,200 feet. The following year a strong Swiss team ascended the Southeast Ridge above the cwm to 28,200 feet. Then, in 1953, Colonel John (later Lord) Hunt succeeded in placing two climbers—New Zealander Edmund Hillary and Sherpa Tenzing Norgay—on the summit of Everest. The next 20 years saw only six successful ascents, but by December 1992 no fewer than a hundred teams had climbed the mountain by ten different routes, and 485 climbers had reached the summit—now measured at 29,028 feet. For many people, Everest has become rather a mountaineering circus.

▲ Sir George Everest, the distinguished geographer after whom the world's highest mountain is named.

The 1924 British Mount Everest expedition. Irvine and Mallory, standing on the left, never returned from an attempt on the summit. ▶

▲ Edmund Hillary and Tenzing Norgay prepare to leave the South Col on 28 May 1953. At 11.30 the next morning they were standing on the highest point on Earth.

The Khumbu Icefall is the first obstacle of an ascent via Everest's Western Cwm. This glacial cataract is in constant motion and its shifting crevasses present one of the most hazardous stages of this route. ▶

▲ The British climber Chris Bonington on the lower part of Everest's long Northeast Ridge. The saddle in the bottom right is the North Col.

TIBET   NEPAL

▲ A rare, aerial view of the North Face of Mount Everest, taken from above Tibet.

PEAKS
1 Mt Everest (29,028 feet)
2 Lhotse (27,940 feet)
3 Nuptse (25,850 feet)
4 Makalu (27,766 feet)
5 Pumo Ri (23,442 feet)

KEY TO MOUNT EVEREST
Ⓐ Khumbu Glacier
Ⓑ Base Camp (17,400 feet)
Ⓒ Khumbu Icefall
Ⓓ Western Cwm

Ⓔ Lhotse Face
Ⓕ South Col (25,938 feet)
Ⓖ South Summit (28,700 feet)
Ⓗ Northeast Ridge
Ⓘ North Face
Ⓙ West Ridge
Ⓚ Southwest Face
Ⓛ Southwest Shoulder
Ⓜ Lho La Col (19,770 feet)
Ⓝ West Rongbuk Glacier
Ⓞ North Col
Ⓟ East Rongbuk Glacier

EXPEDITION ROUTES
① Route from Gorak Shep
② British, 1924, 1933
◈ High point reached by British in 1924 and 1933 (>28,100 feet)
③ British, 1953
④ Chinese, 1960
⑤ American, 1963
⑥ Japanese, 1980
⑦ Australian, 1984

CHAPTER 4

Journey to Lhasa

Ｉ N Kathmandu Caroline collected her mail. 'Look what I've got—your Tibetan visa.'

Caroline had taken visitors to Tibet several times the long way round via China on a Hong Kong visa which enabled her to enter mainland China—of which Tibet was now officially a part. Her friend in Hong Kong had got one for me, but now there were strong rumours that visas for China issued in Hong Kong would no longer be valid at the Nepal–Tibet border. The Chinese wanted to regulate visitors more closely. They did not want a string of impoverished trekkers, only wealthy tourists bearing loads of hard currency.

▲ A terraced hillside in Nepal. Careful terracing such as this is essential to prevent rainwater from draining off the steep slopes and taking most of the soil with it into the valley below.

Everyone we asked agreed. 'Hong Kong visa no good.'

So we evolved a plan which was utterly illegal. It centred on there being very little wrong with our passports, just the lack of a name. They needed a destination written in by the Chinese Embassy in Kathmandu. The words 'Good for Lhasa' would be sufficient.

'Maybe George can doctor them,' I suggested.

George was a Hong Kong Chinese, one of a select group of foreigners at the Kathmandu Guest House whose mysterious comings and goings aroused envy among those tied to plebeian group treks. He and a few carefully selected companions had a scheme to bicycle into Tibet on collapsible mountain bikes with eighteen gears.

George's Chinese calligraphy was exquisite. We persuaded him to help us without much trouble, perhaps because his own plans were as daft as ours. We lent him a pen and the operation took a minute. He examined his handiwork with pride. 'I think that should do.'

'Wonderful!'

One day later we were on our way towards the People's Autonomous Republic of Tibet in a Land-Rover, which was decorated with a board on which was painted HARRY'S JOURNEY. It was an anxious time and we didn't speak much as we drove past skeins of paddy fields with the occasional group of trekkers trudging down the road bearing their rucksacks. With each hairpin bend, the idea of presenting our forged visas seemed less good.

We travelled all day, until we reached a steep valley. Small villages with little terraced fields around them lay clear of the rocks, while a river poured its way down like a spurt of beer released from a bottle. The valley narrowed to a gorge;

overhead the sky was blue, but down here everything was in shadow.

Deep in the gloom was Tatopani, the Nepalese customs post, a scrapheap of a town full of flimsy huts. We crossed the still-unfinished skeleton of Freedom Bridge, which divided Nepal from Tibet. Men and women were breaking stones with hammers and carrying baskets of earth, under the supervision of Chinese engineers in blue uniforms. On the far side of the gorge a waterfall splashed down and higher up were patches of cleared land and a few stone huts. Through vapoury mist, mountain peaks glistened in the sky.

We reached the border town of Zhangmu, a contrast to Tatopani with its brand-new lines of flat-roofed white houses and a large building with a flag waiting to receive visitors. We drove through the entrance onto a concrete ramp where a Chinese soldier stood waiting.

Caroline said, 'I'll do the talking.'

I watched her go up to the window and talk Chinese. I could see an official peering at George's ideograms. For some time nothing happened and there was just the cheep of voices and unexplained silences. Then an officer came out and directed our baggage to the main hall to be examined.

We quickly paid off the driver, and then we were sitting on a bench in the empty customs hall. The place smelt of disinfectant; minutes passed. Then an official appeared and handed back our passports. We were free to go.

We left, carrying our bags. There are no porters in the People's Republic. Although we had pared down everything, the loads were immense: Caroline's rucksack, zip-bags and camera equipment, my large rucksack and an unwieldy

◄ The Chinese-built Friendship Highway, which connects Nepal and Tibet, here passes through the Tibetan border town of Zhangmu. Since 1954 the Chinese have constructed over 12,000 miles of roads in Tibet.

duffle bag marked mendaciously ANNAPURNA EXPEDITION, containing the tent, food, medicine and other useful things. A few steps filled me with bad thoughts about all the weary miles ahead.

The road turned up the hill in a series of dusty loops away from the neat customs house, to where the rest of Zhangmu was jumbled together in a collection of huts, just like its sister town down the road on the other side of the border. We hoped to find a lorry and put a distance between ourselves and the frontier, but we immediately faced problems. In Nepal people still enjoy meeting and helping foreigners, but here we found any attempt to enter into a commercial travelling arrangement met with *No, no, no.* Staggering under our bags, we climbed the hill to more houses, barracks, and more lorries packed with timber

or soldiers staring down. No lifts. It began to rain, then to hail and the road turned to mud.

Caroline said, 'We must find a bed. We'll have to try again tomorrow.'

Just before dark we managed to obtain accommodation in a room full of broken beds, empty except for a Japanese couple huddled together on a stained mattress trying to keep warm. Wind poured through cracks and the roof leaked, making puddles on the floor. We were charged the equivalent of £2 a night; it was not worth a penny more.

Stomach trouble compounded my misery and during the night I had to leave my dirty bed countless times to stumble out into the rain and crouch in the mud. In the morning I felt like a ghost. Caroline gave me a couple of her pills.

We struggled from the hut with our luggage into the steep shanty town, where wisps of malodorous mist hung above the gorge and clung to the pea-green jackets of soldiers. Soldiers were all over the town, a multitude of bright green uniforms and red enamel stars on peaked caps. Here on the frontier the People's Army seemed unoccupied and bored. There were no proper cafés or other garrison amusements. There seemed to be mighty few Tibetans.

Two cars swept around a bend on the way down to the customs post and we had time to glimpse some Caucasian faces. Abandoning our bags we ran down the hill in pursuit. At the post we found two Italians covered in dust and a young Scottish couple.

The Scottish pair told us how they had rented their van with great difficulty in Lhasa in order to see more of Tibet. The problem had been the driver. Throughout the journey he had ignored them and taken no notice of any requests they made. He gave an extra dimension to the concept of rudeness.

Anthony's clipped Scots vowels came through clenched teeth. 'If you've ever really hated anyone, double that again, and you'll get some tiny indication of the way I feel about that bastard!'

The Italians were continuing their journey down to Kathmandu. 'Thank God we leave Tibet! Thank God we go to Nepal! Thank God!' But miraculously Anthony and Jean were returning to Lhasa, since their exit visas only permitted them to leave Tibet through China. There were eight seats in the van.

'You realise it's not very comfortable. Bump, bump, until your backside is splitting.'

'Oh, we don't mind!' We arranged to meet in an hour.

When we returned with our baggage a crowd had gathered round the van, and in among the spectators Anthony and the driver were facing each other, shouting. In his hand Anthony waved the distributor cap he had torn from the engine. 'He's a bastard!' The roar was an octave deeper than the driver's Chinese cries. 'Bastard! Now he says he must have special permission to bring us back.'

'Why?'

'You can speak Chinese, for Christ's sake! Tell him that unless we go now, I keep the distributor!'

The driver spoke to Caroline in the tones of a hoarse budgerigar. Then Caroline began loading our luggage.

The driver had consented to go back to Lhasa with his passengers. Anthony returned the distributor, the crowd wandered off, and to my great joy we were driving up the hill past the shacks of Zhangmu.

On into Tibet

Tibet greets you with wind and silence.

First came snow-covered mountains and then the perpetual, wide, empty gravel plain. There were no houses or trees or people. Everything was caught in an intensity of landscape and sky. The light changed constantly so that the colours of the plain fluctuated from chocolate-brown to brilliant pink and red, while the sky above had a hard enamel sheen. A few waterless ornamental clouds were dispersing. An ochre mountain suddenly became striped like a tiger; a patch of shimmering shale would vanish as you looked.

I sat beside the driver who crouched over the wheel in his padded Mao jacket and green cap, muttering and grumbling to himself. Behind sat the Scots, then Caroline, and behind her a late entry into the van, the Japanese couple who had shared our grim lodgings the night before. We were climbing higher into space, and every so often the radiator of the van belched clouds of steam. The driver would stop, search out a frozen pool of water, open the bonnet and administer a few sharp douses over the engine as one might smack a naughty child. We came to Kose, a derelict village set in the burnt gravel plain with a few strips of green, a rusty corroded landscape where the only life was the movement of black thumbmarks that were grazing yaks. A large mud tower stood quite alone in the gravel, while high on the hill were other scattered ruins and some sort of walled citadel coloured bright red perched on an overhanging escarpment above them.

Here the Japanese got out and left us. All the time they had been in the van they had been taking photographs and collecting information, like squirrels storing nuts for the winter. Nothing escaped them: the speed of the van, rate of ascent, altitude, bird life, blood pressure. They bowed politely as we waved goodbye and went off to photograph the backside of Everest.

We travelled all day through wilderness with dust filtering in through doors and windows. Wearing her face mask, only a nose and eyes showing, Caroline looked as if she was frightening away evil spirits. The Scottish pair had similarly concealed their faces, and I was learning that climatic conditions here dictated that we should dress the part of gunmen in a western. Covered up like that made it hard to talk. I fell asleep and woke to shouts. Anthony was tapping his head with relish.

'Now you can see what I've had to put up with!'

'We want to take photographs!' Jean said.

'What are we paying you for, you bastard?'

'Don't get excited!'

'WHO'S GETTING EXCITED?'

Caroline said in Chinese, 'I will report you to the authorities in Lhasa.'

I felt a little sorry for the driver, who subsided and pulled the van to a halt. We got out and looked to the west edged by a slab of the Himalayas, with Everest among them standing out clearly against the bright blue sky. From this side the range looked diminished compared to the towering mountains above the great, convoluted valleys we had explored with the yaks, for here the table-land seemed to touch their waists.

In the evening we reached Tingri. I had not quite shaken off the dream of arriving at this important religious centre with lamas in their thousands outside their gompas and the air resounding with the braying of horns and rustle of prayer flags. Present-day reality was a flat-roofed compound, the prototype of dozens of similar staging posts scattered all over the country, consisting of four lines of low, mudwalled rooms arranged around a main yard full of lorries.

The driver left us to grab a room and order himself a good meal. Why should that set us all off in another rage? Altitude, altitude! Four hungry, furious foreigners, glimpsing him sitting contentedly at a deal table picking away at

little dishes with his chopsticks, were provoked to another row about food and accommodation, a row which became fiercer with the arrival of a concierge in khaki uniform holding a bunch of keys. Anthony shrieked, Caroline argued over prices, Jean and I nodded in agreement. We should have been ashamed of ourselves.

'She wants the equivalent of six pounds a night!'

'That's quite ridiculous! The normal price for this sort of place should be about two.'

'Oh, let's just accept.'

'Don't be so feeble, Peter. If you let them get away with it, heaven help other travellers coming this way.'

We were brought to an empty hall where a man in chef's uniform dished out ladles of supper through a hatch. After we had eaten, the concierge reappeared and to the accompaniment of much key jingling we were led to a small dormitory furnished with six iron beds, on which were placed rolled-up coverlets and bolsters. Washbasin, towel, candles and a large Thermos of hot water were provided by the state.

A Novel Reveille

At daybreak we were woken by martial music. It was the first time that I had heard this particular way of saying *Good morning, get up*, but Caroline had endured it before and the Scots had had more than enough of it. The squeaky

▲ The Himalayas gleam white over the arid Tibetan plateau. From left to right are the great peaks of Makalu (27,766 feet), Kangchungtse (25,065 feet), Everest (29,028 feet), Gyachung Kang (25,910 feet) and Cho Oyu (26,906 feet).

urgency of the non-stop, marching rhythm vibrating around the little room and rattling the windowpanes set Anthony on a familiar round of curses.

The sleeping compound was in the new Chinese enclave, cut off from the Tibetans, a colonial outpost kept as rigidly separate as the cantonment and the bazaar in Imperial India. There were no gardens, and the houses, built in People's Republic Ramshackle—one storey high with tin roofs—lacked any feeling of permanence.

We did not see much of the Tibetan part of town because the driver treated our request to visit it with contempt, spinning us out onto the main Lhasa road where there was next to no traffic, a lorry every few miles or so, and the odd horseman kicking up dust. We passed shepherds wrapped in sheepskin coats surrounded by their flocks, who swivelled as if they were watching a tennis shot while they followed our bumpy progress. Foreigners were still rarities.

Soon I saw my first real Tibetan village, placed under a crumbling ledge of golden rock, almost indistinguishable from the surrounding landscape. Small brown houses were arranged in layers, each crowned with fluttering pennants and prayer flags, each with its own little courtyard. The windows and doorways were splashed white and the only signs of life were women collecting baskets of dried sticks and turds, which they stored on rooftops.

Everywhere there were ruins, some recent, others the result of the decline of population which had been a trend during the century preceding the Chinese invasion. Impossible to guess their age. Some were roofless, clustered together

The Chinese Invasion of Tibet

IN 1950, ON ORDERS FROM MAO Ze-dong, the Chinese Army launched a well-planned attack along Tibet's eastern frontier. The Tibetans resisted fiercely, often with no more than swords and bare hands, but were no match for the armoured vehicles, machine guns and flamethrowers of the People's Liberation Army. The Chinese overran Tibet, crushed all opposition and installed an occupying army. Then in 1959, after a major popular uprising, they formally abolished the Tibetan government, annexed the country and set about destroying its ancient Buddhist culture.

The Chinese justify their territorial claim to Tibet on two grounds. The first, going back to the seventh century, is dynastic and derives from the marriage of a Chinese princess to a Tibetan king. But the princess was given in marriage by the emperor of China as a peace offering after suffering a major defeat at the hands of the Tibetans. Moreover, her Tibetan husband took other wives, one of them Nepalese, and the government of Nepal has never used this marriage to make any claim on Tibet. China's second reason for asserting the rights of suzerainty is based on their having sent an ambassador as a 'political adviser' to Tibetan rulers since 1710. To the Tibetans, however, these are both very weak reasons for the forcible appropriation of their country.

Chinese armoured personnel carriers enter Lhasa in 1951. ▶

◀ Ploughing with yaks in
the Tsangpo valley.
Tibetan farmers are proud
of their livestock and
often decorate them
elaborately before taking
them out to work.

on the plain. There were great, mudwalled spouts that resembled the open-necked furnaces leading to Hell in the paintings of Hieronymus Bosch. Others clung to the summits of small brown hills, ancient fortresses that looked towards the Himalayas, once designed to guard Tibet against foreign intrusion.

In the afternoon we reached the edges of the Tsangpo valley, the fertile area running across southern Tibet that would become the Brahmaputra valley after it had made a great, thousand-mile sweep into India. Here the views wavered, as the empty spaces and distant aspects of cloud-covered mountains changed into fragile evidence of something a little more domestic. There was an unexpected sight of spring in the groves of sprouting poplar and willow, which were the first trees we had seen, while in stony fields men and women were busy preparing the ground for planting. Most likely the crop would be barley, the staple diet, although here in this fertile area potatoes and other vegetables are grown. They say that in the absence of rats a stored harvest will last for a hundred years, while meat will keep in the dry air for a year.

Ploughmen in long yellow coats, fur hats and dangling earrings followed behind their yaks, pushing a wooden scraper among the stones, and behind them women in long black dresses and coloured aprons similar to the costume worn by Sherpa women threw seeds out of enamel bowls. Now we passed a man who was harrowing, mounted on a wooden board and holding on like a charioteer behind two lumbering spotted beasts. The ground was dust-dry, a tableland that seemed to be composed of ground-up bones, and these agricultural activities appeared to have a measure of faith and theatre.

The yaks were fine-looking creatures, which Caroline and I examined with the air of connoisseurs. It was not merely a trick of the light that made them seem larger than our old friends in Nepal. Tibetan yaks *are* larger. These were all huge with a sable quality to their long black hair that set off the crimson tassels sprouting from their heads, which were in fact dyed yak tails—the things that used to be exported to India to make holy flywhisks. They wore collars from which fell lines of brass bells, occasionally cowrie shells dribbled with the spume from their noses, and they moved with the bulky ceremony of oxen.

The ornate scenes of husbandry, the trappings of the animals, the clothes people wore, perpetually brought to mind scenes from some ancient Book of Hours. The similarities to medieval Europe have been commented on by many observers, who have compared pre-Communist Tibet to France and Burgundy six hundred years ago, with the predominance of monks, the uniformed ranks of the nobility, the structured religion with its extremes of hell, the squalor and the beauty. The confrontation with Communism was bound to be brutal; the new zealots could not approve the outmoded harmony and feudal equilibrium which they set about destroying. There could be no sympathy for the lifestyle evoked by one writer, Fosco Maraini, with its 'medieval feasts and ceremonies, medieval filth and jewels, professional storytellers and torturers, tourneys and cavalcades, princesses and pilgrims, brigands and hermits, nobles and lepers, divine frenzies, minstrels and prophets'.

We halted at Lhazê where we bought cold dumplings from a woman who appeared in the compound carrying a basketful. On to Xigazê where another quarrel blew up when the driver refused to take us to the Tashilhunpo monastery, which is the seat of the Panchen Lama. From the modern town with roofs of tin we could only look up and see a crescent of golden rooftops climbing the hill.

When the sun had gone we reached Gyangzê, until recently the third largest city in the country, whose Jong (or castle) and complex of monasteries were once showpieces of Tibet. Gyangzê had been the scene of the climax of the Tibetan expedition of 1904 when an Imperial force, under the command of Francis Younghusband, had opened up Tibet to English influence. The capture of the Jong at Gyangzê ended a bloody campaign tinged with shame because the Tibetans were so brave and so easy to kill. In the 1950s the Tibetans fought the Chinese in similar spirit against similar odds.

There are other sad memories at Gyangzê. One of Tibet's greatest monastic centres was savagely diminished during the Cultural Revolution. Once sixteen monasteries rose one above the other like golden eggs on the dragon's-back hill, the colour of crushed strawberry. Now there are just two, together with the great pagoda-like stupa—a complex of shrines known as the Kumbum—and the main temple called Palkhor Choide. This destruction has been so neatly tidied up that you simply cannot make out the grandeur that has gone, with all the broken walls carefully scraped away. Reduced by fury, the religious city is a fraction of its original acreage and what is left is shored up for tourists and a few pilgrims.

'Divine Territory'

I walked up the hill to watch the evening shadows creeping over the plain, bordered by the frill of mountains guarding the frontiers with India. Down below I could see some horsemen riding down the main street on thin ponies kicking up dust; behind them were farmers in donkey carts loaded with sticks and sacks of grain. Above me there should have been a fortress, but it had vanished as if a sea had washed it away. Below was what remained of what Byron once described as 'the divine territory of Gyangzê ... land that is a mine of wisdom ...' The Kumbum glinted, a powerful building in ziggurat style with tiered galleries, staring painted eyes beneath a golden dome, and the thirteen golden rings that represent the stages of advancement of Buddhahood.

We stayed in a guesthouse that had the distinction of being purely Tibetan. Behind the upstairs gallery decorated with latticed woodwork were communal bedrooms and a large room for eating and relaxing, with wooden tables and benches on which young soldiers, filling in time from barrack duties, sat wrapped in tobacco smoke, slapping down cards and mah-jong tiles. They played like maniacs in the gloom, banging the tiles and calling out numbers between hawking and spitting and drinking beer.

Part of the ancient, walled monastic complex at Gyangzê. Palkhor Choide is in the centre, while next to it stands the pagoda-like Kumbum, which dates from 1440. ▼

▲ Yamzho Yumco, the
Turquoise Lake, at the
foot of the Kamba La
Pass. Some 50 miles long,
it lies in barren, virtually
uninhabited country.
Because of the Tibetan
reverence for life, its
waters are never fished.

In the kitchen, cauldrons full of soup and lumps of dark-coloured rice were
guarded by an old woman from a number of children who kept jabbing their
hands into the food and running off screaming. They kept a wary eye on us until
our plates were in front of us and then lunged in our direction. Dirt clung to
them in scales like armadillos; mucus hung from their noses. They surrounded
our table and waited; after I had toyed with my fried potatoes and greasy onions
a small boy seized my plate, emptied the remains into his woollen cap and
gulped it down. Others imitated him. Anything left neglected on a tin plate for
an instant was torn from the table by hungry, dirty little fingers. Occasionally a
soldier would get up and chase them out of the room, but they would return.
They put you off eating, and soon we had all handed over our half-eaten dinners
to settle back and enjoy a Thermos flask of rancid butter tea. It was my first
experience of this horrible beverage; I had not yet learned to filter the mud-
coloured liquid through the lumps of grease by drinking it very fast.

Next morning we headed north through mountains on the last leg to Lhasa.
A few miles on we slowed down behind an army convoy, a long line of identical
green lorries with tarpaulin hoods packed with soldiers. Following the English
path of conquest, we wound through the mountains down to Yamzho Yumco,
the Turquoise Lake. Tibetan lakes are generally described as turquoise, and certainly, in their drab brown settings, the startling, South Seas blue stands out. I

don't know if Yamzho Yumco is more turquoise than the rest, but the colour had a sheen as if there were a light at the bottom. The circuit is about a hundred and fifty miles.

We skirted the bright blue water edged with a sandy beach as white as coral which curved through the mountains, its shores quite empty. There were no fishermen or boats, nothing except for a couple of primitive villages and thousands upon thousands of birds. It was dead calm now in the morning, but later on the wind would start, and at any time it could whip up a sudden ferocious storm. That is true all over the country and all lakes are considered dangerous for boats. There is no tradition of fishing or boating apart from river ferries, but this is not only because of the weather, but because water is sacred and fish are sacred. The Chinese have ideas about changing outmoded superstitions and have decided that Yamzho Yumco will do admirably for foreigners to water-ski on. There are plans for a marina where people will be invited to come and fish, if wind and scruples about deeply held religious beliefs are not too much of a problem.

We climbed up to the Kamba La Pass at 15,500 feet, which overlooks the valley of the Lhasa He, the tributary of the Tsangpo that flows by Lhasa. The Lhasa He, the last barrier from the south, 'a river as broad as the Thames at Windsor', according to Younghusband, used to be crossed with old ferryboats which had curved prows in the shape of horses' heads. There was also an ancient suspension bridge of which four rusty chains survive, but it has been replaced with something capable of taking lorries.

This section of the road was still under a feverish bout of construction to get it smart in time for the celebrations later in the year, which would mark the twenty-fifth anniversary of so-called National Liberation in 1959, the year when Chinese occupation became a formal annexation. Along the edges on both sides were lines of tents, while the road itself was a scene of Pharaonic activity with Tibetans and Chinese conscripts in caps studded with red stars all raking, carrying stones, beating stretches of earth and shouting at lorries which had stuck, wheels spinning in the mud.

▲ **Chinese army trucks enter Lhasa in convoy, along a broad new Chinese-built highway.**

Like the Romans before them, the Chinese are amazing road builders. But in Tibet road making has had few problems. Back in 1904 an engineer noted that Tibet was 'the most perfect country for road building; immense level plains, no gradients and a small rainfall'. The trouble was the Tibetan; 'practically all he has to do is to remove the stones to one side and a splendid road is made; but that small amount of energy he is unequal to'.

The Chinese have supplied the energy. Between 1954 and 1977 more than 12,000 miles of road were built in Tibet, and they are still at it. Before National

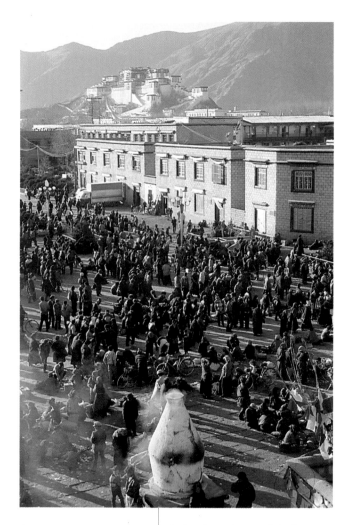

Liberation everything had to be carried up to Lhasa on the backs of animals. The first lorry reached Lhasa on December 25, 1954. (There had been a telegraph link between Kalimpong and Lhasa laid by English sappers after 1904.) Today the road between Lhasa and Xigazê has reduced the journey from a week to a day, more or less.

Arrival in Lhasa

For many travellers, including myself, to see Lhasa has been a lifetime's ambition, but the trouble about the modern approach is the distraction of Chinatown. The noble bulk of the Potala's flowing walls is sullied by the factories in front and the new housing estates spawned all over the green river basin. Now and again I caught a glimpse of other landmarks, reminders of the best of the old life. Hemmed in by drab new buildings, the Norbulingka Palace stood among trees in its walled garden. In the distance I could see the Drepung monastery, once the largest monastery in the world, perched on a hill looking down on the chipped and dirty concrete and the acres of tin.

It was not our business to condemn what we saw—the efforts of the People's Republic to bring housing and industry to an uncomfortable place. The new surroundings of Kathmandu are ugly as well. It was my fault for coming here with the illusion that the old, picturesque feudalism had at least survived visually. I had only myself to blame for my depression as the van bumped over giant potholes and craters, past soldiers bridging a landslide with shovels. By the time we had reached the main street, I was more conscious than usual of feeling tired and dirty, as well as being in a state of shock. The only thing to cheer me was the prospect of parting with our driver. We had been travelling for three days and needed a good night's rest.

Until recently, all foreigners were quartered under an official eye in very expensive government guesthouses and anything outside what were considered legitimate areas of interest was forbidden to them. With boomtime tourism approaching, these restrictions have been eased. We found ourselves in Snowlands, one of the newer and cheaper guesthouses that cater for the new egalitarian class of tourist. A large four-storey building surrounding an open courtyard, it was situated at the edge of the old Barkhor area near the Jo-Kang temple. The Jo-Kang, referred to by bygone travellers as 'the Cathedral', one of the most holy places of pilgrimage in Tibet, still stands in the centre of the old city, which is small, only two-and-a-half miles in circumference within the concrete fringe.

There were no luxuries at Snowlands. A woman took our passports amid the usual frisson that the border authorities at Zhangmu might have realised that we had deceived them. Another woman, clanking with keys, took us along to our dormitory, where guests were furiously washing filthy clothes in plastic buckets. We went off in search of dinner. Caroline led me to the hotel where she had stayed two months ago, a much more lavish place. Down in the basement was a restaurant like a catacomb lit with candles, where assorted foreigners were sitting at wooden tables being served from a big, open kitchen crammed with cooking pots. Smaller plates and smaller helpings than the month before last, Caroline said. We ate and ate and I drank a great deal of Chinese beer. I felt an enormous sense of well-being.

Next morning the deep blue of a Tibetan sky was showing through the window; I was in Lhasa. Down in the courtyard women were washing clothes

◄ The kitchen in the Snowlands government guesthouse in Lhasa. On the right is a brassbound churn used for blending butter and tea, a staple drink in the Himalayas.

around a pump, while from the street came a sound of singing as men and women threw bricks to each other on a construction site.

I went walking. The new main street that runs under the Potala was filled with lorries and horse-drawn carts, as if it could not make up its mind whether it belonged to the old, pre-motor age or to the new. A herdsman wearing a thick sheepskin coat, the wool the same dirty yellow as the sheep before him, his felt boots patchwork red and green like the Pied Piper's, was driving his charges oblivious to blasts from car horns. On the pavement men squatted selling biscuits and clothes, while others sat with sewing machines and cobblers' awls. A horseman came jogging along on a black pony. A blind old woman, in a

▲ Traditional Tibetan jewellery, often worn by men (as here), is rich in semiprecious stones— amber, jade, lapis lazuli, turquoise—together with brightly polished pebbles from the hillsides.

long striped woollen dress and woollen bonnet, crouched spinning a silver prayer wheel.

Among the handful of traditional houses grouped around the Jo-Kang and stretching down to the river, Tibetans congregated in bright clothes, showing evidence of what has been described as a 'convivial serenity alongside a more solid religiousness'. It was moving to see a line of ugly, shaven-headed, ash-covered young men stripped to the waist (with little relic boxes strapped on their backs like the powder-boxes old soldiers used to wear), prostrating themselves along the dusty thoroughfare. They progressed and prayed in unison, rising and falling with the precision of a corps de ballet. This striving for perfection cushions the impact of change. Thubten Jigme Norbu, the Dalai Lama's brother, wrote how 'the only truth that is worth anything to anyone is the truth in which he believes with his heart as well as with his mind, and toward which he strives with his body'.

Other things in Lhasa were new and ugly. As elsewhere, much has been destroyed, but you should try and see things the Chinese way. While they were smashing up things in their own country, a mad contempt for the stately anachronisms of the old Tibetan theocracy was logical. Now they are sheepish about their immediate past and admit it was all an unfortunate mistake perpetrated by criminals. In homage to tourists they are restoring the more important

Sky Burial

For Tibetan Buddhists, who believe in reincarnation, the human body is no more than a temporary home for a person's soul, and is worthless once the soul has departed. It may then be returned to one of the four elements: earth, water, fire or air. In Tibet, where much of the earth is stony and often frozen, where lakes and rivers are also often frozen, and where wood for fires is very precious, returning a body to the air through the ritual of a sky burial is both popular and practical.

Performed by expert undertakers of a low Tibetan caste, the procedure of a sky burial is simple: the corpse is minutely dismembered on a ceremonial rock, the bones are pounded into small pieces, and both are then fed to vultures, which fly up into the sky taking the deceased with them. People unable to afford the expense of a formal sky burial may choose instead to leave their loved ones' bodies out in the open for wild birds and animals to devour.

▲ A rare photograph of the ceremonial rock used for sky burials outside Lhasa.

Sky burials are soberly conducted, with no prayers and few signs of mourning. Relatives of the deceased are present simply to make sure that everything is done properly. A recent witness, the distinguished travel writer Niema Ash, has written: 'What amazed me was that, in spite of the horrific nature of what I had seen, I felt no revulsion. The sky burial fits in with the isolation and strangeness of the setting. Somehow, in that alien environment, it makes sense.'

temples as 'cultural centres'. They have spent over four million pounds, but it does not go far to repair what has been destroyed.

The newcomer can only seek out the vestiges of those elements that combine to make Lhasa unique. The double intensity of light made colours glow and take on importance; the blues were bluer, the reds redder, the yellows yellower with a shocking radiance like a painting by Van Gogh. In the marketplace an old woman would take the amber and turquoise necklace from round her neck and offer the chunky beads for sale. Another cut off the leather strap at her waist holding her horoscope, a little brass dish encrusted with miniature rats and horses and other astrological data, which she sold to me for very little. We were hungry for silver-sheathed knives, amulets, figures of the Buddha, teapots, prayer wheels, jewellery; old Tibet would dribble away in our holdalls.

Buses drove out full of foreigners with cameras to watch sky burials and record low-caste undertakers ripping up bodies, splashing blood all around, crushing bones to powder and mixing them with butter before inviting the vultures to swoop down and snatch the bite-sized pieces. Tibetans do not now bury people unless they are criminals or lepers. The Chinese had ideas of tidying up the bloodstained spot where the undertakers did their work and constructing a viewing platform with telescopes for a distant inspection, so that the vultures would not get nervous of onlookers.

▲ The Norbulingka Palace, light and airy, in contrast to the forbidding Potala, was once the summer home of the Dalai Lama. It and its gardens are now a People's Park for the citizens of Lhasa.

The Dalai Lama's Summer Palace

I visited the Norbulingka Palace, set in a large, pleasant garden surrounded by huge, half-mile walls. I was sorry that the Dalai Lama's car was not on display— the Baby Austin that bore the number plate Tibet 1. But the garden flourishes, very like an English garden up here at 12,000 feet. We were too early for the dahlias, roses, phlox, petunias, hollyhocks and marigolds that bloom late in summer; even the fruit trees were not yet in blossom—apples, apricots and peaches, which do not have a long enough season to bear fruit.

Caroline took me to a studio where a Chinese and a Tibetan worked together as official artists. As we drank beer we inspected their pictures, which were imbued with social realism. Farmers were happily liberated from slavery and harvesting girls looked resolutely towards the east. A soldier seemed a bit odd and elongated, but that was because he had been painted in the manner of El Greco.

'We would be grateful if you would send us books on modern art.' They were tired of the harvesting stereotypes and longed to learn more about artists in the West. Meanwhile they learned from the fragments all round their little studio, pieces of old sculpture and carving they had picked up from sites that had been

▲ A shrine in the Potala Palace, one of hundreds, each one a treasure house of priceless gilded paintings, ancient books and magnificent gold-threaded fabrics.

dismantled by iconoclasts. They gave us each a tiny, leaf-shaped votary tablet made of clay and funeral ashes, stamped with figures of deities and left at some shrine by pilgrims. They were happy and earnest, and moreover they were good friends. The Tibetan was a Muslim, a member of a community that has been in Lhasa for centuries.

I put off visiting the Potala for a couple of days to lessen the deep sense of disappointment I had felt seeing it in its new ugly setting. That was unnecessary; it retains its glory. Its shape has been described as Babylonic. The sloping rhomboid, suggestive of a man standing on a rock with his two legs apart, has its origin in an architecture that imitates mountains. It is more than a building; that is far too weak a word to describe the walls and golden rooftops rising out of the plain. It seems more a work of God than of man. The flights of steps that ripple up and down its sides evoke features of the Himalayas.

The place is classed as a museum and you pay an entrance fee, fearing that you are entering a dead palace embalmed by the state. But the acreage swarms with pilgrims who have travelled here from all over the country and, since religion persists, they come prostrating and mumbling prayers. I watched an old lady scurrying through the Dalai Lama's private rooms, praying as she went, tossing money to every Buddha. There were very few tourists. A Dane with a microphone was squatting beside a prostrate pilgrim dressed in Western clothes, taking down his prayers on a tape recorder.

Apart from the Dalai Lama's apartments, which were painted in saffron tones, every other wall was covered with whitewash which sparkled like phosphorescence and relieved the windowless semidarkness. There are said to be more than a thousand rooms, ten thousand altars and the gilded tombs of eight Dalai Lamas. Huge holy places have a particular atmosphere. The great dark recesses and the innumerable chapels with their frescoes, the lines of statues, had something in common with the interior of a Spanish cathedral. There were statues everywhere, stuck in dark rooms, some enormous, fifty feet high. Some were swathed in khatas, others surrounded by brass butter lamps, Buddhas in every attitude, Bodhisattvas, demonic deities, gods balancing on one foot, some peaceful, some toothily savage. It is impressive now. In the old days it must have throbbed with power and prayer.

Before the Chinese began their programmes of re-education and humiliation, there were 25,000 monks living in the three big Lhasa monasteries of Drepung, Sera and Ganden. Now around 300 elderly men remain. As elsewhere, a lot of the surrounding buildings have been destroyed, like the Great Western Gate that stood below the Potala and hundreds of temples and chapels with their reliquaries.

Next day a notice appeared on the board of Snowlands asking for volunteers to travel to Nepal by bus along the route we had taken with the Scots and the devilish driver. This particular outfit appeared to be as impudent as we had been, travelling cheaply towards the vaguest of destinations.

'Remember your thoughts about Kailas and Lake Manasarowar? Why not just abandon the bus at the Tsangpo and travel west? We could hitch lifts on lorries.'

In for a penny, in for a pound.

Kailas is the holiest place in the world. As far as we knew, no Westerners had visited it for more than fifty years.

In a woolly way we looked at its location on a map, which showed it to be quite near to India.

I said, 'After we've seen it, why don't we just walk out?'

'Those dark smudges in between are the Himalayas.'

There were two recognisable roads to the west. The old southern route which skirted the Nepalese frontier and eventually reached the old trading post that used to be called Gartok, and a new Chinese road which took in a big northerly loop before descending on a provincial town called Shiquanhe. Another road linked Shiquanhe to Kailas.

'Did you know that Kailas is regarded by devout Buddhists as the centre of the universe?' said Caroline. 'That should make things easier.'

On the last evening at Snowlands a New Zealand girl who was travelling on our bus threw a birthday party. Music came from foreign tapes played on a recorder and some Tibetans came in to watch what must have been a novel experience. Foreign boys and girls were shuffling and twisting to the pulsating din. They included two girls, who seemed to be lesbians, in Tibetan clothes, the Austrian who was organising the bus and an American who dressed as a lama in saffron robes and coloured boots. Tibetan ladies sat startled in their stiffened aprons as he whirled in front of them, showing off beads, boots and robes. There was also a proper Tibetan lama, from the Dalai Lama's retreat at Dharamsala, and he, too, was going to venture on the bus. The music roared, the dancers gyrated, a birthday cake got from heaven-knows-where was handed around to the accompaniment of Chinese beer and chang, and everyone got drunk. The Tibetans giggled as they sat and watched the first consequences of the officially decreed tourist invasion.

▲ Tibetans are not solemn people. Buddhism is a joyful way of life, and this dancing figure on the roof of the Potala Palace vividly expresses that joy.

▲ Stripped to the waist, young Buddhist monks prostrate themselves in the dust of a Lhasa street. The boxes on their backs contain holy relics.

Lhasa—The Forbidden City

LHASA (MEANING 'GROUND OF THE GODS') is an ancient city. It first became Tibet's capital back in the 7th century AD, when King Songtsen Gampo built his palace on the great outcrop of rock (the 'Red Hill') overlooking what was then merely a village.

Later social upheavals caused Lhasa to lose its status as capital, but it prospered nevertheless, thanks to its position on ancient trade routes. It finally became the centre of government again in 1642, when the various warring regions of Tibet were united.

The following centuries saw Lhasa growing into a thriving city, both spiritually and materially. Two of its monasteries grew to become the largest in the country: Sera housed over 5,000 monks, novices and attendants, while the great Drepung was home to over 8,000 monks alone. The Potala Palace, the city's most famous landmark, was built between 1645 and 1694, serving until 1959 as the winter residence of the Dalai Lama, Tibet's spiritual and political ruler.

The old city of Lhasa spread out around the Barkhor, the central square in front of the Jo-Kang temple. To this day, this area is composed of narrow, winding, cobbled streets bordered by immaculately whitewashed houses

with black-painted surrounds to their doors and windows, and shady canvas canopies above them. Houses and shops were all no more than two storeys high so that they should not overtop the sacred Jo-Kang. For many years, however, the charms of Lhasa were inaccessible to Westerners. Before the British invasion of 1904, all foreign cultural influences were strongly discouraged, which led to Lhasa being known in Europe as 'the forbidden city'.

▲ The magnificent, golden roof of the Jo-Kang temple, with the Potala Palace gleaming in the distance.

◄ A painted, gilded effigy of the god of wrath lies smashed on a rubbish tip—evidence of the deliberate destruction of Tibetan culture.

▲ A smouldering incense burner in front of the Jo-Kang temple in Lhasa's main square. Ordinary life goes on, despite the Chinese occupation.

Tibetans are enthusiastic games-players. Here a group of men in a variety of traditional costumes take advantage of the country's dry, sunny climate to play pool in the open air, in front of the Potala Palace. ►

◄ The typical colour scheme of old Lhasa—black-framed windows against white walls— here in a section of the historic Drepung monastery.

CHAPTER 5

Bus and Lorry

A FEW HOURS AFTER THE PARTY, at five o'clock in the morning, nineteen foreigners huddled around the doorway of Snowlands. The sky was full of stars, whose sparkle gave some outline to the buildings in the street beyond the ring of light supplied by the bulb in the porch. Occasionally we could make out the shapes of stray dogs moving in search of garbage.

'Has anyone seen Yogi?'

Yogi was the amiable young Austrian who had brought us together with the promise of a bus. Plans had been worked out and we had all agreed on the fare, but we were sceptical as we stood stamping to keep warm, nursing hangovers and beer-ravaged stomachs. No one could recall ever seeing a bus on the Lhasa streets.

Cold and sleepy, we waited for an hour as the stars vanished and dawn began to light up the sky to the howls of the dogs. Every traveller who visited Lhasa moaned about the dogs. Sometimes you saw a pretty little shi-tzu, hairy as a yak, but most Tibetan dogs were fierce and nasty.

The Chinese began a dog-elimination campaign, but to refrain from offending the sensibilities of their Tibetan brothers with regard to the taking of life, their solution was to round up all the dogs and pen them in corrals and leave

Early on a cold, bright morning in Barkhor Square, the main square in Lhasa's old town, the street sweepers wrap scarves across their mouths to take the chill off the bitter air. ▶

them. No one actually killed them; they either starved or ate each other. But there must have been animals that had escaped the dragnet and multiplied; soon it would be time for another round-up.

There was a sudden roar as a very old bus made its appearance and pulled up beside us. The driver got out, followed by his wife, a young boy, and an old man called Chuka, dressed in sheepskins. The vehicle had a scrapyard air of antiquity. The metal body was lined with wood; broken seats had been hastily thrown into lines, the door was held shut with a piece of string, and the big mound of a gearbox stuck with gear levers like knitting needles took up most of the front section of the aisle. The rest of the aisle and much of the available dingy space was occupied by bits of broken metal, coils of wire and cans of petrol and water. We stormed on board, pushing and punching our way forward, since it was immediately obvious that the only seats that retained something pertaining to a springy, undamaged surface were up in front.

Caroline wore combat gear, face mask and black gloves, and the keys in her hat jingled like sleigh bells. 'Quick, quick, don't let them throw you about.' We won ourselves seats behind the lesbians and barricaded ourselves in. It wasn't the best spot to have chosen, because it was much too near the smelly old man in sheepskin. The smell turned out to be mostly yak butter. Chuka was a herdsman, working his way from his pastures in the north to the monastery of Sa'gya to present a large lump of his very own butter to the monks.

Now he poured petrol from a can into the tank on the other side of the aisle while Lobsang, the driver, stood very near smoking a cigarette. Up front Lobsang's wife wrapped herself in numerous shawls and sheets and prepared to be sick.

▲ Yak butter for sale. Huge chunks of butter such as this are often stored and transported in yakskin wrappings.

We drove off through suburbs, past the grey shapes of new houses, a barracks and the scaffolding surrounding the 400-bed Lhasa Hotel, where visitors would be expected to pay the equivalent of £75 a day. The enterprise was wholly Chinese with three thousand imported Nanking workmen being paid oil-rig wages to build it in a year. Tibetans were considered incapable of doing the job, an insulting conclusion considering the Potala was nearby. Everything—windows, air conditioners, carpets, lifts—was being brought up by truck from China. No doubt it would do better than the Everest View in Khumbu.

Breakdown

The route followed a bumpy track along the riverbank over what would soon be the new tarmac airport road. As the bus roared on, everyone became happier. The girls in front hugged and kissed each other.

A few miles after crossing the river, the engine began to smoke. As the bus came to a halt Lobsang's wife, who had been moaning for some time, lurched to the door and undid the string in time to be sick outside. Chuka was delegated to go and look for water, the boy assistant spat and sucked petrol from a can with a plastic tube, while Lobsang tinkered with the carburettor.

The passengers got out and left him. We all walked along the road, which wound up to the Kamba La Pass through brown, barren hills. Sometimes a line of Liberation lorries and petrol tankers would pass us, the uniformed drivers peering down blandly from their cabs at the rich foreign devils. At the top of the pass we gave a cheer as the bus caught up with us; it seemed that Lobsang and Chuka had mended it by stuffing pieces of rag into an oil leak. We climbed aboard again without worrying.

'Everything is now OK,' Yogi said.

Thirteen hours and three lengthier breakdowns later when we limped into Gyangzê, greeted by evening opera choruses from loudspeakers, we had long lost any sense of optimism. It was plain that there was something fundamentally wrong with the engine. Yogi was sad.

'Perhaps she gets us there if we stay in Gyangzê one day. I ask Lobsang to find a new part for the engine.'

We spent the night in the same inn where we had stopped on the way up from Nepal, among the same gambling soldiers and the children, who once again emptied the remains of our meal into their caps. In the morning music resumed from every post and corner, shot through with crackles, howling all over the ancient town. In Beijing and the more sophisticated central areas, the custom of playing 'The East is Red' largely died out in the late 1970s. It only survives in remote regions which are always resistant to change, even drastically imposed change.

While we waited for the bus we could see more of Gyangzê. Dust blew down the narrow streets. 'Bye-bye' was the new greeting when they saw foreigners—no more polite sticking out of tongues except by very old people. Pots of geraniums stood outside windows, children danced around us, old women in long black dresses squatted by a stream, cleaning pots. We looked for supplies. At one time the bazaar held within the monastery walls—mostly razed—was an important centre for the wool trade, carpet-making and the distribution of brick tea from China. The bricks of tea still come from China, and we saw them for sale looking like pieces of turf. We bought rice.

Gyangzê guards the approaches to India and the route to Lhasa. For a time earlier this century an English trade mission was maintained here under the protection of its own small, polo-playing garrison. The mission, one of two—the other being Gar in west Tibet—was among the fruits of conquest. Members stayed at the 'Fort', a solidly built two-storeyed house where they had trouble passing time. One of its commanding officers wrote that he used to wake up each morning wondering what he would kill that day. No nonsense about reverence for life. Gyangzê was considered a dirty hole with a terrible winter climate that got on

▲ Prayer flags by the roadside on the way from Lhasa to Gyangzê. For once the wind is not blowing, and the cheerful message of the flags is temporarily subdued.

men's nerves. No Englishwomen were permitted to stay here with their husbands.

At the entrance to the great stupa, the Kumbum, we were greeted by a very old lama sitting in his small room. There was hardly anyone else in the spooky, deserted galleries and side chapels crammed with frescoes and statues, which one Victorian traveller had condemned as 'gilded images, tawdry paintings, demons and she-devils, hideous grinning devil masks, all the lamas' spurious apparatus of terrorism—outward symbols of demonality and superstition invented by scheming priests as the fabric of their sacerdotalism'. The voice of the Puritan had much in common with the disgust of the image-breakers urged on by the Chinese Government led by its notorious Gang of Four. The lamas are reduced from five hundred in the old days to about a dozen bald, wrinkled old men.

While we were wandering around the labyrinthine rooms and passages, a Chinese delegation got lost. It vanished into a dark interior and a door accidentally closed behind it. I could hear the delegates scurrying around behind the door, knocks, and voices squeaking like mice. When someone managed to prise the door open, they came tumbling out into the light, rubbing their eyes. There were a couple of girls, one with a camera, two men in Mao jackets and a young man in a tailored suit. He caught sight of me staring rudely, and came over at once to shake my hand.

'I am Mr Tung from the Foreign Office in Lhasa. How are you, sir?'

He was on a tour of inspection of the monuments that remained after the

▲ The Jong, or castle, at Gyangzê stands high above the town. Although clearly ancient, its precise age is uncertain: Tibet's unchanging ways down the centuries have made the exact dating of its buildings very difficult.

Cultural Revolution and he seemed delighted to find someone like myself wandering around. 'Your name, please, and country?' I told him, while shaking hands with the rest of the party.

'Irish—good. Now we take photograph.'

We trooped off to the light outside the main door. 'You are my friend,' he kept saying, as photographs were taken of me with my arms around one or other member of the delegation. (What on earth did they do with them?) Everyone was smiling. He took me to the library to inspect stacks of books with carved wooden covers which had survived the despoliation of the monasteries when similar ancient covers were turned into parquet floor, while the manuscripts inside made handy inner soles for boots. Then all together we walked back through the great halls smelling of old butter while statues of Buddha looked down on us. In one shrine an ancient lama sprinkled us with water from a silver ewer. In another a shaven old man chanted to the clash of cymbals, surrounded by paintings of the tortures that faced the damned.

Tibetans love hells. They recognise thousands of them, of which there are sixteen specific regions, eight hot and eight cold. There is one for incompetent doctors, where the victims are clumsily dissected and cut to pieces, only to be reunited and revived so that the process can be repeated. I picked out a suitable hell for the man who had sold me my sleeping-bag.

The Lost Libraries of Tibet

FOR MANY CENTURIES TIBET'S main state printing house stood in the long shadow of the Potala Palace in Lhasa. Most of its output was on religious subjects, but it also produced books of poems, stories and songs. Many monasteries also made books, and as recently as the 1940s Tibetan monks were producing their books entirely by hand, carving the squiggly Tibetan letters in reverse on small birchwood blocks. These were then covered with ink made from a special soot derived from burning yak dung, and afterwards pressed onto hand-made paper.

Tibetan books were not bound, but consisted of loose pages printed on both sides and enclosed between carved wooden covers. They were kept in rich silk cases and treated with great respect. Inevitably, in such a poor country, reading was a skill confined to the aristocracy and the monastic orders. A finely produced book could cost as much as a dozen yaks, and a monastery or a wealthy Tibetan might own as many as two hundred such books.

After the Chinese annexed Tibet in 1959 they restricted printing, destroyed countless priceless libraries and used the wooden backs of the books as parquet flooring. Today very few books on religious subjects are produced in Tibet.

Printing, probably learned from the Chinese, was developed early in Tibet's history. Today Buddhist texts are printed by monks in very much the traditional way. ▶

'This culture is dead,' said Mr Tung, when we emerged from a final group of dark, buttery chapels full of demons rolling their eyes and showing their teeth. 'But now our policy is restoration. We look after old buildings. In Lhasa you see Potala? Very good. Now many tourists come to visit.' He pointed up the hill. 'English people destroy Jong. We restore.' Another photograph. 'Please smile.'

Later Caroline and I walked out to a denuded hill where the religious clutter had been swept away into a vast, dilapidated barn with padlocked wooden door and tiers of little windows. It seemed to be abandoned; then we noticed someone beckoning from an upstairs window. There was a side door into a dusty hall beyond which another door led into a room full of decaying paintings. A Buddha, a patchy Bodhisattva, a demon or two, Yamantaka the Terrible, blue-faced and loaded down with skulls.

No one about. We went up a ladder to a room where an old man sat in a darkened robe copying down mantras onto a piece of parchment paper with the careful flourishes of a calligrapher. He told Caroline that he was the head lama of this empty building.

▲ Yamantaka the Terrible, also known as the Destroyer of Death, has the head of a buffalo and wears a garland of severed human heads.

He must have been middle-aged when this monastery was full. So much gone, and yet he seemed happy living by himself, sitting and praying alone, and looking out of the small window with its view of the plain swept so clean of buildings that had bustled with the ferment of religion, rimmed by snowy mountains. Tibetan Buddhism, developed in a harsh environment, is deeply imbued with stoicism and resignation. What has taken place in the last thirty years is a pinprick in the cycle of human suffering and rebirth.

We piled back into the bus before daybreak. Lobsang had mended the engine, so he said. Chuka was crooning over his butter. Everyone else was morose as we headed in the direction of Xigazê. Then the sun rose, lighting up the remains of old castles perched on rocks above the plain.

A Chuba for Caroline

A strong wind blew across the plain throwing up a golden cloud which tore down the road, ignoring closed windows, filtering in through numerous cracks in the bodywork until everything was covered in a gold film. Particles of dust rattled round the interior, burrowing into clothes, striking behind face masks, hitting hair, lips, throats, making our beards stiff. Lobsang stopped and wrapped a towel round his head, and only Chuka the herdsman lit a cigarette and took no notice. Plenty of weather like this in north Tibet. After the worst had passed, Lobsang resumed the same furious speed.

We drove on to Xigazê over the flat panhandle separating the two cities, where the bus broke down often enough for us to have a worm's-eye inspection of the rich heartland of Tibet: the sight of our first tractor and some indication of modern agricultural methods. We saw nearly as much as travellers of old on foot or horseback. A halt heralded by stuttering jerks as the engine ground to a stop. Another search for water to douse it. A group of men riding donkeys passing slowly, gazing with astonishment. Another breakdown. Xigazê was greeted with ironic cheers.

Coming up from Nepal we had seen little of Xigazê because of the antics of our driver, but now we could wander about at leisure. The Jong, which had resembled the Potala, has been totally demolished, and so has the town. At the turn of the century there were more than 3,800 monks living in the vast compound.

The gilt-topped monastery of Tashilhunpo gleams over the modern town, its roofs shimmering in a series of golden waves. Like many westerners we came with a prejudice against Tashilhunpo because it was the headquarters of the Panchen Lama, China's ally. No doubt this made our reactions subjective. Was the fat lama standing at the main gate really so sour-faced as he demanded an entrance fee?

In the government store, at the far end of a series of long shelves, empty except for packets of instant noodles, Caroline spotted some clothes. Soon she was clad from head to toe in a chuba, an ornate dressing gown with sleeves wide enough to take a Pekingese dog. 'How do I look?' She strutted around, looking like a black heron with striped blue feathers. The chuba is part of Tibetan life, a barrier against weather which can be made out of wool, silk or even sheepskin. It is adapted to the abrupt daily changes of temperature as sun turns to snow and the midday wind gets up. When it is cold, the wearer can be wrapped up, hood and all, like a monk; when the sun shines hot in the thin air, the chuba can be let down so that a man can strip to the waist.

▲ A nomad woman wearing a brightly coloured chuba. This garment is extremely practical and is ideally suited to Tibet's harsh climate. It offers protection from the cold, and can be worn off one or both shoulders when the temperature rises. The baby is wearing woollen trousers, equally practical for a child his age!

We got into the bus once more and drove out into another empty brown land of scattered willows, sparse houses and mountains shining ahead. We were making for Sa'gya, a journey that should have taken three or four hours. Nine hours later we were still on our way.

Sometimes the engine billowed clouds of smoke, sometimes it coked up, and on one of the most lengthy breakdowns it exploded with a rattle of vital parts. Down on the ground, watched by his assistant, his wife, Yogi and a score of impatient travellers, Lobsang struggled for hours. Most times he appeared to fix the problem with his teeth, emerging from his bouts beneath the chassis gripping a piece of metal in his mouth. As we hung around, sighing with exasperation, admiring the view, we failed to appreciate what must have been a mechanical feat of genius.

Long after dark we reached Sa'gya and a wonderful dormitory with candles and the luxury of iron beds. Some women gathered in the shadows to watch the strange sight of assorted foreigners trying to get to sleep, and sleep we did, oblivious to the fact that we were not allowed in this town at all. Perhaps the authorities allowed us to stay because the hour was so late. The reason we had come seemed solely so that Chuka could deliver his butter.

Sa'gya was closed to tourists, and would be until the ruins had been cleared away. Our unexpected arrival appeared to stun the people in charge. One distraught official did think he would try and stop Caroline taking photographs of ruins from a rooftop, but when she snarled at him in Chinese he retreated like a puppy before an angry cat.

There were several acres of ruin. At Xigazê, Gyangzê and even Lhasa, you could only guess about the destruction by reading travellers' accounts or consulting old photographs. There is no evidence of what had gone on. But here at Sa'gya the shocking stretch of broken walls and rubble was still spread over the hillside and the plain, the remains of a great monastic city.

Only the monastery survives, an immense austere building, half-grey, half-red, girdled with a painted white strip. In one of the two great courtyards closed off by high wooden doors, an old man with padded arms and knees, the pads worn thin by prostrations, lay stretched on the ground, while inside the main hall a lama was blowing a conch shell and giving his blessing to the men and women filing past. This was a different sort of cathedral; not a collection of dark shrines smelling of incense and butter, but a hall filled with shimmering colour and light, a place where you felt that life's events had less to do with man than

Tibet's Spiritual Leaders

TIBETAN BUDDHISTS BELIEVE THAT when one of their spiritual leaders dies he is promptly reincarnated (reborn) as an infant who has to be sought out by specially trained monks. Following the death in 1935 of Tibet's most senior religious and political figure, the 13th Dalai Lama, his three-year-old successor was eventually discovered in a distant village, the fifth child of an illiterate peasant family. The official delegation claimed to have been led to him by a holy vision, and he quickly passed the many rigorous tests that proved his identity as the reincarnation of all previous Dalai Lamas.

The 14th Dalai Lama was enthroned in Lhasa in 1940 when he was eight years old. Nineteen years later, following the Chinese annexation of Tibet, he fled the capital on horseback at dead of night with a small band of followers. He crossed into India where he was given asylum and formed the Tibetan government-in-exile. Today he travels extensively, promoting both world peace and his own country's liberation.

Needing the support of a Buddhist leader in the Dalai Lama's absence, the Chinese promoted his second-in-command, the Panchen Lama, and installed him in far-off Beijing, where he played little part in Tibetan affairs before dying in 1989. Significantly, when the Dalai Lama ordered prayers for the Panchen Lama following his death, the Chinese forbade them. As yet no successor for him has been found.

▲ Dedicated to non-violence and obliged to abandon Tibet to its atheistic Chinese invaders, the Dalai Lama heads his country's Buddhist government-in-exile in northern India.

with some higher power. A forest of painted red pillars made from enormous treetrunks reached at least 60 feet up to the roof, and under this big canopy Tantric Buddhism flickered. In the centre young monks were squatting on immense bolsters like woolsacks of yellow silk, intoning mantras. The sound of their voices rose and fell like waves.

Our friend the lama from Dharamsala considered that we were fortunate in seeing Sa'gya before it was cleaned up and the tourists were invited in. In spite of the presence of these young monks, he was deeply depressed about the future of religion in Tibet. When we passed out of the main gateway, there was the old man, still moving along, his hands protected by blocks of wood.

'You will soon see the last of that,' he said.

On the bus the butter had gone; Chuka had left us to take his gift to the abbot. There was general relief at not having to brace ourselves each time before stepping into that smell. Lobsang continued his heroic and epic struggle to keep

us on the road. On our second breakdown we got out and sat under a floating rainbow over another staggering emptiness, and it was easy to understand the Tibetans' appetite for religion.

The Highest River in the World

After Lhazê Caroline and I planned to leave the bus and head west. A few miles away was the Tsangpo where we hoped to get a ferry; once across, perhaps a lorry. It seemed most uncertain; how tempting to continue with our companions into Nepal. Suddenly the old vehicle felt like an ark.

The last morning, we got up hours before dawn. The journey to Nepal was long and Lobsang was eager for an early start.

Just outside Lhazê, Lobsang stopped beside a dusty side road.

Heads fuddled with sleep looked up.

'Good luck.'

◀ Travellers wait to cross the Tsangpo River. Already a formidable obstacle here in Tibet, the Tsangpo flows east and then south for a thousand miles down into India where it becomes the mighty Brahmaputra.

'Rather you than me.'

The string of the door handle was tied up again behind us, and the bus moved on. The noise of the engine, still sputtering, died away.

We stood in the dim morning light with our pile of baggage.

'Can you see the river?'

'It must be somewhere close.'

I could just make out a line of mountains behind Caroline's back. We carried our mounds of luggage down the lane, and sure enough, there was the river shimmering in the dawn.

A steel hawser for the ferry spanned both banks and on the far side, about a couple of hundred yards across, we could see a few houses. Here was the Tsangpo, which would become the Brahmaputra, the son of Brahma, one of India's great rivers. As the Tsangpo, 12,000 feet above sea level, it is the highest river in the world. Downstream, well over a thousand miles away, it completes its giant curve to the Indian peninsula and reaches the sea at Assam.

We waited in silence. After three hours a lorry appeared and the driver got out to stretch his legs. He was a middle-aged man wearing civilian clothes. Caroline hurried over and I watched them arguing away, as the ferry crept over.

Triumph. 'He'll take us.'

The ferry slipped calmly across the river. Besides our lorry driver, Norbhu, there was one other passenger, an elderly farmer in a tattered brown chuba carrying a wooden plough and leading a yak.

North of the river, we had only driven for a few miles before Norbhu stopped at a small house belonging to a friend for a taste of Tibetan hospitality. We were shown into a room with an iron stove in the middle, a shelf with a line of Thermos flasks and cushioned seats all round the walls, which were completely covered with pictures. None of them had to do with religion; instead Chairman Mao was huge, benevolent and garlanded with silk. Mao replaced the Dalai Lama as an icon, and the cult of Mao continues among Tibetans long after their sophisticated Chinese brothers have changed their minds and taken his picture down. Having spent a couple of decades persuading Tibetans of his worth, the Chinese have a problem in re-education.

On one side of Mao was a patchwork of bright certificates showing that our host with the big, almond-shaped smile was a model worker. On the other were posters of Chinese leaders, with ribbons and medals on their chests like smocking, and behind them mountain landscapes covered in big flowers. They had an old-fashioned air, summoning memories of the Irish mountains and streams that used to be worked into advertisements for good whiskey on bevelled mirrors.

Time for Tea

Two men, both with red hair in a plait, one with the startlingly wrinkled face that people here acquire after decades of exposure to wild weather, smiled across at us, while the woman of one of them brewed tea on the stove. Meanwhile Norbhu picked up a bone covered with half-cooked meat that lay among others arranged neatly on the couch beside him. It was evidently the leg of a sheep

because a little cloven hoof hung off at an angle. The red flesh must have been good, for he tore hungrily at the fibrous meat. Good manners required him to finish it completely— my dog Bonzo couldn't have done a better job. While he gnawed away we tackled purple broth and sour butter, and the old man who watched us, checking that we got it all down, produced a leather bag filled with tsampa. The trick was to pour a little into your silver-lined bowl and mix it with the tea, forming a paste that was almost palatable after the butter disappeared into it. In a harsh environment the Tibetan diet reflects a craving for fat and animal protein at variance with religious beliefs.

A final exchange of fraternal smiles and we were on our way, leaving the lonely little house buffeted by the wind. We drove on through tawny brown country north of the river set with an occasional lake like a blue glass eye. This was an ancient route, once a rough track that was part of the most elevated highway in the world. The road-making was perfunctory, with the dusty track almost indistinguishable from its surroundings. In places someone had built a little pile of stones to indicate the way forward, or a dip was filled in with rocks, but the road had done nothing to change the landscape which was still wilderness where the sky and the land met each other in a burning collision of wind and vibrant colour.

The wind blew constantly, sending dust to cloud the windscreen and ping against the sides of the vehicle as we moved through the same biscuit-brown

▲ A sandstorm seen across the Tsangpo River. For much of its length the Tsangpo flows through wild, barren country: wind-scoured hills and dusty plains populated only by hardy willows.

land, empty for miles and miles, and then a few tents and shepherds and little sheep like crumbs on a carpet. The emptiness was oppressive. There was no water, no vegetation. Once we passed a thermal spring, steam rising out of rocks and pools of bubbling water. In the distance a mountain peak glimmered in the sun, then vanished.

▲ The author poses between Norbhu, the driver, and an elderly farmer who was also hitching a ride. It was a squash for the three of them and Caroline inside the cab, but an improvement on the draughty old bus.

After the bus, sitting in the comfortable little cab was wonderful. Like everything else in Tibet the lorry belonged to the past, a more recent past conjuring up wartime images of supply lines coaxed along by the voice of a BBC newsreader. The Chinese motor industry is home-grown. There has been no development in design, and these Liberation lorries are utilitarian, old-fashioned, reliable and weatherproof.

At nightfall we stopped at the home of another friend of Norbhu's, who lived in an equally tiny house that beamed a welcome in the wilderness. We were given rice and tinned pork washed down with tea, and afterwards Norbhu and his friend smoked cigarettes under pictures of generals on rearing horses. Outside the wind howled, really howled; inside, the little room lit by the flickering stove was warm and comfortable. Laws of hospitality, the first to go when tourism comes, still prevailed here. Our host gave us breakfast—stinking tea is a terrible way to start the day—and after a battle of smiles refused to take our money.

We set off through another sandstorm towards Saga, where we hoped to find another lorry. The roaring wind covered the plain in whirling dust that blotted out the sun. Half an hour later we emerged into a bright blue sky, bumping along another vast, chipped gravel plain, which turned into stripes of colour as the sun hit it. Bands of black, white, pink, gold, purple. A mountain in front had a touch of snow. Along the way was one solitary huddle of chocolate-brown nomad tents with goats and sheep, guarded by ragged figures resigned to wind, hail and sand. Then suddenly a barracks. Here was Saga, a large dusty square the size of a college quadrangle, filled with men, mainly soldiers, staring. Norbhu threw down our bags, took our money and made off as quickly as he could. Dust from his exhaust was the last we saw of him.

'Get a room quickly! Take the bags!'

Around the square were bleak lines of mud apartments. A woman took her keys and opened up one which smelt of urine. Behind us a dozen faces peered in, watching Caroline.

But among them was an officious young man from the Public Security Bureau with a dreaded accomplishment—he spoke English. He was dressed in a blue zipper jacket, track trousers and rubber-soled jogging shoes, which in these parts are a sign of modernity and authority.

'You have permission? Passports?'

He flipped the pages to the forged visas and examined them with the concentration of the shortsighted.

'Who say you come here? This frontier area. No foreigner. I found out from higher authority. Please stay.'

We watched him strut across the square towards a small office followed by the crowd of Tibetans, who appeared to have satisfied their curiosity about Caroline. He had left our passports behind.

'Let's get out of here.'

We retrieved our luggage from the dirty room and carried it as nonchalantly as possible down to the main road. There was no sign of the Public Security Bureau man. But a long hour passed. Then a welcome roar and another green lorry identical to the one in which we had travelled from the Tsangpo.

We did not go very far, just a few miles back along the road we had originally come on, getting dumped in a place called Raka. Birds of prey circled over another compound empty of vehicles, with a well in the middle and the usual square of small rooms.

My thoughts were still in Saga where the Public Security Bureau man would have found out that we had vanished. In such an exposed and empty land it would be easy to find us. Caroline did not agree.

'In China no one will take responsibility. They pass the buck. We've moved on out of his orbit and he's not going to worry about us now.'

We acquired another cell. Two beds with their coverlets, a broken-down stove, half a candle and a large Thermos flask. All over the country these lorry stops differ only in their degree of cleanliness. They link with a very old tradition when every camel stop in central Asia had its quadrangle offering accommodation, frugal comfort and shelter against the desert. Apart from the change from animals to vehicles, they remained remarkably similar, with their lack of heating and only the central well in the square providing water.

The tough little man who ran this Holiday Inn lacked a suspicious mind. It helped that he had never seen a foreign passport before. He cooked our noodles over an open fire while we waited at a rickety table, and a lot of nomads wearing blackened sheepskin coats over trousers, and pigtails dangling down from under rakish fur hats, sat and grinned at Caroline.

▲ Tibetans love bright colours and dress up their drab working clothes whenever possible with sumptuous jewellery.

They had plenty of time to hang about and watch the gorgeous Foreign Devil. We were marooned in Raka for five days as unhelpful lorries came and went.

A Long Wait

Outside the compound was only the harsh lunar plain, smooth and empty, stretching away to an assortment of distant mountains which, for a Tibetan horizon, were comparatively meagre. Overhead were always birds of prey or carrion; beneath them the smaller birds they sought sang constantly. Whenever I walked out across the gravel towards the nomad tents in the middle distance, I would see big hares bounding away, and other little gopher-like animals the size and shape of guinea pigs, which must have been mouse hares. One day I came upon a stream edged with ice, where I frightened two large golden ducks with white heads that dashed away over the desert. There was never any rain. The morning clouds were empty of moisture; perhaps to the Buddhist mind they were an omen of the vanity of human wishes.

The worst thing was the wind. Regularly by midday it began blowing, and it increased until you had to fight it, together with pelting particles of dust, in order to stand up. It was my first prolonged experience of a landscape with a degree of desolation that made it unreal. We were at about 15,000 feet and wherever you looked you saw the same flat scree of rocks and shingle with the sharp ridges of hills rising in the thin air, and rising out of them like a dream the distant snowy crests of mountains. There was a link between this landscape and the great Buddhist shrines I had seen, where the flames of butter lamps illuminated dark interiors and gilded Buddhas stared out of the dark.

On the fifth day, as I lay in my sleeping-bag trying to keep warm, I heard a roar and four lorries turned into the compound.

Caroline leapt out of bed and into her chuba. 'You stay here, I'll talk to them.'

By now I was used to the routine. We would be refused, either with an excuse—most times no room—or without. Chinese drivers bring rudeness to a fine art.

But no. Caroline demonstrated her powers of persuasion and found a driver who would take us for 50 yuan.

We squashed in the back with half-a-dozen other passengers. A man's head was jammed against my knees, and beneath me a piece of metal stabbed my back. After five days at Raka it was a pleasant sensation.

These lorries belonged to a cooperative in Gêrzê, to which they were bringing seed potatoes and other provisions from Lhasa. Passengers are not officially allowed to be taken on, but in a land where transport is so limited the rule is generally ignored. Like other drivers, this one appeared to welcome his windfall, especially since foreigners could be charged at least double the normal rate.

The misery of travelling across Tibet in the back of a Chinese lorry is considerable. Imagine a small, cramped space packed full of groaning people, kerosene drums, pieces of machinery, wooden planks, plastic cans of petrol, sacks of potatoes and sharp things like spades and axes all tumbling about. Imagine a pitted, dusty road on which a wild driver is going at sixty miles an hour behind a comrade who is throwing up dust, which pours down your throat. Occasionally one of the other travellers sends a well-aimed globule of spit in your direction—not from malice since even here, amid the discomfort, they aim a wan smile at you as well. Otherwise there is little movement as they sit about seemingly dead, wrapped in their own personal suffering.

At noon the convoy stopped among rocks to make a meal. Ample provisions from Lhasa, tins of meat, rice and vegetables, were cooked on a species of

▲ Butter lamps burn like bright, flickering spirits in the dark interiors of Buddhist shrines.

blowlamp; everyone took out their own chopsticks. One Chinese, taller than the others, wearing an officer's fur-lined coat, came and sat down beside us.

'Why do you come here?' he asked in English.

Caroline put on her disarming smile. 'We wish to see more of Tibet. It is so beautiful.'

He put down his chopsticks and gazed at us dumbfounded.

'But there is nothing here. I would like to see California.'

He was an interpreter who had learnt his English in some Chinese academy before joining the army and being posted to western Tibet; it was like going to Siberia.

Hours later, we stopped beside a stream and everyone climbed out.

'We go fishing,' the interpreter said. 'This river good for fish.'

The sparkling mountain stream wound through a wasteland of sand and rock with an unexpected pale-green edging of thin grass on each bank. Four men walked upstream for a hundred yards or so and then ran back. Suddenly there was a spout of water and an explosion.

When the ripples had died away, all the Chinese pulled up their trouser legs and waded around in the freezing water picking up corpses, soon to be gutted and fried in a pan by the blowlamp.

The previous year I had reverently tried to pull some fish out of Lough Mask, while Caroline spun a rod on the Dee. Now we were unsporting enough to eat our fill with our hosts. The trout were very good. Only the Tibetans did not join us.

'Silly people,' said the interpreter. 'Such old-fashioned attitudes.'

Tibetans might gnaw and kill yaks and lambs, but veneration for life, evolving from the central doctrine of reincarnation, meant they did not like to kill

A yak herdsman in a sheepskin chuba. Somehow, even here in the arid Tibetan mountains, this nomad will find enough fodder for his beasts. ▶

little things with souls. They were pragmatic: one slaughtered yak equalled the souls of several fish or birds. So every stream was crammed with fish, while the plains teemed with hares and gazelle and the sky overhead was filled with unshot birds.

The Late Show

We moved on in darkness, and after twelve hours of driving we reached a little settlement called Coqen—at least, that was what it sounded like.

Everyone vanished. It was as if the earth had opened up and devoured them. Caroline eventually routed out an old man who had been left behind like the lame boy in *The Pied Piper*.

'He says they've gone to the cinema. Typically Chinese.'

For the next two hours we hung around in the cold, as the entire population of Coqen enjoyed a video whose music was relayed through loudspeakers out onto the moonlit landscape. All the rooms were shut and locked and there was no way we could get a bed.

It was almost twelve o'clock when the music was switched off and a few dim figures emerged into view. A door was unlocked and we were shown into a room containing four beds, and the standard smells of tobacco smoke and urine.

Next day the troupe left the gravel plains and climbed into a land of towering mountain peaks and immense, dried-up valleys. We were up at 19,000 feet for lunch. Just above where we stopped, a herdsman and his daughter were erecting their tent in a waste of gravel before a mountain background. Their dogs barked at us, massive brutes that were tied down during the day. It must have been lonely and tough in this world of snow and rocks; the two of them watching their herds in a routine unchanged since the days of Abraham. They sat outside the tent, beside a stream edged with jagged pieces of ice, watching us scoop meat and noodles and vegetables with our chopsticks. They watched spellbound as the lorries roared away; all the time there had been no communication or greeting.

At four o'clock the lorry stopped in Gêrzê, home town and final destination of the convoy. Time to pay off the driver.

Gêrzê was a frontier-style town with some official buildings within its mud walls, nomads without, camped on the edge of the desert surrounded by their animals. The place was big enough for officials and queries about permits. Caroline sought out another lorry travelling west, and with her touch of the miraculous immediately managed to find a driver who said that he would be leaving early next morning. We spent the night in the back of his lorry.

The driver had said that he planned to leave early, but by seven o'clock he was still shunting backwards and forwards around Gêrzê collecting people and things. A load of long wooden planks was shoved on top of us, some sacks and tins of petrol, and then half-a-dozen passengers, including the interpreter. With so many people and so little room to move, space was contested as in a gannetry, and any incursion into someone else's territory was met with a kick.

We lay in our sleeping-bags, very cold, hardly moving for stops and starts and pauses to cool the radiator. We reached Gê'gyai eighteen hours later, and a crowded dormitory where Tibetans were chewing legs of raw mutton covered with long black hairs.

In the morning I woke and lay listening to the sounds around me—bubbling throats, wheezes, rattles, heavings, gaspings, dry barks and long harsh series of early-morning evacuation from the lungs. Every Tibetan appeared to have a respiratory problem. Two soldiers were pulling up a bucket from the well in the middle of the compound, the big creaking winch letting down a long leather thong and bucket into the depths to draw up the precious water for cooking and washing. A hen ran across the yard; a litter of small black pigs came out from beneath the wheels of a lorry. The soldiers carried their bucket across the dust to some mud cabin. There was a potent sense of exile. Tibet is officially regarded as a hardship post, with six months' leave every two years.

At ten o'clock it was time to climb back on to the lorry, and for the next three days we continued to travel towards the wave of mountains, by way of Shiquanhe and Gar. Perhaps as a sign that we were approaching holy places, we noticed hares, little deer scurrying over the stones, and small birds dipping their wings and playing like porpoises around us. Pairs of eagles soared overhead; herds of sheep and yak increased in size.

Then the driver stopped and pointed to a glistening white cone.

'Kailas.'

To reach the holy mountain, the focus of what has been called the greatest and hardest of all earthly pilgrimages, we had travelled westwards for sixteen days, across a series of desolate and noble landscapes.

Tibet—The Wind-Swept Plateau—and its People

L YING ON A VAST PLATEAU at an average elevation of almost 14,000 feet above sea level, Tibet covers an area of approximately 472,000 square miles. The northern half of the country is virtually uninhabited desert known as the Chang Tang or Northern Plain, entered only by occasional hunters and salt-gatherers. South of this is a wide, mountainous region in which groups of nomads graze their herds of sheep, goats and yaks. Living in black, animal-hair tents, these people follow a way of life that has probably changed little over 2,000 years.

Most Tibetans, however, live settled lives in the far south of the country, in the valleys irrigated by the great Tsangpo or Brahmaputra River and its tributaries. Here they grow the country's staple crops of barley, wheat and pulses, and keep domestic animals such as horses, goats, sheep and yaks. Here too are all the country's large towns, such as Lhasa, Xigazê and Gyangzê, though none of these has an exceptionally large population. Before the Chinese invasion of 1950, Lhasa's population is estimated to have stood at about 25,000; now it is nearly four times as large, owing to the deliberate relocation of Chinese people here, in addition to the sizeable presence of the Chinese army and civil administration.

Before 1950, Tibetan society was largely feudal, consisting of aristocratic landowners, peasants, nomads and merchants, as well as an enormous monastic clergy, comprising as much as a third of the population. Nowadays most traditional ways of life have broken down, or been 'modernised' by the Chinese. The country's characteristic religious culture has all but vanished, though there are signs that it is being allowed to re-emerge a little—if only, cynics might say, for the benefit of tourists.

▲ A peasant woman near Tingri in southern Tibet.

▲ A horseman of the plains in festive costume.

Lush fields surround a tiny farming village in a river valley near Lhasa. ▶

▲ A nomadic yak-herder's wife wearing her finery: a colourfully patterned chuba and silver ornaments in her elaborately plaited hair.

▲ Life at 15,000 feet for a poor but proud nomad family, their smoke-blackened tent situated in the corner of their yak pen.

▲ In spite of the many green and blue cotton uniforms sprinkled among this crowd attending a festival, many Tibetans clearly still value traditional ways of dressing.

CHAPTER 6

Kailas and its Lakes

T HE HOLY MOUNTAIN OF KAILAS is unique in its shape and symmetry. It is one of those rarities in nature, a perfectly regular form, four sides of a crude pyramid facing the four corners of the compass, as sharply defined as if they had been chiselled by an axe. Traditionally it is said to be composed of crystal and different jewels, but in fact the mountain is geologically significant as the world's highest deposit of tertiary conglomerate. In other words, it is a giant mound of cemented gravel.

Remotely placed near the world's largest snow barrier among the headstreams of four mighty and holy rivers—the Ganges, the Indus, the Brahmaputra and the Sutlej—the mountain of Kailas and the oval lake of Manasarowar beside it, both sacred destinations of pilgrims, present in geographical fact the images of natural harmony that are essential to Tibetan and Hindu philosophy. The union of balancing and opposing forces is here for the pilgrim to see.

We were deposited, together with our baggage, a couple of miles away from the line of red foothills. The sacred mountain spire loomed in the distance behind a row of splintered orange hills which seemed sharp as sharks' teeth. The sun was blindingly hot. Caroline took up one pack and I took the others, carrying some baggage forward, going back for the rest and taking that beyond the load in front. We moved very slowly along the track.

After a few hundred yards Caroline said, 'I think I'll go on. You bring up everything.'

I watched her bound away towards a little building surrounded by an encampment of huts, behind which Mount Kailas showed over its guard of foothills. I followed on slowly with a backstitch gait. After about an hour I reached a rough road where groups of women carrying enormous loads were striding along, and a lorry went by crammed with nomads who looked like Red Indians. These were pilgrims. A pretty girl caught sight of me and came rushing down to pick up some of the bags and toss them easily up on her back. Further on I could see Caroline standing outside the gate of a walled enclosure that surrounded a low building. She was talking to two men.

When I at last came to the gate I was met by a Tibetan and another oriental, a plump, middle-aged man in a bright

The area around Mount Kailas and its two lakes, showing the routes of the two parikramas (circumambulations) traditionally undertaken by pilgrims. ▼

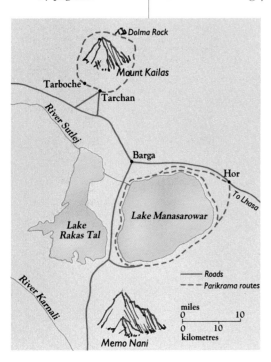

blue jacket and yellow cap. The Tibetan was Dorje, who ran the Tarchan Guest House for pilgrims. The other was Dr Kazuhiko Tamanura, Professor of Tourism from Doshisha University, Kyoto, Japan. Kazi, as we came to know him, smiled and shook hands, dismissing the girl who had carried my bags with a few sweets.

Dorje helped us bring the bags inside and assigned us a room. This very ancient pilgrimage centre was originally built by a king of Bhutan for the benefit of pilgrims from outside Tibet. Controlled by the Bhutanese for centuries, Tarchan ignored any directives from Lhasa. The lamas who ran it were called Dashok, and they seem to have had a certain style. When Colonel Sherring visited Tarchan in 1905, everyone in the place was drunk; twenty years later, when Colonel Ruttledge journeyed here across the western Himalayas, the Dashok still appeared to be drunk.

Before 1981 the pilgrimage had been suspended for a twenty-year period, during which any manifestation of Buddhist ceremony was forbidden. Now religion was acceptable once more, and the resthouse had been rebuilt specifically to accommodate Indian and Nepalese pilgrims. A trickle had already journeyed here across the Himalayas during the three years since the parikrama (ritual circumambulation) and festival of Kailas had been resumed, but until this year no foreigners from the West had been here for at least thirty-five years. This year a number of outsiders had made the journey to Tarchan: one American, and one Austrian, who both got official permission by paying thousands of dollars to China Travel; Dr Kazuhiko from Japan; two impoverished Irish travellers.

The room we were assigned was simple—no washbasin, no beds, just sacks filled with dried pellets of sheep dung. But it was our first room since leaving Lhasa that did not smell of urine and on the whole it was clean.

▲ These pilgrims have halted their truck at the first sight of the holy mountain of Kailas to pay homage to it by the roadside. The mere sight of Kailas would be a blessing for them.

In the evening the Japanese professor entertained us. First, he gave us a glass of Japanese whisky, and then out of a large cardboard box he took packets of dried seaweed, prawn chips, dried vegetables and strips of processed beef, which we heated on a gas burner.

'Perhaps you like green tea?' he asked, as various Tibetans crowded round the door to have a look. Kazi was a member of the Chinese–Japanese Friendship Mountaineering Expedition, which at this very moment was engaged in climbing Memo Nani, a virgin peak in the Gurla mountain range which we could see from the guesthouse. The Japanese had worked for almost twenty years to get here; negotiation was sweetened by staggering sums of money paid, so Kazi assured us, by the richest man in Japan.

'You see, we must each pay twenty thousand dollars for the permission. We also give four new Japanese Landcruisers as a big bribe. The Chinese are clever people and climbing mountains is political. Already a celebration dinner is planned in Beijing. Very good for Japanese–Chinese trade.' The food we were eating was part of the expedition's general supplies.

Before we retired, Kazi lent us an extra gas stove and that night we enjoyed a cup of tea.

It was strange to get up without the feeling of 'Oh God, can we find a lorry today?' At Tarchan there was peace and no prospect of officials strolling around in green jackets asking awkward questions.

Nomadic tribesmen bring their sheep with them when they come on a pilgrimage to Mount Kailas. The chorten they are passing marks the start of the parikrama. ▼

Behind the pilgrims' resthouse were the remains of the old gompa surrounded by tents with the cone of Kailas shining behind its back. One morning I investigated the old building, which for centuries must have been the only solid habitation for scores of miles that had a roof and walls. Until the resthouse was built in 1982, this important centre for pilgrims had been allowed to decay. I walked through the small, bare rooms where the lamas had lived and prayed and got drunk, where shepherds now camped down with their meagre possessions: a few battered tin pots, or a tea churn with a long, elegant, brassbound stem. A sheep peered at me from a doorway and an old woman wrapped in a bright, Aztec-patterned shawl was cooking over a fire. She smiled and said something, but I couldn't stay; the smell of burning dung and damp earth and years of unwashed communal life was overpowering. I felt as if my head was on fire and each short breath made me gasp. In the next dark room a rickety ladder led upwards, and in seconds I was out on the roof, breathing the rarefied cold air, looking down on the shimmering golden plain with the lakes of Manasarowar and Rakas Tal, and the background of the Gurla mountains. Behind them I could see more lines of mountains, the Himalayan barrier which was like so many breaking waves.

▲ Kailas cannot be circled in a single day so pilgrims set up their own little camps; they do not fear discomfort and their needs are few.

The New Tolerance

The lamas had gone. Would the Chinese let any trickle back for the sake of the pilgrim trade? People give you different figures. One estimate has about 120,000 monks in Tibet in 1959 and 2,711 monasteries. At present, nine or ten monasteries with lamas remain in the whole of Tibet.

Perhaps things would change with the new tolerance. Here was Tarchan rebuilt and functioning as a hostel. This was its third year. Most of the rooms would remain empty until the end of June or the beginning of July, when small contingents of Indians and Nepalese would come this way after the passes were free of snow. Tibetan pilgrims did not aspire to stay indoors, but camped all around outside. At this time, during the final week of May, Tarchan accommodated, besides ourselves, Kazi, Dorje, Dorje's aunt and another old lady with cracked blue-tinted glasses and a face as wrinkled as W.H. Auden's. Witchlike, she was followed everywhere by a small brown cat.

Dorje, a small, sinewy man with a cast in his eye, could just remember the old unchanged Tibet, warts and all, before the Chinese swept in in 1950. He fled into exile in India, where he learnt English, returning to his own country in 1970 to look after his sick father. During the Cultural Revolution his ability to speak English was regarded with the greatest suspicion.

'They said I was a spy.' He did not enlarge on his personal experience of

persecution during the years when thousands were killed in a period of unprece-
dented violence, and much of the social and cultural fabric of Tibetan life was
destroyed. The memory is recent, but like so many other Buddhists Dorje displayed a lack of bitterness almost incomprehensible to Westerners; the passive
acceptance of suffering is an intrinsic part of the Buddhist path to perfection.

'It is not that we do not care. But our beliefs make us realise how little time we spend in this world.'

'And those who died?'

'They have their reward.'

All around us were nomads with their animals. In the early morning I watched them milking their sheep before letting them go free on the mountains, absorbed by the daily spectacle of hundreds of bleating ewes and the gaudy clothes of those who tended them. Getting the ewes into parallel lines for milking, facing each other, heads interlocking, took time and expertise. Later, when the sun got up, people and animals vanished into the hills. A man or woman with a staggering number of sheep would fade away, expressing a potent force of freedom. The Chinese have had little luck with cooperatives in Tibet.

▲ Traditionally, ewes are roped together, their horns interlocked, for milking. This stony field offers, in Tibetan terms, a rich pasturage.

A Pious Question

Often Kazi would invite us for a meal. Why wasn't he on the mountain with the rest of the Chinese–Japanese Friendship Expedition? He was engaged on important research on pilgrims. While his colleagues were busy on their virgin peak, he was a star turn down at Tarchan. He walked around armed with notebooks, sketch-books, index cards, typed questionnaires and flipover counter-check lists, tape recorder and Polaroid camera.

The Polaroid was part of his irresistible interviewing technique. After he had questioned his pilgrim with Dorje as interpreter, he immediately photographed him, giving him a free colour print, while keeping a second picture to be filed with his notes. Most people had never seen photographs of themselves before. All day long the little courtyard was filled with eager interviewees, monks and shepherds, nomads and merchants from Lhasa, mountain men with their families, who had come from all over the country to the spiritual heart of the Himalayas and the mystical centre of the universe. The pilgrimage to Kailas was the fulfil-ment of a lifetime's ambition, which the coming of Communism had not dimin-ished, and Dr Kazi was one of their rewards.

When the Polaroid was produced, the pilgrim would go off and change into his best clothes. Here were four young nomads with their wives, swashbuckling figures in embroidered hats and cloaks, brandishing ornate daggers. The wives in long black dresses, their hair braided to the height of mantillas, stuck out their tongues and giggled. A tall youth displayed his new cloak edged with fox fur, an old man in a shaggy chuba appeared dazed as he held the little piece of card and watched his figure slowly emerge.

Then Kazi decided to do the parikrama, or ritual circuit, around Kailas in the steps of his compatriot, Ekai Kawaguchi, who circled Kailas in 1900.

There are three paths of pilgrimage around the mountain. Most pilgrims take the widest and lowest. One tour is adequate, but many do three or thirteen, a particularly holy number. Those who complete twenty-one parikramas are considered worthy to attempt the middle circuit high across the four faces of the mountain. There is a higher route still, only attainable by those who have achieved an advanced state of Buddhahood, culminating in the hundred and eighth circuit, which is said to ensure Nirvana.

One circuit would do for Kazi. We watched him depart with his two porters and return two days later exhausted, to receive our congratulations before collapsing in his room.

We planned to follow his example. Dorje found a young brother and sister who were willing to carry our bags. Pusu Seren Urju and Pusu Chorten were a handsome pair with apple-red cheeks, who thought it hilarious to be working for foreigners. Their laughter was uproarious as we showed them our rucksacks, bags, tents, provisions, all to be taken along. First the girl was loaded, and then the boy, everything tied on and balanced by straps across the forehead.

Our porters led us round the edge of the hills. Pale yellow flowers bloomed among the rocks and, as the sun came up behind our backs and warmed us, the light picked out details like a probing torch: a mani wall of stones, elaborately carved with sacred texts and figures of Buddha; hares bounding across the grass, tame as dogs; a young man prostrating himself along the route. He wore the uniform of prostrating pilgrims, the protective sheepskin apron and wooden blocks strapped to his hands. It would take him about twelve days to complete the circuit, following the prescribed rules for covering the ground. There is the way to stand and lift your arms, the way you pause and pray; and the way you measure your length. The distance around Kailas is about thirty-three miles, much of it over snow and rocks and stones.

Protected by a canvas apron and mittens with wooden blocks on their palms, this woman pilgrim prepares to prostrate herself. She may do this as many as 20,000 times during her circuit of the sacred mountain. ▶

All morning we followed the traditional route towards Kailas, a dusty trail marked out with little piles of stones and chortens stuck with blue, white, red and yellow flags. Pilgrims were walking and praying around each one. At midday we turned our backs on the plain at a place where another chorten, covered in tattered flags, marked the first important point of the circuit. It stood at the foot of the high, buff-coloured hills that guarded Kailas; now the holy mountain itself towered in front of us.

Around the Holy Mountain

As we walked towards a gorge, with Kailas above our heads, two horsemen were riding towards us, the hard wooden saddles of their ponies placed on embroidered saddle cloths; their plaited manes and tails were tied with pink bows. The riders, wearing fur coats, fur hats and high, decorated fur boots, spurred their mounts beside a stream known as God's River, trotting on what appeared to be bright green grass. But when we came closer and the ponies were urged past us, the green dissolved and, like other spectacles in the thin air, turned out to be hallucinatory; all I could see were specks of burnt foliage among the rocks.

A little further on we came to Tarboche, where a huge wooden pole was covered with coloured yak skins; streamers of prayer flags tumbled from its head, giving it the look of a giant maypole. In a land without trees, the sight of such a giant, which must have been carried up painstakingly from the forests of the Himalayas, was a startling herald to the entrance of the gorge and the start of the parikrama proper. Inside, the path followed a dark, cold valley; above our heads, one side was crossed with moving shadows, while the other sparkled in light where the world of snow and ice began above the crests of stone.

Occasionally there was the thunder of an avalanche, a distant puff of snow and a long silence. Beside us the murmur of the little river continued undisturbed, a burble like monks praying in the dark.

We joined a group of pilgrims camping under a mani wall glistening with butter spread over the years. Two men and their wives, one with a parcelled baby, welcomed us and offered us tea. They had lit a small fire using the same sort of pellets of sheepshit on which we had been trying to sleep for a week. The smallest and most ordinary things would keep them alive on the parikrama: ground-up barley meal taken from a leather bag, rancid butter swirling in the bowls of lukewarm brick tea which they shared with us.

After we had swallowed tea and tsampa in the cold, the family went ahead, while we continued more slowly among the stream of pilgrims who walked and prayed, spun prayer wheels, or carried poles or staves, usually with prayer flags tied to the tips, to help them over the rocks. There were also a number of Nepalese pilgrims carrying umbrellas. Now we reached another chorten where pilgrims stopped and prayed, circling it in the prescribed clockwise direction. Here was the family who had given us tea going round briskly, baby bundled on his mother's back, reciting their mantras and religious texts while we gasped for breath. This chorten had an imprint of the Buddha's foot, the next one along decked with flags contained the bones of a holy man, and now we were passing a cave revered as a place of particular sanctity because it was once the abode of an ascetic. It may well have been one of those where in the old days lamas were walled up for a grim bout of meditation.

We continued to follow the track beside God's River, our porters trotting many yards in front, occasionally stopping so that we could catch up. Along the way groups of pilgrims travelled with us, many passing us, others stopping to pray or picnic, the occasional dogged prostrator inching his way up the valley. Above us was still the steep line of corrugated brown peaks that guarded Kailas, and from time to time the holy mountain would emerge from a cauldron of clouds with snow running down its shoulder like custard on a Christmas pudding.

Late in the afternoon we camped beside the frozen riverbed. Kazi's stove did not work. Beyond the river the track twisted in a gentle bow and the valley widened as we started to climb towards the Dolma Pass. Among the weeping spires of ice and frozen waterfall, we came across a large herd of yaks, big Tibetan yaks with fringes over their eyes and rivers of hair falling down to tiny protruding legs. Some were golden, others spotted or dappled with white, but most of them were black as ebony. What did they live on? Moss, perhaps, lichen? There was nothing visible for them to graze on in this wilderness, certainly nothing in the way of grass. How spoilt Sod and Mucker had been, compared to their cousins snatching meagre grazing beneath Kailas.

By dusk we had been walking for almost twelve hours; the gleaming sides of Kailas were directly above us and it was very cold. In the old days there used to be four monasteries along the route to shelter travellers— three were near the summit of the pass. But up here nothing remained to welcome pilgrims, and we were lucky to erect our tent inside the shelter of what seemed to be a run-down

▲ **A rock beside the pilgrims' trail, painted to represent Kailas.**

▲ A major focus for devotion, the Dolma Rock at the top of the Dolma Pass is decorated with prayer flags, holy texts and pilgrims' offerings.

yersa situated beside an abyss. A campsite for ascetics—no prospect of keeping warm as icy winds rattled the tent's sides. From time to time we heard outside a song or the hum of a mantra. At 19,000 feet up at the summit of the Dolma Pass, our porters were softly praying.

Their prayers may have kept them warmer than I was in my sleeping-bag, for at dawn brother and sister appeared none the worse for wear. Nor did the pilgrims who climbed with us, without visible sign of camping gear.

The sun ascended slowly as we walked in Indian file towards another snow-field. The crowd of pilgrims was becoming denser, and more and more were prostrated on the wrinkled, icy surface of the pass.

By midday we had reached the very top of the pass, where the Dolma Rock marked the culmination of the pilgrimage. The polished appearance of the bottom part of this came from butter smeared on the sides as high as human arms could reach. Numerous small objects were embedded in the grease. In the old days a pilgrim would smear a bit of butter on the stone, pluck out a lock of his hair or even a tooth and slap it into the butter. Today's offerings were a lot less grisly—just coins and banknotes, flags, a few sweets and nuts, a piece of chewing gum and a photograph of the Dalai Lama.

We were in a state of immense exhaustion, as mountain sickness increasingly claimed us with shortness of breath and a headache that made me feel that my skull was much too small to contain my brain. Kazi's stove failed us again, and for a long time we sat gasping, watching an endless line of pilgrims pass, praying and touching the great rock. The sight of so many trudging through the snow, waiting to make their devotions at the shining, black, butter-smeared, flag-hung rock standing in snow and ice, was sublime.

We were intruders, myself and Caroline with her camera. No doubt the next thing would be a film crew. I wondered how much longer Kailas would remain isolated from outsiders and non-believers. Would foreigners travel this way in the numbers that wandered under Everest, to mingle with the great queue of the devout below us?

Time had fled and we had recovered enough to begin the descent from the pass through another steep, slippery valley of snow and ice. A line of pilgrims was holding hands to try and stop slipping since there were no aids to safety, no guides or ropes or handholds. I watched men and women of all ages, arm in arm, slithering down the bone-breaking ice. Slowly, slowly we made progress down the slippery trail, and then Kailas was behind us with all its ice and mystery. We came to a different world, a windy valley free of snow through which a stream bubbled over rocks. With muted green, brown and grey colours predominating, it resembled a glen in Donegal, except that yaks were grazing with the sheep and there was not a blade of grass to be seen. The bright greens that shone with a quality of stained glass were lichens and moss.

At the point where the valley opened up to the plain we found a small, derelict gompa where the sole inhabitant was a very old lama with whom we drank tea. This was the only holy building left on the parikrama. Although this one remaining temple was a bleak little place without holy pictures, shrines or gilded Buddhas, it appeared to have a future—workmen were repairing it after the long night of the Cultural Revolution.

We reached Tarchan in the evening when the rays of the setting sun were touching the distant mountains; snowy peak after peak was caught in the light before vanishing suddenly in darkness.

The parikrama of about twenty-eight miles had taken us two days.

'I was worried about you,' Dorje said. 'Such an old man walking the round.'

▲ A Nepalese mother lifts her son up to the Dolma Rock so that he may receive its blessing.

Raising the Pole

We felt a sense of achievement, having joined the select group of foreigners who have made the parikrama of Kailas. Even our porters were pleased that we had achieved the greatest of earthly pilgrimages. For the whole time they had been with us there had been no acrimony. I felt my own inadequacy; how can people who endure so much always remain friendly and cheerful?

Summer and the birth of the Buddha were being celebrated at Kailas. The great, garlanded pole we had seen at Tarboche, marking the beginning of the parikrama, would be replaced to the accompaniment of all kinds of rites. For Dorje, the most important thing about the festival was that it was taking place at all. For seventeen years, from 1966 to 1983, it had been prohibited, and a whole generation of people had grown up without being able to take part in it.

For the next few days he organised the arrival of the thousands of pilgrims who descended on Tarchan. Every few minutes another pilgrim group would descend from a lorry to be told where to pitch their tents or find water and other provisions. Dorje was everywhere, directing mothers with crying children, or sorting out a group of nomads carrying daggers, their chubas peeled back to reveal tough torsos, who strode into the courtyard making demands in harsh, grating voices.

Besides sorting out pilgrims' problems Dorje arranged the ceremonies. He had invited along a young lama who had made twenty-two circuits of Kailas and hoped to do at least a hundred.

From early morning we could hear the lama chanting away in Dorje's section of the guesthouse, which had been rearranged. Dorje, the two old ladies and the calico cat crowded into the front room; while the small room behind was converted into a temple. In spirit, the lama's presence reminded me of a priest coming to do the Stations of the Cross in a farmer's house back in Ireland. The cupboard acted as an altar, a flickering butter lamp was balanced on an empty cocoa tin and a small drum hung from the ceiling. The lama sat crouched against a wall, reciting mantras, seemingly oblivious to the pilgrims perpetually

Pilgrims at Mount Kailas

PEOPLE OF MANY FAITHS have for centuries regarded both Mount Kailas and Lake Manasarowar as sacred. For Hindus this is the place where Lord Siva, the creator and destroyer, dwells; for Buddhists it is the Lord Buddha's abode; for members of the Indian Jain religion it is where their first great teacher, Tirthankar Rishabhadev, attained Nirvana or enlightenment; and for the Bonpa believers of Tibet it is the home of their gods Daimchowk and Dorje Phangmo.

Consequently, pilgrims from all over Tibet, Nepal and India congregate at Kailas to make a parikrama (a circumambulation, frequently including ritual prostrations) of the mountain and sometimes of the lake as well. For many, this pilgrimage

and parikrama, possible only during the few short months of spring and summer, will be one of the most important religious events in their lives.

It is at Tarboche, near the foot of Mount Kailas, that the parikrama of the mountain begins. And here, each year in early summer, at the full moon of the fourth Tibetan month, a great pole is raised, in honour of the Buddha's birth, death and enlightenment. The pole supports many prayer flags, each one inscribed with holy texts, which are believed to be blown on the wind far across the world for the benefit of all mankind.

A young Tibetan monk, with prayer wheel and holy scriptures in hand, sets out on a devotional circuit of the holy mountain. ▶

crowding in. When he finished one page, it was taken out and replaced by another, and in spite of his zeal in reciting there was a pleasant casualness about the scene. If a man came in during the prayers and talked to him in the middle of his reading, he was not at all put out. Someone would be passing around chang, while next door the old women endlessly pounded churnfuls of tea. For an hour or so we crouched on the floor sharing offerings of little cakes made in the shape of Kailas and painted bright red. There were plates of nuts and sticky sweets, thimblefuls of barley grain and a sickly sweet drink served in a silver-rimmed skull.

The next day we all set off for the ceremony of erecting the new pole of prayer flags.

The morning was windless and perfect, the sky deep blue, the mountains white and golden, the plain tinged with sapphire and emerald. The colours of the landscape were echoed in the pilgrims' clothes, for everyone was wearing their best and the strong, clear colours were attuned to their surroundings. Much in evidence were long, shocking-pink robes; embroidered cloaks and dresses and wonderful hats, some lined with fur and perched on women's heads like embroidered cushions; bonnets of snow-white wool and stiff Gretchen caps. Among the men was a great variety of cowboy extravaganzas in black and brown, with immense brims which had the effect of dwarfing the proud wearer's face until it resembled a nut or a berry.

▲ A rare scene in today's Tibet: lamas gather in their traditional red and saffron robes and elaborate, crested hats.

Dorje was wearing a long gown of chocolate-coloured silk and had brought along a camera. 'We must take three photographs of everything,' he said, focusing on some pilgrims circling a chorten. The figure three, representing the trinity of Buddha, Dharma and Sangha, was auspicious. To Caroline it seemed a waste of good film.

From every direction groups of pilgrims were walking towards the gorge. As we rounded the last hill we could see scores of tents in front of us. Some were little conical erections with spears for tent poles, others were more elaborate and rectangular and looked like Noah's Arks. Flags were everywhere. So much of the picturesque quality of Tibetan life has disappeared: the robes of higher officials, the mulberry silk gowns, the embroidered undercoats, the wide-brimmed papier-mâché topis lacquered with gold, the yellow woollen hats shaped like centurions' helmets; such frivolities have given way to green uniforms. But here was a glimpse of a fast-vanishing world.

It was a time for prayer and enjoyment for pigtailed nomads, yak herders, shepherds, lamas, nuns, battered old men and women and plenty of giggling girls, many wearing make-up, since pale complexions are desirable. Both sexes were loaded with jewellery, silver necklaces set with egg-sized lumps of turquoise and the warm chestnut of amber beads. A line of ponies and yaks was being driven up, the ponies mincing along, the big black yaks lumbering, followed by nomads in fur-lined coats and coloured boots, their left arms swinging free as they swaggered along. Many of them carried spears and old flintlocks decorated with coral and silver balanced from girdles. Portraits of the Dalai Lama hung from pilgrims' necks.

The great pole lying on the ground, eighteen times a man's length, was being dressed by groups of pilgrims. Two men sat outside a tent sewing together coloured prayer flags donated by the devout, including a string that had been brought up by a party of Nepalese. Others decorated the shaft with strips of yak hide, a blacksmith hammered at the huge metal chains, men and women walked around it praying, and a lama blessed the work by throwing handfuls of rice over the stump.

Time passed; two Japanese Landcruisers drove up containing members of the mountaineering team which had just succeeded in climbing Memo Nani, together with the first-ever Chinese television team to come into this area of western Tibet. Now that religion was respectable, it was possible to entertain Han comrades back home with picturesque views of ceremonies in far-flung corners. A microphone was thrust under my chin.

'You are from where?'

I admitted to Ireland, but answered other questions with a Gaelic shrug.

The pole-raising ceremony did not take place that day, and as evening approached the cameras were packed away. We walked back to Tarchan, where the resthouse had become inundated with Chinese. In addition to the cameramen, a couple of journalists and some geologists, a mysterious Mr Su had arrived, who, we learned, worked for the government in neighbouring Burang. For the first time since our arrival, we began to feel vulnerable.

This pilgrim woman has put on her finest jewellery. Hanging from her necklace is a portrait of the Panchen Lama.

Next morning we made our way over the rocks back to the site of the ceremony. Once again, preparations were being made to pull the pole upright into position by its four chains. At first the ceremony seemed to be proceeding smoothly, and by ten o'clock the carpenter had given his signal for the teams standing at the end of each chain to begin pulling. As the cameras recorded the event, the huge treetrunk, bigger than a telegraph pole, was raised foot by foot over the heads of the crowd. From every tent and from every corner, the people watched this vernal emblem of their religion rise into the western skies under the holy mountain for the third springtime since the ceremony had been revived. A group of lamas were chanting prayers, men and women prostrated themselves and a lonely shepherd, watching the event from the top of a rose-coloured rock, stopped whistling to gaze across.

And then everything went wrong. Although the pole had been raised without incident for the past two years, after the seventeen-year gap the actual

mechanics of leverage had still not been worked out with confidence. Enveloped in skins, streamers flapping, a yellow-painted basin on its top, the pole stood upright for twenty seconds; then it began to totter. Before anyone could call out there was an almighty crash and it came down, missing me by a couple of yards. There it lay, splintered in two.

Miraculously, no one in the huge crowd was killed. A woman, slightly hurt, was surrounded by well-wishers while the lamas chanted mournfully outside a tent. The gaiety was extinguished. What had gone wrong? Many reasons were given. The chief lama was said to have hurried the prayers. Perhaps the failure was a portent of irrevocable change signalled by the presence of the cameras and by our own intrusion.

For the rest of the day the crowd waited around anxiously while the broken halves of the pole were tenderly lifted into place and the carpenters began to splice the pieces of wood together, working at the join in the same way as an old sailing ship damaged in a storm is fitted out with a jury rig.

While waiting, we were invited into a tent for tea and tsampa with a lama and his friends. He had a bad leg; with a smile he pulled up his gown for us to see the livid flesh, and to receive a dab of antiseptic cream from us. Stoicism is still needed in a land without medicines.

Another tent, the smiling host and hostess stoking up the fire with a handful of sheepshit, dispensing basins of tea with odd hairs floating on top and offering

▲ A group of herders and their yaks near Kailas. Tents and other household belongings are strapped to the yaks as they are driven from one pasture to another.

us a bone. We became adept at hesitation. Another invitation, another smoky interior with altar, icon and smiles, a cosy dung fire, a briquette of tea, more bowls of swill to be surreptitiously emptied behind a mat or cushion and then insistently refilled. One traveller has compared the taste of Tibetan tea to water in an oriental harbour.

▲ The second attempt to raise the pole garlanded with prayer flags, now carefully mended after its disastrous fall. On this occasion the ceremony was a complete success.

Just before dusk the broken pole was spliced. Now it rose again under Dorje's direction, and this time there was no mishap and everything was properly secured. But the joy and excitement of the festival had gone with the sense of shock and dismay and the silence when it fell.

As we walked away from the gorge, the pole with its prayer flags was being circled by the crowd, while the light fell behind the mountains. Other pilgrims were moving in prostration or setting off on the parikrama. The festival was a particularly auspicious time to make the round, and one circuit now was the equivalent of thirteen made at another time.

Back at Tarchan next day we got a signal that we would have to move on when the geologists invited us into their room for lunch. Halfway through the noodles and the affable conversation, one of them produced from his inner jacket pocket the essential travel permit for western Tibet and asked if we had similar ones. There was an exchange of smiles as Caroline put on a brilliant display of not quite understanding what he was saying. He put away his document and picked up his chopsticks again, having given us a kindly warning.

Meanwhile, though, Caroline had managed to beguile Mr Su, the government official from the administrative capital of Burang, and persuade him to give us a note asking the police or anyone in charge for their help. Her foresight meant that we now had an important, scribbled piece of paper signed by a bona fide government official, which was the first legitimate piece of authorisation we had acquired since leaving Kathmandu.

'What happens when he finds out about us?'

'We'll probably never see him again.'

The Sacred Lake

In the morning we were ready with all our bags. Fortune was kind to us. We only had to wait a couple of hours before a truck arrived with pilgrims and the driver agreed to take us to Hor, the nearest village to Manasarowar where we hoped to hire horses and tour the lake.

With great sadness we climbed into the cab. I watched Tarchan vanish behind us, the pilgrim tents and sheepfolds, and the small place of refuge where we had spent happy weeks. Dorje stood by the gate and waved.

The distance to Hor was around eighteen miles over a golden plain rippling down to the two lakes, Manasarowar and Rakas Tal, one round, one in the shape of a crescent moon. Our first stop to let the engine cool down was at a small settlement with high-walled enclosures like something out of *Beau Geste*. Around and about were a few dirty tents. Beyond the rocks and the sand that blew up thick as custard and the dingy prayer flags rattled by the wind were patches of bog, which perhaps heralded the presence of the lakes.

Another hour's drive brought us to our destination at Hor. We were instantly surrounded by another jostling crowd; someone took up one of Caroline's bags and she snatched it back. A man came out of one of the mudwalled rooms wearing a Western-style jacket and trousers, the sign that he was an official. Caroline presented him with our paper from Mr Su and a host of problems—accommodation, horses to hire for travel around the lake, a guide.

Followed by an interested crowd, we retired to his small office where over lidded pots of tea we were told swiftly that horses were no good for making the round of the lake, since there was no grazing on the other side and no hay on this side. Although Mr Su mentioned that this was the first time that foreigners had come to Hor, he was ready for us. He announced that, if Caroline wished to use her camera out in the countryside, the fee would be 10 yuan a photograph. The idea of fees for photographs was taken for granted in Lhasa and other tourist centres—but this was the first time we had come across such entrepreneurial spirit in western Tibet.

The landscape around Hor, lit by the setting sun. Prayer flags adorn the little bridge on the left. ▼

'Outrageous,' she muttered, as we were shown across the dusty compound past a group of men playing cards towards one of the few mud dormitories that did not have broken windows. Two ragged men were curled up on sacks, and a woman with a sick child sat on a pile of litter.

'Let's camp!'

Just a few yards beyond the village was the sacred lake of Manasarowar beside a green meadow with the mountains beyond. There were two shepherds' tents and, apart from them, solitude and peace. The only sounds came from nature, the murmur of a small river and the cries of birds skimming over the water or feeding on the grass. Birds in their ten thousands with little to fear from hunters, ducks, geese, herons, dense flocks of waders in three or four sizes, and multitudes of screeching black-headed terns. Big hares bounded in the emerald-green grass and everywhere larks were singing. The lush landscape was filled with herds of grazing sheep and yaks, with the occasional horse. A few miles off, the green oasis by the lake faded away once again into the spare pasture that supported the nomad herds we had been watching for weeks; burnt stretches of rock and clay and the orange hills that rose before the distant cone of Kailas.

We camped peacefully that evening beside the calm lake. A group of shepherds came over to inspect us. Their tents, made from thick yak hair, were cavernous like battleships; in comparison ours must have seemed as fragile as an egg. They

Lakes of the Sun and the Moon

NO ONE CAN VISIT MOUNT Kailas and its two lakes—Manasarowar and Rakas Tal—without being overwhelmed by their beauty. In the thin air of the Tibetan Plateau, at over 14,000 feet above sea level, colours are intense and the light is clear and pure. Seen from the south at sunset, the snowcapped mountain is brightly lit by the orange glow of the sun, while the two lakes in front of it gleam a rich turquoise. Then, as night approaches, Kailas appears as a silvery peak across the lakes' darkening waters.

Pious pilgrims who have performed one or more parikramas of Mount Kailas sometimes go on to the sacred shores of Lake Manasarowar to complete their spiritual journeys. Buddhists and Hindus both regard Manasarowar

as a profoundly holy place, and believe its waters to be full of healing properties. Prayer flags on poles around its shores mark places for special devotions; and these, if fully observed, can make a single, 64-mile circuit of the lake take two weeks or more.

By contrast, Rakas Tal, the smaller lake, is shunned by most pilgrims. Sickle-shaped beside Lake Manasarowar—the moon to its sun—Rakas Tal is taken to symbolise all that is mysterious and threatening. It is said to be a moody, brooding place: a fitting home for the demons that are believed to inhabit its depths.

• •

A pilgrim prepares to prostrate herself on the shore of Lake Manasarowar at a special place marked by a pole covered with colourful prayer flags. ▶

felt the thin green material and stood around riveted by the sight of our small domestic cares: Caroline brushing her hair, myself cleaning tin plates in an ice-edged stream. We sat on the grass as the sun set over Manasarowar in an orange ball and the mountains turned from white to gold until the last snowy peak shone like a star. Then the darkness drifted down and the only sound was the rustling of sleepy birds.

Although the headman of Hor had said that we could not make the full circuit of the lake on horseback, he provided two thin steeds for a day's hire. They stood waiting for us in the yard, horses that had suffered a hard life before being fitted with high wooden saddles that felt like sitting on knives and very short rope stirrups that pulled up our legs like flat-race jockeys. When I mounted, I seemed to be doing penance for the whole suffering animal world. They were so enfeebled, they needed a guide to pull them along by a rope halter.

We left the village at a pace that made Sod and Mucker seem Derby winners, and our original idea of travelling around the lake lunatic. After an hour of torture, disregarding the pleas of the guide, I dismounted and handed him the rope. Freedom never seemed more pleasant. Caroline followed my example.

We walked across a sand dune to the great blue pool of Manasarowar, and for the rest of the day wandered along the curve of empty strand. There were no houses or boats or people, just space filled with the sound of water and birds, mostly screeching terns. In places there were huge sand dunes along the shore, and by the edge of the water was a ridge of dark, chocolate-coloured weed. It could have been any familiar seashore, grey waves with terns weaving and calling and the chill of an ocean wind, except for that unique rippling light, and always, whenever you lifted your eyes, snowcapped mountains—ahead, the Gurla range with Memo Nani among them.

The sixty-four-mile circuit of the lake used to be as important a part of the pilgrimage to holy places as Kailas. For Hindus, Brahma himself made the lake, and pilgrims who come here are expected to follow the precepts laid down by the ancient sacred writings, for like the banks of the Ganges the shores of Manasarowar are a good place to die. But we found no pilgrims circling the sacred lake as they had been rounding Kailas. Perhaps after the long period during which religious practices had been forbidden, the lakeside parikrama had not been resumed. Perhaps the time of year was wrong.

Without inducement we had no urge to do the circuit ourselves, and ambled instead for some hours on what seemed a seaside walk. We realised that the headman of Hor had been right and that horses—certainly not those horses—could not find sustenance beyond the fertile strip where we were encamped; for the land turned once again to gravel and there was no grazing even for the hardiest ruminant. The shores were totally devoid of human habitation.

The slap of water continued on the sand and the air was shrill with the cries of birds. Nothing disturbed them; Manasarowar, rippling in blue light, was surrounded by an empty ring of sand.

▲ The Himalayan blue poppy has evolved a brilliantly coloured flower to attract the few insects that live at high altitudes. Its spines are there to discourage browsing animals from eating it.

▲ Spring in the Himalayas; wild flowers blossom at 11,200 feet in a valley in the Everest region.

◄ This distinctive high-altitude plant has tiny yellow flower heads on an insulating cushion of woolly leaves.

The magnificent rhododendron, Nepal's national flower. ▶

Mountain Flora

PLANTS IN THE HIGH mountains have a hard time of it. They must pit themselves against scourging winds, long periods of being covered by snow, and summer temperatures that swing between intense daytime heat and freezing night-time cold. This is why many grow small, hug the ground and insulate their flowers in cocoons of fluff.

Those that grow on the eastern slopes of the Himalayas have another problem to contend with: torrential monsoon rains. Some plants have learned to cope by closing the petals of their flowers at the first hint of rain and then reopening them again within minutes of the sun's reappearance.

As the 19th-century botanist Joseph Hooker discovered, the lower slopes of the Himalayas are a veritable treasure trove of flowers and shrubs, many of them now staunch favourites of gardeners the world over: plants such as hydrangea, buddleia, clematis, and azalea. But the pride of the area are undoubtedly the numerous varieties of rhododendron, which range in size from the tiny dwarf carpeter to the tall rhododendron tree, and whose blooms can be any colour from scarlet to pure white.

There are also magnificent forests of spruce, larch, fir, evergreen oak and chir pine. At higher levels grows the distinctive juniper, whose berries are used medicinally by local people and its leaves burned as incense. Higher yet are birch forests, which mark the tree line at approximately 13,000 feet.

The unmistakable, gnarled juniper tree high above the Kali Gandaki gorge. Its leaves are burned by Buddhists for incense. ▶

▲ Birch trees at 10,000 feet, bent by the weight of snow that they have to support every year.

◀ The effects of heavy monsoon rains can be seen in the network of exposed roots of this tree in eastern Nepal.

CHAPTER 7

Return to Nepal

On our second evening encamped outside Hor, we went to bed in spring and woke to midwinter. During the night, snow had gently covered the world. Outside the tent was a blinding white light and the ochre hills in front of Kailas had become a glittering white line. Snow lay on the grass and on the lakeshore; the small river was completely iced over and the only signs of life were the dark, humped shapes of yaks. The lake remained blue in its white setting.

We had decided to make for the Tibet–Nepal frontier, since, even discounting the blank spaces and inaccuracies of our map, Nepal was close by. Beyond the Gurla mountains was the frontier post at Burang.

The headman announced that a lorry was leaving Hor that day. He spoke with an enthusiasm that suggested he had had his fill of foreigners. Caroline bargained with the driver, the usual uniformed Chinaman: another tough guy—120 yuan for the five-hour journey to Burang, the equivalent of two months' salary, and travel in the open back. The snow? No, we could not join him in the cab.

The snow came in fits and flurries as we followed the narrow isthmus between Manasarowar and her sister lake, Rakas Tal. The sanctity of Manasarowar is counterbalanced by the evil associated with the sickle-shaped stretch of water beside her. At the same time, the shape of Manasarowar represents the sun and is synonymous with wisdom and compassion, while the crescent of Rakas Tal stands for the moon and enlightenment. One is good, one is evil; one is a bride, the other a groom; they are yin and yang.

Most travellers feel a spiritual uplift from the physical contrast between the lakes, with Kailas making a trinity. Lying in the back of the lorry with half a dozen Tibetans, and with snow flurries, dust and sand raining down on us, we felt no mystical experience. Now we were driving by the Gurla mountains and could see Memo Nani, their highest peak, and even make out the Friendship mountain camp up on a buttress of ice, a bleak spot surrounded by boulders and open to the winds. No wonder Kazi preferred to work with the pilgrims in Tarchan.

More snow fell on us. We lay among muffled figures and worried about our arrival in Burang with its customs and checkpoint.

The nearer we got to Burang, the more it became obvious that it had a noosehold on travellers crossing the frontiers of Nepal and India. It guarded the western approaches and for hundreds of miles there was no other way south over the Himalayas.

After we had left the Gurla range behind, the countryside changed dramatically. One moment we were surrounded by snowy peaks, and in five minutes we were

among groves of poplars and small, terraced fields with burgeoning green crops. (But in winter this area must be as desolate as elsewhere. One traveller mentions a poultry farm which prospered in the summer, but in the cold weather the fowls' feet froze and they became crippled.)

In a landscape that was lush and green we were passing a small village, with flat-roofed houses, prayer flags and stacks of dung. Then a small gompa with a curved golden roof looking down on the River Karnali and the honeycombed cliff below it. The caves were homes for a number of people whom we could see standing beside their white-painted doorways, rubbing their eyes as they came out into the light. We stopped at a flimsy suspension bridge guarded by lounging soldiers; above them some shepherds were guiding their flocks, which grazed around clumps of violets growing among the rocks. The roar of the ice-blue river drowned out all other sound.

The lorry moved forward towards the outskirts of the town. Once again we were at the mercy of a driver; although we banged helplessly on the roof of the cab, he swept us into the centre, past a barracks with a decorated gateway, a line of official residences, and into a large compound where, to our consternation, Mr Su was waiting for us among neatly trimmed flowerbeds, staring officials and senior army officers. The black leather jacket, sneakers and dark glasses were those he had worn when we met him in Kailas.

▲ A market at Pulan where salt and wool, transported by sheep, are traded. Note the cave dwellings of local people.

He greeted us shyly with every wish to please. 'Welcome to Burang.' Handshakes after we had climbed off the lorry and retrieved the baggage. 'I was expecting you here, there is wash house and good restaurant. No problem.'

Carrying our bags, our minds filled with visions of corrective camps, we followed our mentor down a gravelled path between flowerbeds filled with geraniums and salvias to one of a series of chalets that brought to western Tibet the air of a Butlin's holiday camp. The usual woman with the keys appeared, and took over from Mr Su, who retired with smiles and the announcement that dinner would be ready in an hour.

Mr Su and Mr Sung

We were in a bedroom that offered us the nearest thing to luxury that we had found in Tibet, a room which had its own basin, mirror and two comfortable beds with clean linen. It was a bewildering new experience to wash with a decent amount of water while Caroline unzipped her bags and went through her housewife performance. Outside, groups of women with yard brushes were sweeping, while a gardener worked among the flowers. China was in charge of a routine that was clean and ordered.

There was a discreet knock, and outside the door stood Mr Su with an older official wearing a tight, buttoned-up blue tunic, whose name was Mr Sung. He spoke no English, but smiled a lot.

Mr Su said, 'Mr Sung, Head of Security.'

We discovered that Mr Sung had only been here for ten days and had not adjusted to Tibet.

'Not interesting,' Mr Su translated. 'What is there to see?'

We explained our problems. 'We wish to travel to Nepal.'

'Sure. I will see to everything.'

Mr Su and Mr Sung took us to the small shop where we were able to buy provisions for the journey ahead. A girl produced the usual noodles, biscuits and a pungent Chinese sausage like a shrivelled bar of soap.

'You can charge them more,' Mr Sung said in Chinese.

'A good seventy per cent more,' Caroline said later.

That evening we invited Mr Su and Mr Sung to join us for a meal. In the canteen—dining room would be too elegant a word to describe the barnlike structure full of metal tables and chairs—we discovered a number of burly Chinese and Japanese mountaineers from the Friendship Expedition. Among them was Kazi.

He came over and joined us. 'You go tomorrow?' Caroline smiled and nodded and he realised that we were in a very delicate position.

Appetising smells seeped in from the kitchen next door where we glimpsed chefs in white hats and coats bending over cauldrons. The arrival of our little party galvanised the staff into activity and waiters jostled to bring in a series of dishes that demonstrated the best of Chinese cooking, served in the land of tsampa and mutton bones. We feasted on bowls of thick egg soup, glazed sauces, creamy sauces sprinkled with herbs, and kebabs, strips of pork, bean curd, crinkled stalks of an unfamiliar vegetable, dishes of boiled rice, fried rice, sweetened rice, noodles. Many of the ingredients of the feast must have been carried across the high plateau in lorries. There was beer and two fish cooked in their skins, complete with heads; something like carp, they were delicious.

Caroline smiled sweetly at Mr Su. 'When I was in Beijing last November, I stayed in the vice-presidential suite.'

While she was describing the lavish sitting room and bathroom provided for members of the higher echelons of socialist administration, Mr Su's tired face gazed at her over his chopsticks with an awestruck expression.

In the morning we made our way to the dining room to renewed feasting as tasty dishes were served up: pickled cabbage, spicy sauces and something in gelatine like sheep's eyes. Around us the mountaineers were eating heartily as if they had never gone to bed, their appetites hard to satisfy after their exertions.

We were spooning gruel soup when Mr Su bustled in. 'Good morning, good morning. You sleep well?' He sat down at our table and lit a cigarette while once again Caroline recalled her privileged sojourn in Beijing. I was wondering if she was overdoing it, when the swing doors burst open again to reveal another young army officer. There was something familiar about him, about the sharp glare with which he picked us out from the other diners, his slight stoop as he walked towards us. It was the interpreter. The last time we had seen each other was hundreds of miles away on the road to Shiquanhe.

'The Director of Police wants to question you.'

We abandoned the breakfast and returned to the bedroom.

Four more men in uniform were waiting.

'Passports.'

We sat on our beds while they crowded in and handed the passports around to one another, examining them page by page: first the message from the Minister for Foreign Affairs in Ireland, then the place of birth and *signes particuliers*, then the horrible photographs, then the pages with stamps.

A ratty little man turned to me and flipped a page. 'What is this?'

'It must be an exit stamp from Greece.' Evidence of a package holiday on Corfu.

'Ah. This?'

'Dover. A port in England.'

'Ah.' The passports were handed back, and we couldn't look at each other.

One of the officers was carrying a large parcel wrapped in brown paper. There was a long moment of silence before he began to open it.

'We would like to present each of you with a beautiful calendar of our country.'

He spoke officially, watched by three smiling colleagues. The calendars, large as prayer mats, were unrolled to reveal bright pictures of Tibet: the Potala, blossom in the Norbulingka, a couple of mountainous places, a blue lake, a shaggy man on a shaggy pony, some girls in distinctive clothes dancing near a flowerbed.

▲ **A Chinese policeman in a Tibetan street market. Tibetans are never allowed to forget that their country is now officially considered by the Chinese to be a province of China.**

Caroline was the first to regain her voice and wits.

'You are most generous.'

'It is nothing.'

Many smiles and handshakes. No mention of baggage and currency. They saluted and walked out of the room.

In a state of euphoria we congratulated each other.

Maybe it was the vice-presidential suite. Maybe they thought we could obtain every Chinese in Burang a visa for California. Most likely they were kind, friendly, hospitable and unable to believe that we had no permission to travel here.

We could start for the border right away, and Mr Su and Mr Sung had ordered us a jeep. Like visiting royalty we had to make our goodbyes. There was Kazi saying farewell all over again. Then the mountaineers, whom we found in their dormitory, all reading copies of *Playboy* as they lay on their beds passing the time. Heads nodded over the nudes as more smiles were exchanged.

Escape from Burang

Mr Su and Mr Sung told us they would accompany us all the way to the border. It was their duty. A small fee was agreed for the journey and, hardly believing our luck, we watched the jeep being loaded with our bags. After we paid our bill, Caroline took group photographs of the best of friends. There was Mr Su, his dark glasses removed, grinning in his ritzy black leather jacket. Click. There were Mr Sung and myself with our arms around each other. Then we all got into the jeep with two security men and the driver hunched up in front.

From Burang the route followed the edge of the river, lined on either side with small terraced fields, while across the valley lines of snowy mountains caught the sun. Since the roadmakers had not been this way, the route remained more or less a path for track animals. Even with four-wheel drive, the jeep found it very rough going, negotiating places where the track had been washed away or a vertical stretch of hill that had to be navigated inch by inch in first gear.

'Tibet is very poor country,' Mr Su apologised for any discomfort. 'Much better in America.'

Although the jolts and bumps were painful and hard to bear, we knew that every yard took us further away from Burang and its telephone link with Lhasa. An hour later we bumped to a stop in a small village with flat-topped houses surrounded by the usual high mud wall, set in a patch of greenness and fertility like nothing we had seen for months. This was Khojarnath, which Dorje had described to us—it had an important gompa built by Indians, which Indian pilgrims to Kailas always made a point of visiting.

Even at this final stage of our journey the two security chiefs felt obliged to show off Tibet's heritage. Mr Su rooted out the lama in charge. 'Five yuan each to see.' He himself did not want to go in. Both Mr Su and Mr Sung disapproved of anything to do with religion, manifestly a backward step into the past. On the whole they seemed to find little to enjoy in these parts. Mr Sung had a cold and Mr Su complained about the problem of the headaches that had afflicted him ever since he arrived. I remembered how Manchu officials a century ago regarded their tours of duty in Tibet as a thankless penance, usually a punishment for some massive misdemeanour.

▲ A bundle of incense sticks hangs near the top of a brightly decorated pillar in a Tibetan monastery.

The old lama to whom we gave our money seemed well used to tourists. Like every monastery in Tibet, Khojarnath is much reduced from the days when it used to harbour sixty monks and about a dozen nuns. At the beginning of this century a fire destroyed much of the interior, but the place was soon redecorated in the most gaudy style, and the gay interior with red wooden pillars and giant statue of Buddha remains cheerful.

Mr Su and Mr Sung were waiting outside the main door. 'You like?' But Mr Su was not really interested in our opinion. 'Please, there is some small trouble. Jeep cannot go on.'

We hardly dared to ask. 'What's the matter?'

'Road no good. We learn from headman here. Better take horse—I have given orders.'

We waited, trying to appear unconcerned, inspecting the small market under the village walls where a few people squatted in the dust, offering dull things for sale on pieces of cloth—plastic-framed mirrors, photos of Chinese leaders, hair ties. Then the horse arrived, poor creature, another wretched, skinny pony with an angry-looking old man dragging it along.

'Tibet very primitive,' Mr Su apologised, as the man began to strap our bags over the saddle.

Goodbye, goodbye. Many thanks. 'One moment please,' Caroline said, as Mr Su and Mr Sung were climbing back into the jeep. 'I suggest you write a letter for our porter, which we can show if we meet a checkpoint.'

'Of course.'

'Thank you. Goodbye. We are most grateful.'

The jeep drove away. How nice Mr Su and Mr Sung had been, and how glad we were to see the back of them.

The Frontier

A cold wind blew up as we followed the horse down a narrow, sunless valley with the river thundering at our feet and the promise of mountains ahead.

We had asked Mr Su the distance to the frontier. 'Perhaps two hours. Perhaps five.' He had changed the subject. Either he had not been there or, like the man who had made our map, he had been defeated by this vast empty world just beneath the clouds.

The track rose and fell over the rock, mile after mile. Mr Su was right: no jeep could have made the journey. The horse with our baggage had to be cajoled all the time, dissuaded from stopping and snatching at weeds. Its owner continued to look angry. We had been travelling for three or four hours and were descending towards the river and a long bank of shingle, when we noticed men coming our way. One moment the world was empty except for our gruff companion yanking his horse along by a rope, the next we were surrounded by a group of chattering pilgrims on their way to Kailas.

Two Hindu pilgrims on their way to Kailas pause by the roadside. The man in the background is a saddhu, a holy man. ▼

They told us they had come up from Simikot, the government headquarters of a province of western Nepal, which we knew very well was out of bounds to foreign trekkers. But from here Simikot would be hard to avoid; in any case, it had a small airfield where we might get a flight to Kathmandu.

We watched them walking away in the direction we had come, the porters with their conical straw bags whistling and singing to each other in encouragement under the heavy weights they carried.

A voice called back. 'Remember Nepalese nice people. We like English people.'

An hour later we reached a small village hanging over the gorge in a nest of trees surrounded by a few little fields. In front of us the valley had narrowed to what appeared to be a cul-de-sac, and the mountains faced us, rising straight up and threatening. Far below I could make out a small wooden cantilever bridge.

That must be the frontier. Our porter immediately started taking our bags off his horse with great haste.

'Go on,' Caroline shouted in Chinese, and then in English. 'Nepalese border.'

He shook his head and our bags continued to pile up on the ground.

Some men and children came out to watch him escape. He was away; Mr Su's letter did us no good, and we would have to get from here to the frontier on our own. It was not far off, but the bag of provisions, my Annapurna bag and Caroline's effects all had to be moved.

'I'm going on.' Sinking under the weight, I plunged on down the path, Caroline following slowly.

'There's something wrong with me,' called out Caroline behind. 'I think I'm getting a heart attack.'

'It'll have to wait.'

I left her to her own devices and she managed to persuade several young girls to take her things.

I looked down on the ice-blue river cutting through the valley. I was almost there. Nothing to indicate a border, not even a chain at the rickety little bridge, just a few tottering steps across the wooden planks with the river roaring its welcome.

'Nepal?' I shouted, as one of Caroline's porters lurched into sight. 'Nepal?' The girl nodded and thoughts of a Chinese prison finally faded.

▲ The cantilever bridge by which the author crossed from Tibet to Nepal. The characters carved on the stone proclaim the territory in the foreground to be Chinese.

Caroline crossed. 'I still can't believe it.'

'How's the heart?'

'I really didn't feel well, Peter, and I must say I got very little sympathy from you.'

We sat on a Nepalese rock and munched our last chocolate bar, feeling like gods.

We had crossed in the late afternoon, and now we pitched the tent on a narrow shoal of shingle just above the river. Two of the girls who had carried down Caroline's bags came back to see the foreigners put up their tent and parade their camping utensils. When they understood that we intended to travel in the direction of Simikot, they needed little urging to join us. They had relatives there.

We lit Kazi's burner beside the bridge on the border and contentedly ate a sausage we had bought at Burang while we watched the sun sink behind the mountains. The girls, who must have been about fourteen or fifteen, came down again with some coarse blankets to sleep in, which they stretched beside a fire made from scraps of brushwood and yak dung. After Kailas I felt no qualms about them not sharing our tent.

Later, listening to the roar of the river, I thought of the places I had seen— Gyangzê, Xigazê, Sa'gya, all diminished, Lhasa, tarnished, but all places of beauty and mystery. And deserts, moonscapes, mountains, blue lakes. Kailas and Manasarowar. We had left behind the roof of the world with its remaining monasteries and black tents and conquering Chinese. In their bottle-green uniforms and Mao hats they were busy—busy making roads, improving health, constructing factories, building houses, pulling down the past, tempting tourists and organising their colony. Poor Tibet.

▲ Caroline and the author celebrate their escape from Tibet. Caroline holds out a genuine Nepalese pebble, as proof that they are on safe soil.

Although we had received much kindness, it was still with a great sense of relief that I was in Nepal once again. No matter how much the Chinese try to project their new open policy towards foreigners, no matter how much they emphasise the improvements that Communism has brought, there is still the overwhelming sense of visiting an occupied country.

We were woken by the sound of thousands of scurrying feet.

Dazed with sleep, I poked my head outside. In the dawn light I could make out the two girls squatting beside their fire, trying to relight it with wet sticks. But something else was going on; slowly, like one of Kazi's Polaroid pictures, the scene became plain. An army of sheep was pouring down the mountainside towards the bridge across the river. Our small camp had become submerged in animals. More and more continued to thunder through.

As the light increased, I could make out how each sheep or goat—there were goats mixed up with them—was fitted with a pack saddle. Most likely, these would contain rice or grain, although I could see that some animals had small pieces of wood sticking out from the pouches. Each sheep carried roughly thirty pounds.

It took more than an hour for them to hurry past; thousands of bony bodies covered with rough wool, thousands of angular heads with curving horns. Through the foghorn of bleating I could hear the shouts and whistles of the drovers, who were whirling around as the immense flock formed a pushing, moaning traffic jam at the foot of the bridge. On the other side, high up towards the Tibetan village, a continuous line of animals covered the narrow track in a moving grey ribbon.

At last they had gone and there was silence. We made tea and shared some biscuits. The sun was skirting the tops of the mountains, and Caroline was brushing her hair, each stroke followed intently by the girls. A little later, our party was increased by an old man. After the tent was struck and bags distributed, we all set off at a spanking pace, the man and two girls, each in a Mao hat emblazoned with a red star, scampering ahead.

A Long Walk

After being asphyxiated in the back of Chinese lorries, I found something magical in making a journey on foot. This was a fine lonely place, and if we were going to get anywhere we would have to cross a good many hills and a good deal of forest. The track rose straight up from the river into the sky, through tawny

Traders from the fertile Nepalese lowlands transporting food for remote mountain villages on the backs of pack sheep and goats. ▼

rocks up to the first drifts of snow. In spite of carrying no baggage, we were soon gasping for breath. Ahead, the girls were having a last look back at their home, the small village on the edge of a cliff above the thin divide of the river.

In another hour that particular river was behind us, and so was Tibet. We had reached a divide in the Himalayan landscape which was like stepping off a high terrace into space. Here was another world, of snowy mountains as dramatic as those we had seen when we travelled near Everest. But no trekkers or tourists came to the Humla district of western Nepal. Here the travellers were shepherds, traders and other nomadic wanderers.

Now that the short summer season had begun, when the passes were free of snow, people were bringing their caravans of goods and animals up from Nepal into Tibet. This was a very ancient traffic. In the nineteenth century it was already old when foreign travellers noted how gold dust, borax and salt were carried down on the backs of animals, while cooking utensils, pots, pans, earthenware and foodstuffs were brought up from Nepal. I had read that, when the Chinese moved in, much of this trade had ceased, and the traditional nomadic life of the Bhotias who wandered between Nepal and Tibet had been drastically curtailed. But we were witnessing how the old ways had survived.

▲ Informal trade is vital to the border towns of Tibet and Nepal. Here a yak caravan, taking advantage of the summer weather, descends a narrow pass between the two countries.

We came out into a fold of mountains with another steep gorge falling beneath our feet, where looking up we could see a flow of people and animals descending in our direction. Another long sheep caravan took half an hour to float past us, each laden animal kicking up dust; ten minutes after they had gone by, I could still hear the clang of bells and the shouts and whistles of the shepherds. Behind the sheep jogged some horsemen, oblivious to the precipice that edged the track. Then, higher up, I could see approaching a column of yaks with valuable planks of wood strapped lengthways along their backs, the ends sticking out far beyond their bushy tails like bowsprits on old sailing ships. They, too, passed in dust, big shaggy Tibetan yaks balancing like tightrope walkers—one false step would be fatal—an impression of flaring nostrils puffing out steam, massive heads lolling downwards, musky body scent, the creak of wood, and then they were gone.

Behind the yaks came another line of porters: small men in tattered white pyjamas, so different from Tibetans with their thick, furry clothes. These men were bent double under the same massive wooden planks the yaks had been carrying, and climbing slowly step by step. Their ordeal seemed terrible.

Far ahead, another steep escarpment fell thousands of feet below. Although Himalayan trails may seem giddily dangerous in photographs, when you are actually walking along one, the danger of falling over the side somehow appears less. New instincts of balance take over like those of flies climbing up window-panes, and much of the time your feet stick to the shaly surface without slipping.

By midday we had reached a point well above the snow line where black clouds rolled over our heads and the air was wintry. Here were more sheep. A sheep caravan moves along slowly—I believe that it averages about four miles a day. This makes for great difficulty in keeping the animals in some sort of formation without breaking ranks. The idea of dogs as herders has no place here, and the men who coax up and down the mountains hundreds of erratic beasts, straying and snatching at ragged pieces of grass as they move along, channelled for miles along steep, narrow tracks beside precipices, have a tremendous task. These drovers were returning from Tibet, bringing down sacks of salt as their ancestors had done for thousands of years with the same perils and misfortunes. I watched a man pick up a sheep carcass and throw it over a cliff away from the

▲ Only a few hundred feet below the top of the pass, winter aconites bloom in a patch of snow.

tracks, as sailors consign their dead to the sea. The body rattled over rocks and stones until it vanished, while another shepherd took out a small mouth organ and played a wheezy lament.

After another backbreaking climb we reached the head of a pass marked out by a chorten with strips of flag cracking in the wind. Far below us another valley, a gulf closed in by mountains. Wherever you looked the peaks clawed into the sky, wave after wave, with the Tibetan Plateau a lost world behind our backs.

With the freezing wind blowing up and tearing at the flags, the pass was no place to linger, and we followed our porters who had galloped down the other side, our bags bobbing on their backs, the old man keeping up with them. As we went gasping down the track, suddenly instead of menacing lumps of rocks and snow and pools of ice we were walking among green specks of vegetation and bright yellow flowers. A herd of yaks was grazing on a mountainside, birds were singing, and a rivulet splashed beside the path. In a hundred paces it was spring. We had missed all the blue poppies and yellow roses of Tibet that do not bloom until late July. The flowers waited for us here. We had seen spring below Everest and lost it; now we found it again high up in western Nepal. The air had a greater warmth and smelled of pine trees; primulas and hyacinths grew at our feet.

Perhaps the thin mountain air increased the sense of well-being, sharpening smells, increasing the delight for the eyes. I was resting, sitting in the sun enjoy-ing my charmed surroundings, so different from the wilderness which was the world of the Tibetan nomad. Suddenly the sun was blotted out by a shadow, and I looked up to see an eagle flying over my head. Around it were five others effortlessly sailing over the valley floor, taking advantage of swirls in the air with an ease I had only seen in gannets. One of them, a big brown bird which seemed as large as a hang-glider, swooped down and landed on a rock not far away—I could make out a yellow eye. Eagle? Lammergeyer? Here, more or less safe from guns, they were in the concentration that nature intended.

We came to a small, thatched house surrounded by flowering bushes, where a group of men were playing cards in a yard outside. Two of them wore khaki uniform, and it seemed that we had arrived at our first Nepalese checkpoint.

'Yes, please... what do you want?' One of the uniformed men looked up from his cards. His command of English seemed to give him and his friends great satisfaction.

'We have come from Tibet. Do you wish to speak to us?'

They didn't particularly. We were an interruption. They went on throwing down cards as if we didn't exist.

There seemed to be no point in staying here, since no one wanted to inspect our credentials. We had been walking for almost ten hours, and were feeling hungry. We would move on and camp.

Wage Negotiations

While we had been watching the play, our porters had taken off their loads and were sitting together with the old man in a conspiratorial group talking to each other. Now, as we got up, one of the girls went over to the card-playing group where she started to argue and wave her hands. At last there was a pause in the

The Bone-Smashing Lammergeyer

▲ The lammergeyer with its distinctive, droopy moustache.

THE AIR ABOVE HIGH MOUNTAINS is home to birds of prey, many of which are carrion-eaters, and scavengers; for the perils of life near the snow line—either from predators or from the merciless cold—provide them with a constant supply of carcasses. This food supply attracts the huge griffon vulture, and its even larger cousin, the rare bearded vulture or lammergeyer ('lamb vulture') with its magnificent 10-foot wingspan.

Unlike other members of the vulture family, the lammergeyer has feathers on its head and neck, and so should really be considered an intriguing link between true vultures and the eagles. In fact, with its dramatic swept-back wings and long wedge-shaped tail, it looks very like an enormous falcon. The lammergeyer lives in high, rugged areas, mostly in Asia, eastern Europe and parts of Africa, where it is one of the world's fastest and highest-flying birds, capable of diving at around 80 mph from heights of over 26,000 feet. It also has the peculiar habit of carrying the bones of quite large animals high up into the air and dropping them onto the rocks below, in order to smash them open and so get at the marrow within. These birds have been driven to the edge of extinction, largely by people who refuse to believe that they do not feed on living prey.

game as the conversation with the officers became more heated.

The traveller's constant problem. Baedekers are full of advice about dealing with porters. No doubt Marco Polo had similar problems.

'They say more money,' the soldier told us. 'They won't go further.'

'We made an arrangement.'

All anyone wanted to do was to get back to the game. After much shrill chat, it was agreed that the porters would bring our bags down to the checkpoint at Yari a few miles on. There we would find a senior official to sort things out.

We marched down to Yari, a cluster of houses by the track, where we found more soldiers, some policemen in buckled khaki, and a flagpole on a small terrace. No one knew what to make of us. A portly officer came out of an office and stared disbelievingly.

▲ A group of Nepalese woodcutters take a break from their strenuous labour to enjoy a game of cards in a secluded spot.

'Tell these people there is no way we will give them any more money.'

The police chief brought us all into his office where an ancient crank-handled telephone stood against a wall. We all crowded into the small room, our three porters, the police chief and most of his staff. Everyone was talking at once; the arguments were paraded amid a long exchange of translated abuse.

'Tell them I'm not the sort of person to deal in blackmail,' Caroline yelled, and I had rarely seen her so angry. 'I'm not having any more arguments.' Then all of a sudden she got up and pushed the Tibetans out of the door. We never saw them again.

Immensely impressed by Caroline, the police chief gave us tea and cakes, and later directed one of his men to help me pitch the tent in a field beside the station. It was a perfect site, looking down on a valley full of sheep grazing among bushes of thyme and lavender and scattered flowers. On the far side the vegetation and tree line soon gave way to screes of rock, and above and beyond was the sharp white line of peaks.

Western Nepal was a place of hardship. 'We are a poor country, a poor country,' intoned the man who had helped me erect my tent and now, together with the others, stood watching me cook. 'In Simikot no doctor. What shall we do?' Simikot was two days' travelling away. Did the poverty and isolation of Yari and the surrounding province confirm the theory that, although Nepal is one of the most subsidised countries in Asia, much foreign aid intended to bring medicine and education this way vanished somewhere to the east?

The same man told me that this was the territory of the snow leopard. 'Leopard no good. Come down in winter.' The beautiful, endangered feline did not confine its prey to wild sheep in the remoteness of the mountains, but sometimes sought easier prey in the form of domesticated animals.

Living at heights where prey is scarce and the weather merciless, the magnificent snow leopard has always been rare and is today threatened with extinction. ▶

None of the policemen had been in Tibet. One said, with perversity, 'Tibetans look happy, but they are sad people. They were right to get rid of their temples and the lamas. We should do the same.'

A Hardship Posting

All night I could hear the patter of rain falling on the tent and worried that the monsoon was here. But next morning the sun was lighting up the snowy peaks and the valley exhaled scents of herbs and flowers.

We asked if we could find more porters. Perhaps even a horse?

Like Mr Sung in Burang, the Chief of Police at Yari had only taken up his appointment a few days before. He was clearly depressed at the prospect of enduring life in such a remote place, especially since he had spent time in Kathmandu, and already dreamed of returning to its queasy delights. No entertainments here, no civilised company.

He told us that the trail to Simikot was difficult and very dangerous. There were falling rocks and landslides and every kind of wild animal—tigers and leopards in every tree. As a special favour he would try and arrange other porters, but he couldn't be sure of obtaining them. 'These people do not even respect the police. I give orders and they do not do as I say.' He changed the subject. 'I have bad stomach.'

Caroline produced her pills, and soon found herself dosing everyone in Yari. The pills made everyone more disposed towards helping us, and suddenly the police chief took more positive action. A whistle blew and his men lined up shoulder to shoulder on the little terrace beside the flagpole.

'I will give you two men as far as the next village and they will take some of your baggage. Please divide it into four parts.'

The dilemma of what to do with us had been solved without anyone having to inspect passports and visas.

The police, carrying almost everything, shot ahead rapidly while we followed towards another snowy mountain, a barrier rising above the forest pine and juniper. We walked among jasmine, honeysuckle, flowering hawthorn, yellow dog roses, potentilla. There was lavender, peppermint and thyme. A cuckoo called.

We were walking down a pathway above the river through a country garden in early summer. There were sulphur-coloured butterflies and black and yellow swallowtails, with enough flowers and flowering shrubs here to gladden any collector and fill every garden in the British Isles.

I had a dip in the stream, plunging into the ice-cold water of a deep pool. We lazed for a while in the sun, before continuing beside the little brook which took strength and shape as it was fed by melting snow and glaciers from up above. Soon the trickling brook of a few miles back had become a torrent and we rested again beside a sandbank speckled with hovering butterflies seeking moisture. Occasionally dragonflies the size of birds lunged across the water.

In places the main stream divided, forming islands with cataracts splashing between the rocks, and lower down we had to cross over a small wooden bridge balanced between two boulders. The trail became confused and split into numerous small tracks. But before we became totally lost, we walked into a group of shepherds sitting in the shade of the shining green foliage of a walnut tree, their woollen packs stacked behind them, their sheep and goats scattered while they concentrated on their gambling. Arcadia with playing cards. I recalled that such is the Nepalese passion for gambling that they devote an annual feast day to it. Surely a Nepalese version of Monopoly would be successful—perhaps with Everest in place of Park Lane?

A player looked up just for a second and pointed the way up the hill where the policemen had gone. We climbed after them through the pale green forest, the moss at our feet another series of luminous greens, every bush in flower, and everywhere birds, butterflies, dragonflies, bees, beetles and lizards. Larger animals kept away, as they usually do in forests. Higher up we came to a terrace containing a long, low building which turned out to be a school. This was Muga; one of the teachers gave us a delicious cup of tea, and here were our policemen. In Nepal everything seemed easy.

We pitched the tent in a small hollow full of wild flowers beside a stream that bubbled out of a well. The night was cold and we wore every garment we possessed. The tent smelled of thyme and mint.

The Walking Rucksack

At six o'clock, as the first trickle of pack sheep was passing us, we were woken by their bells. The policemen stood outside the tent with a man and a boy they had recruited as porters to take our baggage to Simikot. The father, dressed in cotton pyjamas and jacket, was grinning; the boy looked about ten.

▲ Butterflies flourish in summer on the fertile lower slopes of the Himalayas. Here, a Nepalese Blue butterfly takes nectar from a delicate mauve geranium.

'These men very strong.'

The day was cool with mist rising over the river and, above the cloud cover, white mountains. The policemen set out on the return journey to Yari, and we loaded up the porters. The boy vanished under luggage so that you could only see his legs; we referred to him as the Walking Rucksack. His father too seemed impervious to weight.

The valley which we had been following for two days seemed to come to a stop in front of a wall of steep, forested hills and a background of snowy mountains. We realised that we had come to the entrance of a narrow gorge whose cliffs formed a funnel through which the water of the river roared so loudly that we had to shout to hear each other. Another herd of sheep came towards us over a terrible suspension bridge, followed by two shepherds who appeared as if by magic through what looked like an impenetrable wall of rock. It was very hard to see how men and animals had come this way, but once we were over the bridge we found a sheep's path on the far side, which rose dizzily upwards over cliffs and rocks. Then it descended to the river and up again, spiral-ling upwards to another thin ledge—along a bit, then down and around, and up and along and down, never more than three feet wide, with a wall of moss

▲ Nepal's natural forests, now only a fraction of their original size, are full of magnificent trees, often draped with lichens. The mountains, as always, are never far away.

and slimy rock on one side, and a drop on the other.

We paused for breath, while father and son continued sturdily ahead of us. I felt as people do when they ride in a rickshaw. Our porters were so much smaller than we were, and they were going up and down a three-foot-wide path carrying our burdens at a tireless pace, whistling through their teeth. There were many stretches of path where, if they made one false move, they would fall hundreds of feet.

Mist and spray from the river made the trees grow huge. The massive oaks, festooned in mistletoe, had trunks that would do for the roofs of palaces; the towering maples and chestnuts were draped in moss. In the higher places above the spit of spray we walked among junipers and tiers of pines reaching upwards to the snow line. But, if the trees were spectacular, it was the river that domi-nated this narrow enclosed world, giving it a presence and a life, the milky flood gathering speed and strength as it thundered its way through rocks.

Around midday we came to a village on a ledge where the river turned south. We had been walking for five hours, and I remember feeling a sense of awe that people could live in such isolation, with the path that we were following as their only communication with the outside world. Their lives were passed to the accompaniment of the roar of water louder than the human voice.

The river valley was all around us, flecked with green foam. Over our heads there were still white-capped mountains rising out of trees, and everywhere a muffled sound of running water. Terraces painfully carved out of the forest fell steeply in broken frills down to the river, each stretch of green barley dotted with women working in bright red dresses. Everything was stirred and put in motion by icy draughts of mountain air sweeping through the gorge. Grass bent double, the tossing trees and swathes of green corn were caught by the wind and moved endlessly. From far away came the crack and roll of thunder.

We stopped in a small square with a chorten in the middle. In the pretty villages of other regions the architecture was gradually being moulded by the demands of tourism, but here the village had taken centuries to grow out of the forest. The houses, hewn from the surrounding trees, were made from massive blocks of wood ringed by a couple of balconies, which had the look of creepers and were linked by a series of notched ladders leading finally to the flat rooftop, from where a number of people were gazing down at us. Others were gathered beside the chorten. It was a shock to see how most of them were ill and undernourished. There were goitre pouches under thin faces, and here and there a set of features retarded by lack of iodine. Unsmiling children had stick legs and pot bellies. The scalloped fields round about that looked so rich provided insufficient harvest for the apathetic groups who were watching us go by.

It was a short climb and descent to the next village, a similar group of high houses with notched logs leading to terraces and galleries, carved pillar posts blackened by smoke and small, dark interiors made from great slabs of wood. Even the dogs and goats wore wooden collars. Similar paradisiacal surroundings

A typical village in western Nepal in which houses made of wood and mud are stacked one above the other and linked by staircases hewn out of massive treetrunks. ▼

▲ As the valleys widen out, the forests are left behind. Here, in fertile farmlands, Nepalese villagers use water buffalo to thresh their rice harvest.

beside roaring water, more dark-eyed, sick-looking children staring down at us. There are plenty of other remote places like these in western and central Nepal, where food shortages threaten starvation and poverty is exacerbated by the difficulties of communication.

The depression induced in us by this poverty could not last. The forest green elated and refreshed us. In only a couple of days we had left behind the wind-scoured Tibetan Plateau and, although we had descended a considerable distance, it still seemed astonishing how the physical world could have changed so dramatically in such a short period of time. No matter how stark and noble the Tibetan landscape had been, those gaunt stretches of wilderness were places for ascetics or saints or artists with a feverish vision. We found we were more attuned to succulent tones of green, bushes, flowers and trees. Above us a water-fall curved in a rainbow spray with a couple of extra silver plumes watering moss and ferns, and filling up dark golden pools.

'I bet there's good fishing here.'

We camped in the evening beside the steep drop to the water's edge from where came the river's roar, drowning out every other sound. It had grown monstrous from the small, ice-edged trickle in the snow to an irrepressible force cascading through the rocks. It made different sounds that became a chorus, some muted where it eddied and turned into a quiet pool, then again a low hum like a man greeting the first good day of spring, and somewhere where the valley narrowed a noise like a cry of pain.

There could be few places in the world where it was such a pleasure to camp and wake, watching the first glow of light stealing over the hills and listening to birdsong while drinking your first cup of tea. Caroline picked flowers: roses, honeysuckle, rock roses and fragrant herbs. Along with the sounds of water, the gorge was full of flower scents. The noise of water made many other sounds inaudible. Down through the trees I could see the creamy torrents of the river breaking over the rocks.

Soon after we began walking, the gorge opened up and suddenly there were a lot fewer trees and a lot more people. We passed fields with women at work wielding scythes; we were down now in a place that was ready for harvest. The great shadowy forest was behind us, the land here was cleared in burnt-out patches and the weather was getting hot.

By now we were impatient for journey's end. 'Simikot?' we kept asking the man who carried our bags, and he would point over the next range of hills. People and animals had changed. Instead of the pack sheep with their Roman profiles, now in the heat there were buffalo and Brahmini cattle.

We had accumulated other travellers who were going the same way. A bearded, monkish man in a threadbare chuba walked barefoot behind us; a military-looking man with moustaches suddenly appeared from behind a tree. We sat and rested in a small village under a grove of walnut trees harbouring monkeys with furry black faces and bushy tails. On a rooftop some women were flailing corn with paddles; I watched their arms rising and falling and listened to the chorus of cicadas. The heat also seemed to rise and fall in waves.

It was almost a week since we had left Tibet and stepped off the great tableland into the Himalayas. In Manasarowar it had been snowing; at Yari spring had lasted for a day before we descended to the heat of full summer. We had seen the sprouting green fields of barley, then the thick golden heads of ripening corn, and finally we had watched the harvest.

▲ Nepalese women bringing in the harvest by traditional means. Wheeled vehicles are few and far between in many parts of the Himalayas and their foothills.

It was now really hot, and we walked through a vaporous soup of steaming air that clogged the valley in a wet, sticky embrace. We rested and shared tea with some cattle people living here with their Brahmini bulls and cows on the edge of the forest. There was a look of India about the men in their loose-fitting white clothes and the women in their brilliant saris, and a different sort of jewellery from the Tibetans' and the hill people's—the heavy elaborate necklaces had given way to a lot more jingling of silver bangles and earrings. The subcontinent loomed.

We had been walking through one of the world's most magnificent surviving forests. Now, as we approached Simikot, we could see it being destroyed. Stretches of ruin where the primeval jungle had been gutted and charred into pools of grey ash covered the hillsides as far as we could see. At some places, where the bare eroded ridges stuck out from the trees behind, the next to be felled, the ground was still smoking.

The trail had risen again, and we were climbing into the shadows. As the last strokes of sunlight faded, they were succeeded by the bright orange tongue of forest fires lifting up clouds of dense black smoke. Everywhere you looked the forest was being burned; as we walked in the twilight the pall of smoke was supplemented by prickles of orange flame catching the crackling trees.

Then we came out on top of another steep rise, and down below were electric lights. Simikot.

Flying Out

An hour later we reached the outskirts of the town, dim shapes of houses threaded through with muddy lanes, and then a long stretch of grass which was the airfield.

'Please come in,' said the young airport official. 'I fear we are not too comfortable.' There was, however, a plane coming in the following day and we could change at Nepalganj for Kathmandu. If we had come a week or so later the monsoon would have been upon us. Then the airport would have been closed down except for emergency flights and we would have had to use our feet.

The Blessing of the Monsoon

SWELTERING IN THE SUFFOCATING 125°F heat of early summer, the people of southern Asia, from the Arabian Sea to China, long for the coming of the monsoon, their annual period of overcast skies and torrential rain. Although they are accompanied by mildew, leaking roofs, landslides and sometimes disastrous floods, the monsoons also bring blessedly cool winds, which allow the people to breathe freely again.

What happens is that the landmass of southern Asia heats up dramatically in summer, while the sea off its coast stays relatively cool; and because winds always blow from cooler towards warmer regions, there comes a point in every Asian summer when powerful, moisture-laden winds surge inland off the sea. The moisture in these winds condenses into rain as they cross the hot coastal plains and reach the higher, cooler land beyond. Darjiling, for instance, in the foothills of the Himalayas, receives an average of 24

▲ In typical monsoon conditions, even the hardiest trekker is glad of his umbrella.

inches of rain in the month of June alone. Further inland, however, the life-giving rains peter away; the huge bulk presented by the Himalayas and the

Karakorams blocks off the monsoon winds, so that to the north of these great mountain ranges less than 3 inches of rain may fall in an entire year.

'I think it would have taken you a month to the nearest place where there is a bus. We have no cars or buses or motor traffic here.'

No one could have been more hospitable than the airport staff at Simikot on whom we had descended without warning, putting them to great inconvenience. The cook prepared our remaining supplies and two of them insisted on moving out of their small bedroom for us.

At eight next morning Simikot's links with the outside world appeared as dots in the sky and a small crowd gathered to watch two small planes land in dust. The turnround had to be quick, for by ten o'clock the atmospheric conditions made flying in the mountains impossible. Another farewell. We had paid off the Walking Rucksack and his father the night before. Now they came to see us off and shake hands. After we got on board they lingered; I could see them through the small porthole window, the boy's head enveloped in my orange balaclava. The old man was smiling; he hadn't seen a plane before. Later they would struggle back upstream to their small house in the flowering forest above the ice-blue river.

The takeoff was a hair-raising exercise, which our young Nepalese pilots managed with assurance. They fly these small planes through the mountains and foothills with a skill and experience which has to measure turbulence as the sun heats up the waves of mountain air, wicked crosswinds and monsoon showers that can strike out of a velvet sky. Among the peaks there is no level land to put a plane down. At one moment we were placed precariously on the shelf of land on which Simikot was built; the next we had shot over an abyss with a quick glimpse of roofs of baked brown houses and paths zigzagging up and down ravines. After Simikot fell away, there was nothing but bare mountains where the big trees had been cleared.

We changed planes at Nepalganj, a small town which has the reputation of being the hottest place in Nepal. We sat in the canteen watching a couple of pilots eating curry, sweat dripping down their faces.

In Kathmandu swollen grey clouds that covered the valley belched a welcome. Rain pattered on the corrugated rooftops of the Rana palaces, ran down the Corinthian columns and soaked the bright flowers. It poured on the rose-brick houses of the old city, the new garish villas, shoddy commercial blocks and lines of Indian-style godowns. It fell on the ferroconcrete monuments and fountains, on the camellias and mauve bougainvillaea, on the bronzed, helmeted head of Jung Bahadur astride his horse, on the rickshaw wallahs crouched under the flimsy hoods of their cabs.

'Monsoon early this year,' said the taxi driver as a crack of lightning was followed by a roll of thunder.

In the Kathmandu Guest House I was pointed out like Dante with his singed beard back from Hell.

'You must have been in Tibet,' said the dhobi when I handed him a large bundle. 'I have never seen such dirty clothes.'

Preparing to Go

Practicalities Independent travel is feasible and rewarding in parts of the Himalayas, where expenses are very low after the initial cost of the flight. Pre-booking tours from home may smooth the way considerably, but costs will be rather higher. Bear in mind that large areas are sometimes temporarily closed or unsafe for tourists.

Travel Kabul is the usual port of entry for **Afghanistan** when the country is open to visitors. The only way to fly into **Bhutan** is to take a flight from Calcutta to Paro, which is otherwise two days by road from India. The most convenient international airports for the Himalayas are Delhi in **India**, Islamabad in **Pakistan** and Kathmandu in **Nepal**. These can all be reached from Asia, Europe and elsewhere. An exciting route into **Tibet** is by road from Kathmandu to Lhasa. Otherwise, the main approach is by air into Lhasa from China, though this is difficult for independent travellers to arrange.

Visas Nearly all nationals need to obtain visas for Himalayan countries before arrival; these usually last for three months. **Afghanistan** and **Bhutan** are difficult to enter. Chinese embassies issue visas for **Tibet**, as well as Alien Travel Permits, which are necessary for certain parts of the country. **Nepal** also insists on permits (available from the Central Immigration Office) for entry to particular areas.

Language English is the most useful language in Bhutan, India, Nepal and Pakistan. Nepali is spoken in Nepal, Urdu in Pakistan, Tibetan and Mandarin in Tibet, and a variety of local languages in the Indian Himalayas.

What to take Days can be very hot, and nights bitterly cold. A down- or fibre-filled jacket, a sweater, a large water-bottle, iodine tablets, sunglasses, a daypack and a good sleeping-bag are essential for trekking. Sunscreen and photographic film may be difficult to obtain locally. Serious trekkers should take well-broken-in walking boots with good soles and ankle support; trainers

▲ **All the excitement of a Tibetan folk opera, performed here by a touring dance–drama group in Nepal.**

may be adequate for the easiest treks. In some trekking centres, particularly Kathmandu, it is possible to hire or buy secondhand equipment.

When to go Himalayan winters get very cold and have heavy snowfalls. In spring, the wild flowers are at their best; rhododendrons are especially fine in **Nepal** in April. October to April is

Amid magnificent surroundings on the Everest trail: a trekker camp below the monastery at Thyangboche. ▼

generally a good time to travel here, although climates vary from area to area. **Bhutan** has a particularly pleasant spring and autumn climate. **India**'s hill stations are lovely during the summer (from April to June) when the plains are oppressively hot, but trekking in India is possible from April to October, with September and October seeing the least rainfall. The trekking season in northern **Pakistan** is July to September. **Tibet** is best from spring to late autumn; its climate is generally dry, though light rain is common from July to early September.

Health Travel insurance is essential. Take a comprehensive first-aid kit, with iodine tablets for purifying water and medicine for diarrhoea—a notorious problem in many areas. Drink only bottled, boiled or purified water, and avoid salad and unpeeled fruits. Take precautions against malaria, and obtain inoculation against hepatitis, tetanus, typhoid, diphtheria and yellow fever. Have a medical check before going and consult your GP on the latest health matters concerning the region you intend to visit. If you intend to trek, train beforehand with some reasonably energetic walking. Altitude sickness is a real problem, so pace your itinerary carefully. If you are stricken, descend at least 1,000 feet as quickly as possible.

Trekking Organised trekking is big business, especially in Nepal, where there are numerous trekking agencies, many of which are linked to tour companies worldwide. Treks can be chosen to suit your fitness and interests, taking you through villages or into wild mountain scenery, for instance. Although trekking is not mountaineering, participants should be reasonably fit. Gradients are often quite gentle, but the altitude can make them hard work. Most treks involve shared rooms, dormitories or camping. Arranged treks include porters, who carry food and equipment.

It is quite possible to organise your own trek, especially in the more well-trodden areas. Porters and guides can often be hired locally.

Hassles Touts home in on tourists to sell them souvenirs, accommodation, tours and more. This practice can be annoying, but it is seldom aggressive, and is often useful. Expect to bargain for souvenirs, taxis and rickshaws.

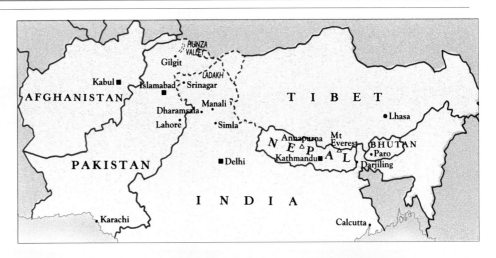

Where to Go

Afghanistan Rarely seen by foreigners, Afghanistan can be very rewarding for the intrepid traveller. Kabul, the capital, is not especially interesting, but the Hindu Kush is rich and varied, both in its scenery and its people.

Bhutan This small kingdom is not open to independent travellers, and group tours are expensive. However, for those with time and money, it offers a chance to see a country largely unchanged by Western influence, with wonderful festivals in spring and autumn.

India There is much to enjoy here for both casual visitors and trekkers, but check on the current political situation in northern India before leaving: not all areas may be open or safe for tourists. In the northwest, Simla is an appealing hill resort with echoes of the Raj, while Manali and Dharamsala make good trekking bases. Srinagar has a charming lake abutting it, with accommodation on houseboats, and the splendid Mughal gardens. Ladakh, to the west of Srinagar, and known as Little Tibet, is set in bare mountains with a striking beauty of their own. Treks in this region take in waterfalls, lakes, caves and glaciers. In eastern India, Darjiling is a sedate hill resort, famed for its mountain railway.

Nepal The most popular trekking routes are in the vicinities of Annapurna and Mount Everest. Licences are required to climb most peaks. There is an arduous 21-day trek from Kathmandu to Everest Base Camp, which involves almost 30,000 feet of ascent and descent. However, there is the option of flying to Lukla, about two

days' walking south of Namche Bazar, and proceeding to Everest from there.

For non-trekkers, the Kathmandu Valley is compact, has good public transport, and a great heritage of temples and shrines. Kathmandu itself has lively festivals in October and November, and is excellent for souvenir shopping (notably carpets and Tibetan artefacts). A trip to Royal Chitwan National Park, southeast of Kathmandu, enables visitors to view rhinoceros from an elephant ride, and to go white-water rafting (best in October).

Pakistan Pakistan offers outstanding trekking in the Hindu Kush and Karakorams. The Karakoram Highway is one of the great scenic roads of the world, passing through deep gorges, arid desert scenery, colourful villages and stupendous mountains. It is especially impressive where it runs through the Hunza valley. You can follow the Highway from Islamabad, or fly to Gilgit and pick up the route from there.

Tibet The Chinese are promoting expensive group tours; as a result, Western-style hotels have appeared in Lhasa. The authorities are not keen on independent backpackers, and trekking can be a rough experience. The food and accommodation require high levels of tolerance, and the language barrier is very strong. Tibet lies mostly on a high plateau, from which the Himalayas appear less snow-covered and more austere than from the south. In remote areas there is often little to see. However, adventurous travellers might encounter lonely monasteries, herds of wild yak, nomads on horseback and breathtaking mountain scenery.

Index
and Acknowledgments

Note: page numbers in *italics* refer to captions for illustrations. Peter Somerville-Large is referred to as P.S-L throughout the index.

Acknowledgments

The editors gratefully acknowledge the use of information taken from the following books and articles during the preparation of this publication:

'At the Crossroads of Kathmandu' by Douglas H. Chadwick, *National Geographic*, July 1987

The Encyclopaedia Britannica

Flight of the Wind Horse: A Journey into Tibet by Niema Ash, Rider Books 1990

Foreign Devils on the Silk Road: Search for Lost Cities and Treasures of Chinese Central Asia by Peter Hopkirk, Oxford University Press 1984

The Great Game by Peter Hopkirk, Oxford University Press 1991

Hidden Tibet: The Land and Its People by Roger Hicks, Element Books Ltd 1988

The Himalayas by Nigel Nicolson and the Editors of Time-Life Books, Time-Life 1975

Kailas: On Pilgrimage to the Sacred Mountain of Tibet by Russell Johnson and Kerry Moran, Thames and Hudson 1989

'Kathmandu's Remarkable Newars' by John Schofield, *National Geographic*, February 1979

'Ladakh—The Last Shangri-la' by Thomas J. Abercrombie, *National Geographic*, March 1978

Mountains of the Gods by Ian Cameron, Century Hutchinson Limited 1984

Mountains of the Middle Kingdom by Galen Rowell, Sierra Books 1984

My Tibet by His Holiness the XIV Dalai Lama, Thames and Hudson 1990

The National Geographic Society: 100 Years of Adventure and Discovery by C.D.B. Bryan, Phaidon Press Ltd 1987

Nepal edited by Lisa Choegyal, Insight Guides, APA Publications 1992

Reader's Digest Great Illustrated Dictionary, The Reader's Digest Association Limited 1984

Reader's Digest Library of Modern Knowledge, The Reader's Digest Association Limited 1981

Sagarmatha by Sir Edmund Hillary; 'Insight Topics', The Himalayan Trust 1991

Tibet by Ngapo Ngawang Jigmei et al., Bestseller Publications 1981

The Tibet Guide by Stephen Batchelor, Wisdom Publications 1987

Tibet: The Lost Civilisation by Simon Normanton, Hamish Hamilton 1988

Trespassers on the Roof of the World by Peter Hopkirk, Oxford University Press 1983

Picture Acknowledgments

T=top; *B*=bottom; *C*=centre; *R*=right; *L*=left; *I*=inset

Cover *Spine* Trip/Ian Corse, *L(T-B)* Caroline Blunden; Tibet Image Bank/Sean M. Smith; Royal Geographical Society/Norma Joseph; Still Pictures/M. Harvey; Royal Geographical Society/Norma Joseph; *R* Patrick Morrow, **2** Ace Photo Agency/Andrew Conway, **3** John Miles, **5** Cephas Picture Library/Nigel Blythe, **6** Tony Stone Images/Mike McQueen, **7** Caroline Blunden, **8–9** Stone Routes, **12–13** Ardea, London/Richard Waller, **13** *T* Impact/Caroline Penn, *BL* Stone Routes, *BR* Cephas Picture Library/J. Brereton, **14** *T* Patrick Morrow, *B* Oxford Scientific Films/David C. Fritts, **14–15** Patrick Morrow, **15** Oxford Scientific Films/Martyn Colbeck, **16** *C* Wilderness Photographic Library/John Noble, *B* Eye Ubiquitous/Julia Waterlow, **16–17** Wilderness Photographic Library/John Noble, **17** Royal Geographical Society/Jim Holmes, **18–19** Bruce Coleman/Gerald Cubitt, **20–21** *T* John Miles, *B* Robert Harding Picture Library/Nigel Blythe, **21** *T* Panos Pictures/Cliff Venner, *CR* Royal Geographical Society/Norma Joseph, *BR* Eye Ubiquitous/Chris Gibb, **22** *T* Life File/Barry Mayes, *B* Britstock-IFA/Bernd Ducke, **23** Impact/Mike McQueen, **24** *B* The Bridgeman Art Library/British Library, London, **24–25** Museo Nacionale, Napoli/Photo Scala, **25** *BL* The British Library, Oriental and India Collections/Artist, James Atkinson, *BR* Trip/Helene Rogers, **26** *R* Livre des Merveilles, Bibliotheque Nationale, Paris, *C* Royal Geographical Society/Jim Holmes, **26–27** *T* Mountain Camera/John Cleare, *B* Mountain Camera/John Cleare, **27** Viewfinder/Martin Puddy, **28** Cephas Picture Library/Nigel Blythe, **29** *T* Pictures Colour Library/Chris Caldicott, *B* Tibet Image Bank/Anders H. Andersen, **30–31** Russell Johnson, **32** Punch Publications Ltd, **32–33** Royal Geographical Society/The British Mission, 1903–1904, **33** *BL* The British Library/Oriental and India Office Collections, Unknown Artist, *BR* Viewfinder/Robin Adshead, **34** *TL* NHPA/E.A. Janes, *CR* Royal Geographical Society/Bruce Herrod, *BL* Bruce Coleman/Hans Reinhard, **34–35** Ardea, London/Charles McDougal, **35** Oxford Scientific Films/Stanley Breeden, **36** *I* Royal Geographical Society, Mount Everest Expedition, 1922, *B* Mountain Camera/John Cleare, **36–37** Mountain Camera/John Cleare, **37** Oxford Scientific Films/Doug Allan, **38** The Image Bank/Ricardo De Aratanha, **38–39** Royal Geographical Society/David Constantine, **39** Magnum/Steve McCurry, **40** *BL* Royal Geographical Society/Bruce Herrod, *BR* Ardea, London/Richard Waller, **40–41** Viewfinder/Robin Adshead, **41** Patrick Morrow, **42–43** Robert Harding Picture Library/Thomas Laird, **44** The Image Bank/Wanda Warming, **46–47** Impact/Mark Cator, **48** Ffotograff/N.C. Turner, **49** Impact/Mark Cator, **50** Rex Features Ltd/John Shelley, **53** Sonia Halliday Photographs/John Dewar, **54** Wilderness Photographic Library/John Noble, **55** Cephas Picture Library/Nigel Blythe, **56** Robert Harding Picture Library/Gavin Hellier, *I* Patrick Morrow, **58** Mountain Camera/John Cleare, **60** *TL* Robert Harding Picture Library/Gavin Hellier, *C* Stone Routes, *BL* Images Colour Library/Alfred Gregory, *BR* John Miles, **61** *T* Royal Geographical Society/Bruce Herrod, *BR* Robert Harding Picture Library/Tony Waltham, **62** Viewfinder/Martin Puddy, **64** Genevieve Leaper, **65** Patrick Morrow, **66** Britstock-IFA/C.L. Schmitt, **67** The Hutchison Picture Library/Sarah Errington, **69** Oxford Scientific Films/Richard Packwood, **71** Robert Harding Picture Library/Thomas Laird, **72** Viewfinder/Martin Puddy, **74–75** Tony Stone Images/Colin Prior, **76** Magnum/Steve McCurry, **77** Viewfinder/Martin Puddy, **78** Patrick Morrow, **79** Mountain Camera/John Cleare, **80** *BL* The J. Allan Cash Photo Library/Roger Divito, **80–81** Wilderness Photographic Library/John Noble, **81** *TR* Richard Madden, *CL* Viewfinder/Robin

Adshead, *CR* Magnum/Bruno Barbey, *BL* The Hutchison Picture Library, **82** Royal Geographical Society/Bruce Herrod, **83** Impact/Olivier Follmi, **84** Caroline Blunden, **87** Tibet Image Bank/Sean M. Smith, **88** Caroline Blunden, **89** Patrick Morrow, **90** Caroline Blunden, **91** Eye Ubiquitous/Jason Burke, **92** Viewfinder/Martin Puddy, **93** Patrick Morrow, **95** Robert Harding Picture Library/Bill O'Connor, **96** Royal Geographical Society/Bruce Herrod, **97** Chris Bonington Picture Library/Chris Bonington, **98** Patrick Morrow, **99** Impact/Mark Cator, **100** *L* Royal Geographical Society/Elliot and Fry, *R* Royal Geographical Society/Alfred Gregory, *B* Royal Geographical Society/Captain J.B. Noel, **100–101** Chris Bonington Picture Library/Chris Bonington, **101** *R* William Thompson, *L* Mountain Camera/John Cleare, **102** Eye Ubiquitous/Patrick Bouineau, **103** Patrick Morrow, **107** Mountain Camera/John English, **108** Tibet Image Bank/Tibet Information Network, **109** Quest Picture Library/Robin Bath, **111** Britstock-IFA/Bernd Ducke, **112** Robert Harding Picture Library/Simon Westcott, **113** Tibet Image Bank/Sean Sprague, **114** Tibet Image Bank/Mike Tibbetts, **115** Caroline Blunden, **116** *T* Royal Geographical Society/Maurice Joseph, *B* Niema Ash, **117** Stone Routes, **118** Robert Harding Picture Library/James Strachan, **119** John Miles, **120** *BL* Caroline Blunden, *BR* Robert Harding Picture Library/Peter Ryan, **120–121** Robert Harding Picture Library/Nigel Blythe, **121** *T* Images Colour Library/Sue Gregory, *C* John Miles, *B* Robert Harding Picture Library/Gavin Hellier, **122** Tibet Image Bank/Sarah Murray, **123** Royal Geographical Society/Maurice Joseph, **124** Tibet Image Bank/Irene Kristalis, **125** Robert Harding Picture Library/Gavin Hellier, **126** Quest Picture Library/Robin Bath, **127** Quest Picture Library/Robin Bath, **128** Robert Harding Picture Library/Tony Waltham, **129** Magnum/Raghu-Rai, **130–131** Eye Ubiquitous/Julia Waterlow, **133** Robert Harding Picture Library/C.C.D. Tokeley, **134** Caroline Blunden, **135** Magnum/Marc Riboud, **136** Royal Geographical Society/Norma Joseph, **138** Magnum/Marc Riboud, **140** *TL* The Image Bank/Harald Sund, *BL* The Image Bank/A. Seiden, **140–141** Tibet Image Bank/Zara Fleming, **141** *TL* Mountain Camera/John Cleare, *TR* Robert Harding Picture Library/Tony Waltham, *B* Impact/Asupi/Visions, **143** Russell Johnson, **144** Russell Johnson, **145** Caroline Blunden, **146** Royal Geographical Society/Norma Joseph, **148** Russell Johnson, **149** Morrow Photography/Baiba Morrow, **150** Russell Johnson, **151** Russell Johnson, **152** Russell Johnson, **153** Stone Routes, **154** Royal Geographical Society/Norma Joseph, **155** Tibet Image Bank/Robert Beer, **156** Caroline Blunden, **157** Tibet Image Bank/Hamish Horsley, **158** Russell Johnson, **160** *TL* Mountain Camera/John Cleare, *TR* Bruce Coleman/Gerald Cubitt, *BL* Royal Geographical Society/Bruce Herrod, *BR* Life File/Wayne Shakell, **161** *TR* Royal Geographical Society/Bruce Herrod, *BL* Patrick Morrow, *BR* Ardea, London, **163** Tibet Image Bank/Sean Jones and Brian Beresford, **166** Magnum/Marc Riboud, **167** Royal Geographical Society/Norma Joseph, **168** Patrick Morrow, **169** Caroline Blunden, **170** Caroline Blunden, **171** The J. Allan Cash Photo Library/John Blower, **172** Ardea, London/Richard Waller, **173** The J. Allan Cash Photo Library/Arthur Spencer, **174** Oxford Scientific Films/Eyal Bartov, **175** Wilderness Photographic Library/John Noble, **176** Still Pictures/M. Harvey, **177** Tibet Image Bank/Rose Lewis, **178** Impact/Mike McQueen, **179** Royal Geographical Society/Bruce Herrod, **180** Mountain Camera/John Cleare, **181** Quest Picture Library/Robin Bath, **182** Patrick Morrow, **184** *T* Magnum/Ernst Haas, *B* Britstock-IFA/Jenny Hager

SEPARATIONS Litra Limited, Edenbridge, Kent
PAPER Townsend Hook Limited, Snodland, Kent
PRINTING AND BINDING Mohndruck, Gütersloh, Germany